Guide to Information Sources
in the Physical Sciences

Reference Sources in Science and Technology Series

Judith A. Matthews, Series Editor

A Guide to the Zoological Literature: The Animal Kingdom. By George H. Bell and Diane B. Rhodes

Guide to Information Sources in the Botanical Sciences. Second Edition. By Elisabeth B. Davis and Diane Schmidt

A Guide to Field Guides: Identifying the Natural History of North America. By Diane Schmidt

Guide to Information Sources in the Physical Sciences. By David Stern

Guide to Information Sources in the Physical Sciences

David Stern

Yale University

Series Editor

Judith A. Matthews

Michigan State University Libraries

2000

LIBRARIES UNLIMITED, INC.

Englewood, Colorado

Libraries Unlimited, Inc.
P.O. Box 6633
Englewood, CO 80155-6633
1-800-237-6124
www.lu.com

Library of Congress Cataloging-in-Publication Data

Stern, David, 1956 Dec. 30-
    Guide to information sources in the physical sciences / David Stern.
      p. cm. -- (Reference sources in science and technology series)
    Includes bibliographical references and index.
    ISBN 1-56308-751-0
    1. Physics--Bibliography. 2. Reference books--Physics--Bibliography. 3.
Physics--Information services--Directories. 4. Physics--Databases--Directories. 5.
Physical sciences--Bibliography. 6. Reference books--Physical sciences--Bibliography.
7. Physical sciences--Information services--Directories. 8. Physical
sciences--Databases--Directories. I. Title. II. Series.

Z7141 .S74 1999
[QC5.35]
016.53--dc21   99-045970

Contents

List of Figures

Preface

This book is intended to serve as a guide to the major trends and information resources in physics. It will be helpful for both new researchers in the field of physics and working physicists in need of additional information resources outside their normal spheres of study. It will also serve as an introduction and daily resource for beginning librarians seeking information about physics.

The literature of physics is vast and rapidly expanding. There are older sources that provide quite impressive comprehensive listings of the previously published physics resources (see the Bibliography chapter). The scope and coverage of this monograph will provide a strong overview, but this is not an exhaustive list of all physics sources. Selectivity was used to create an annotated list of major tools and representative examples of new technologies. Further, the chosen tools are primarily in English, with a few titles in other languages included when of great significance. The prices are included for those items still in print. Significant attention is placed on the new electronic resources available via the Internet.

Kristine K. Fowler, Mathematics Librarian at the University of Minnesota (and well qualified with a master's degree in physics), has contributed chapter 12, "Important Works in the Development of Physics, 1600–1900." This chapter is included to help physicists and librarians rediscover some of the most important primary literature in the field of physics.

I would like to thank the many people who have helped me understand the rapidly changing world of information science. Among those I need to specifically mention are the members of the Physics-Astronomy-Mathematics Division of the Special Libraries Association, Kris Fowler, Andy Shimp, Lori Bronars, and Kari Lynch.

Finally, I would like to thank my wife Susan for her support, patience, and understanding.

Introduction

Physics (from the Latin term *physis*: growth, nature), "a science that deals with matter and energy and their interactions" or "the physical processes and phenomena of a particular system," can be broken down into the following traditional branches: classical and relativistic dynamics, gravitation, electromagnetism, heat and thermodynamics, statistical mechanics, and quantum physics. Other classification schemes involve the treatment (theoretical v. experimental) or the scale of matter and energy levels studied (e.g., high-energy or particles, medium-energy or neutron physics, large-scale molecular physics or surface science). Librarians and physicists have adopted a number of classification schemes, and these are described below.

Subject Classification Schemes

Scientists and librarians have devised a number of subject classification schemes for the field of physics. These hierarchies of physics are used for the description of specific documents or concepts within a document. Such descriptive indexing, or metadata, can then be used for storage and retrieval purposes. The major schemes are PACS (Physics and Astronomy Classification Scheme), LC (Library of Congress), and Dewey Decimal; explanations of these three schemes follow.

PACS Codes

The standard physics community subject hierarchy, the Physics and Astronomy Classification Scheme (PACS), created by the American Physical Society and used in the major indexing and abstracting tool (*Physics Abstracts*), can be found at http://publish.aps.org/PACS/pacsgen.html.

This tool is used by authors to assign subject headings at the point of manuscript submission. Many disciplines ask authors to assign keywords beyond those found in the title and abstract, but few ask authors to assign context descriptors. This added author information complements that of the professional subject indexers working for the commercial abstracting and indexing services. It would be interesting to determine if this philosophical step produces any significant results in terms of novel perspectives.

The major PACS headings are listed below.

1998 PACS—Hierarchical List

00.   SUMMARY OF PACS SCHEME
01.   Communication, education, history, and philosophy
02.   Mathematical methods in physics
03.   Classical and quantum physics: mechanics and fields
04.   General relativity and gravitation
05.   Statistical physics and thermodynamics
06.   Metrology, measurements, and laboratory procedures
07.   Instruments, apparatus, components, and techniques common to ...

10.   THE PHYSICS OF ELEMENTARY PARTICLES AND FIELDS
11.   General theory of fields and particles
12.   Specific theories and interaction models; particle systematics
13.   Specific reactions and phenomenology
14.   Properties of specific particles

20.   NUCLEAR PHYSICS
21.   Nuclear structure
23.   Radioactive decay and in-beam spectroscopy
24.   Nuclear reactions: general
25.   Nuclear reactions: specific reactions
26.   Nuclear astrophysics
27.   Properties of specific nuclei listed by mass ranges
28.   Nuclear engineering and nuclear power studies
29.   Experimental methods and instrumentation for elementary-particle
      and nuclear physics

30.   ATOMIC AND MOLECULAR PHYSICS
31.   Electronic structure of atoms, molecules and their ions: theory
32.   Atomic properties and interactions with photons
33.   Molecular properties and interactions with photons
34.   Atomic and molecular collision processes and interactions
36.   Studies of special atoms, molecules and their ions; clusters
39.   Instrumentation and techniques for atomic and molecular physics

40.   FUNDAMENTAL AREAS OF PHENOMENOLOGY
      (INCLUDING APPLICATIONS)
41.   Electromagnetism; electron and ion optics
42.   Optics
43.   Acoustics
44.   Heat transfer, thermal and thermodynamic processes
46.   Classical mechanics
47.   Fluid dynamics

90. GEOPHYSICS, ASTRONOMY, AND ASTROPHYSICS
91. Solid earth physics
92. Hydrospheric and atmospheric geophysics
93. Geophysical observations, instrumentation, and techniques
94. Aeronomy and magnetospheric physics
95. Fundamental astronomy and astrophysics; instrumentation, techniques and astronomical observations
96. Solar system
97. Stars
98. Stellar systems; interstellar medium; galactic and extragalactic objects and systems; the Universe

LC Subject Classification

The most common subject heading hierarchy used by the North American library community for book material is the Library of Congress (LC) Subject Headings. Within the Science categories is the heading for Physics. These subject categories have related "call numbers" that are used for shelving materials in a logical arrangement that allows for both quick shelving and for browsing through similar subject materials. The physics call numbers begin with QC and are followed by the general subject area. Example: The call number for a book on radioactivity would start with a number somewhere between QC 794.95 and QC 798.

The major physics subject headings in the LC system are listed below.

Physics QC

Dewey Decimal Subject Classification

An earlier library subject arrangement for book materials still used by smaller U.S. public libraries, and modified by many other worldwide libraries into a different Uniform Decimal Classification (UDC) scheme, is the Dewey Decimal scheme. The DDSC is used for shelving materials in a logical arrangement that allows for both quick shelving and for browsing through similar subject materials. The physics call numbers begin with a specific number that relates to the general subject area. Example: The call number for a book on radioactivity, found as a subheading under the major heading Physics, would start with the number 530.4.

The major physics subject headings in the Dewey system are as follows:

530   Physics

531   Classical mechanics; Solid mechanics

532   Fluid mechanics; Liquid mechanics

533   Pneumatics (Gas mechanics)

534   Sound & related vibrations

535   Light & paraphotic phenomena

536   Heat

537   Electricity & electronics

538   Magnetism

539   Modern physics

There are other classification schemes in use; however, these are the major hierarchical arrangements most researchers will encounter. Each scheme has strengths and weaknesses. It would be easier for recall if one classification system could be used for the searching and arrangement of paper documents. The increased and enhanced use of online documents in the near future will create additional requirements for identification, validation, and classification standards.

Characteristics and History of Information Resources in the Physical Sciences

The physics literature is composed of both paper documents and new electronic resources. It would be impossible to describe the domain of physics information without including all media types. This book will integrate these sources by classification but will also have a separate section highlighting some of the most useful, interesting, and provocative electronic resources.

A Short History of Physics Publications and Information Distribution

Society Publications

The history of physics literature closely parallels the history of science and physics. Early science was investigated by people of leisure as an intellectual pursuit as opposed to for economic interests. The scientific method was used to provide reproducible experimental results to confirm theoretical models of nature. The reports of these ideas, discoveries, and proofs were presented at meetings of societies such as the Royal Society of London. The discussions at these meetings served the purpose of peer review. The publication of the minutes of these meetings served as the means of distributing new ideas to worldwide audiences of interested individuals and societies. There were always questions about the effectiveness of this means of distribution. Some society publications were not easily available to all interested readers. The language barrier may have presented problems for readers. Many publications were not even known to potential readers. The quality of the peer review behind these publications was also a concern. However it appears that papers from lesser society publications could on occasion be known throughout the major reader populations, an example being recognition of the work of Benjamin Franklin, which was published in relatively minor U.S. publications.

Commercial Journals

The increasing institutional and national control of science, primarily through the increasing development of universities, changed the dynamics of scientific publishing. The need for quantitative and qualitative evaluation of researchers and teachers created tenure and promotion requirements. This requirement for recognition in order to obtain economic and social advancement led to a proliferation of journals, editorial boards, and manuscript submissions. The rapidly increasing number of educational positions meant an ever-greater number of subdisciplines and manuscript submissions. Journals continued to expand in size and number. Commercial journals began to appear and to skim a profit from larger and more dependent reader populations.

The societies either could not, or chose not to, compete with these commercial producers, and over time a large percentage of the number of articles and books produced in certain fields was distributed on a commercial basis. The question of whether the quality of commercial publications is equal to that of society publications goes on to this day. This debate has included legal challenges and has resulted in higher costs for all scientific publication; for information on a particularly difficult battle between the publisher Gordon & Breach and the American Physical Society (et al.), see http://barschall.stanford.edu/. This debate focuses on the methods used to measure the surcharges and the added value contributed by commercial publishers.

The competition between commercial publishers has not resulted in competitive pricing, as the small world of scientific publishing is dominated by only a few commercial publishers and is not subject to normal market factors. Exacerbating this problem is the fact that most authors are unaware of both the high costs and the long-term financial and distribution effects of giving up their copyright to the commercial publishers. The continued commercialization of the distribution of nontrade scientific information will unduly hamper the spread of science now that there are technical means of spreading peer-reviewed material in a much less expensive and more rapid manner.

Factors in Increasing Publication Costs

Other factors in science have had effects on the publication of scientific information. The improving technology used by researchers has resulted in significantly more research material. Improvements in transportation have resulted in more conference programming, and these proceedings tend to be published as either journal issues or monographs. Support costs for legislative lobbying and other political and continuing education issues (public relations, training, etc.) have been loaded onto the cost of institutional journal subscriptions. The "publish or perish" system developed in academia has created a situation that encouraged the Least Publishable Unit phenomenon—the replacement of one journal article by the creation of multiple journal articles composed of the smallest amount of material that can be considered an article. This attempt by scholars to appear to create more publications for promotion and tenure purposes ultimately increases the cost of publication and slows down the entire publication process. This is not to mention the frustration created for readers who want a concise reproduction of a concept in one logical paper.

The publish or perish situation has been treated in other fields in more creative ways. The education community attempts to allow distribution of certain materials through the development of a less-expensive cooperative clearinghouse for materials: ERIC, the Education Resource Information Clearinghouse. This collection of ERIC reports and ERIC documents is searchable as an online database and considered part of the academic warehouse. Copies of these documents are available from many library microfiche depositories. In many ways ERIC fulfills the same role as the Los Alamos preprint database (see entry 28) in providing a quick and inexpensive way to store, search, and distribute scientific information relating to education materials. The related ERIC Clearinghouse for Science, Mathematics, and Environmental Education is a gateway to information about teaching and learning resources, and is located at http://www.ericse.org/.

Specialization

Historically physics literature was more clearly divided between pure and applied research than many other scientific disciplines. Many other fields continue to have all their subfields published in one journal. The physics literature has been regularly splitting these new or developing fields into ever-smaller subdisciplines with either their own journals or new sections of existing journals. This has been done in both the society and commercial journals and allows researchers to obtain personal subscriptions to smaller journals. However, it means that these journals are compartmentalizing the literature and creating a greater need for indexes and abstracts if researchers desire a comprehensive coverage of their field. In these times of tight budgets it is much more difficult for libraries to subscribe to new journals than to simply increase their allocations to expanding titles.

Interdisciplinary Research

An increase in cross-disciplinary research, in areas such as surface science and chaos, has resulted in new collaborations that create tensions when deciding where these research manuscripts most logically should be published. The appropriate funding of cross-disciplinary journals is a challenge to librarians working with budgets that are allocated along traditional subject disciplines. Identifying the most appropriate citation databases for searching and retrieving these materials is an increasing challenge for researchers.

New Electronic Publications

Physics journals are now appearing in electronic formats. These electronic journals, or e-journals, are produced in various formats with a variety of features. Some e-journals are simply online reproductions of paper journals; some are moderately enhanced with links to supporting material; and others are fully integrated multimedia products. Many e-journals are novelty items located on small and often isolated publisher websites. Some publishers attempt to send e-journal information to individual scholars via e-mail—in some cases in direct opposition to library current awareness tools and intentions. Some individual e-journal titles are even split according to year of publication on different aggregator systems with completely different interfaces and options.

The eventual goal is to have these e-journals seamlessly linked to the larger information network of abstract and index (A&I) finding tools such as the INSPEC (see entry 35) and Science Citation Index (see entry 40) databases.

Some publishers and gateway services are attempting to integrate traditional abstracting and indexing with more proactive gateway functions such as online file cabinets and commenting features. Book and journal material has been distributed on CD-ROM for quite some time, and CD-ROMs may serve as a reasonable platform in certain small-scale environments. The first practical online book products are now being demonstrated.

In addition to the historical publication mechanism of paper journals and books, the new electronic networks provide many additional communication channels. There have always been alternative scientific networks such as the "Invisible College," the informal network of scholarly communications, which used formal preprints and informal personal communication. These channels have increased tremendously with the introduction of e-mail, listservs and electronic discussion groups, chat rooms, individual websites, and departmental and institutional websites. New media types (photographs, digital images, video, audio, online simulations, etc.) have also been added to the mix. Decentralization of information sources has become a problem for those interested in comprehensive searching. The introduction of important non-peer-reviewed information (e.g., teaching tools, software and hardware clearinghouses) has made the database and the search process even more complex. Variant formats (RevTeX, LaTeX, PostScript, PDF, HTML, etc.) have made the display of this information a major challenge for the typical researcher on a personal computer without technical support.

The Library's Role in the Electronic Future

This information explosion, when combined with the new media format possibilities and the increasing network characteristics, has led to user confusion and/or misinformation. The library and information science community has the responsibility to collaborate with researchers and information producers to design a seamless Knowledge Database that is at once easy, powerful, and logical. Otherwise we may end up with another Internet gopher scenario in which powerful navigation tools are developed by computer science personnel without any logical classification and organization principles. The most important issues that need to be addressed are those of federating independent and autonomous databases; creating normalized indexes to search across all databases simultaneously; developing metadata to identify context-specific descriptors across and within disciplines; enhancing filtering techniques for limiting results; including weighting techniques for filtering results; enhancing natural-language search interfaces; incorporating linking between articles and other documents; integrating personalized preferences, commenting capabilities, and filing systems for individuals, laboratory groups, and class purposes; and devising and implementing long-term archiving and migration technologies for the new electronic materials.

The future of physical sciences information transfer will include the present information channels and tools plus the creation of subject-specific information systems (Knowledge Databases; see chapter 11). Through the collaboration of librarians and information specialists with researchers, we will see the integration of both descriptive and content databases allowing search, retrieval, and postsearch manipulation of data. Personalized current awareness tools will provide automatic screening and notification (referred to as "push" technology; see chapter 2) to scholars when relevant ideas and content are added to databases in their areas of interest.

Until this seamless system is designed, users will need to consult library tools and librarians in order to identify the full range of literature resources. This book provides an overview of some of the most important tools for a physicist in search of published (and in some cases unpublished) information. A more comprehensive listing of paper resources can be found in the bibliography books listed in Chapter 1.

Further Reading

For an interesting and somewhat radical review of e-journal publishing ideas see:

John W. T. Smith. "The deconstructed journal—a new model for academic publishing." *Learned Publishing* 12(2), April 1999. ISSN 0953-1513. Available: http://libservb.ukc.ac.uk/library/papers/jwts/d-journal.htm (accessed May 4, 1999).

Chapter 1

Bibliographic Sources

This section includes selective listings of previously published guides to the literature, both physics-specific and for the general sciences; physics bibliographies and catalogs; history of physics sources; and special bibliometric reference tools and their uses. Many newer bibliographies no longer include listings for older publications; for this reason earlier editions are included for some major tools. See also chapter 12, "Important Works in the Development of Physics, 1600–1900," by Kristine Fowler.

Guides to the Literature

Physics

1.   Shaw, Dennis F., ed. **Information Sources in Physics**. 3rd ed. London: Bowker-Saur, 1994. 507p. (Guides to Information Sources). $105.00.

The definitive bibliography containing the most current and comprehensive coverage of the physics literature. An in-depth critical analysis of the literature in rather specific subdisciplines. Each section is written by research scientists, and coverage includes short field descriptions, journals, reference tools, and key textbooks. An excellent guide to the print literature for librarians and researchers when exploring materials outside their normal areas.

1a.   Shaw, Dennis F., ed. **Information Sources in Physics**. 2nd ed. London; Boston: Butterworths, 1985. 456p. (Butterworths Guides to Information Sources).

An earlier edition of the above title.

1

2. Arny, Linda Ray. **The Search for Data in the Physical and Chemical Sciences**. New York: Special Libraries Association, 1984. 158p. $45.10.

This volume provides sources and concepts used in the identification of numerical measurements of specific physical and chemical properties of well-defined substances or systems. Discusses compilers, sources, and important agencies and programs. Part 2 focuses on the data compilations of the [former] National Bureau of Standards [now the NIST, National Institute of Standards and Technology]. The index to selected NBS data compilations provides a very useful table of terms found in the literature that is cross-referenced to appropriate NBS publications.

3. Coblans, Herbert. **The Use of Physics Literature**. London; Boston: Butterworths, 1975. 290p. (Information Sources for Research and Development). ISBN 0408707097.

This work begins with five chapters on library methodologies and a physics literature overview. The remaining contributed chapters contain short reviews of the field and selected annotated sources in the following areas: patents and translations; history of physics; theoretical physics; astrophysics; mechanics and sound; heat and thermodynamics; light, electricity, and magnetism; nuclear and atomic physics; crystallography; instrumentation; and computer applications. The dated nature of the work makes the highlighted textbooks less useful, but the remaining information is still valid.

4. Whitford, Robert H. **Physics Literature: A Reference Manual**. 2nd ed. Metuchen, N.J.: Scarecrow Press, 1968. 272p.

A survey of physics literature at the college level, representing a working collection, and including an outline of library methodology. Divided into information-seeking realms: biographies, experiments, mathematics, education, terminology, and disciplines.

General Science

5. Hurt, Charlie, D. **Information Sources in Science and Technology**. 3rd ed. Englewood, Colo.: Libraries Unlimited, 1998. 346p. $55.00. ISBN 1563085313 (pa.).

An excellent resource guide for librarians and researchers covering the broad range of science.

This edition does not include much printed material before 1990, so keep the earlier edition on the shelf beside this book. Includes informative annotations, important URLs, and excellent indexing. A short section with the major physics tools is included. Best used for multidisciplinary subject coverage.

5a.   Hurt, Charlie Deuel. **Information Sources in Science and Technology**. Englewood, Colo.: Libraries Unlimited, 1988. 362p. (Library Science Text Series). ISBN 0872875814.

An earlier edition of the above title.

6.   Chen, Ching-chih. **Scientific and Technical Information Sources**. 2nd ed. Cambridge, Mass.: MIT Press, 1987. 824p. ISBN 0262031205.

Descriptive annotations of more than 400 post-1977 titles. Arranged by type of publication and then by subject. A very good tool for beginning librarians.

6a.   Chen, Ching-chih.   **Scientific and Technical Information Sources**. Cambridge, Mass.: MIT Press, 1977. 519p. ISBN 0262030624.

An earlier edition of the above title.

7.   Malinowsky, H. Robert. **Reference Sources in Science, Engineering, Medicine, and Agriculture**. Phoenix, Ariz.: Oryx Press, 1994. 355p. ISBN 0897747429.

Another excellent guide to resources across the sciences. Includes a brief section of evaluative annotations on the major physics tools. Best used for multidisciplinary subject coverage.

7a.   Malinowsky, H. Robert, and Jeanne M. Richardson. **Science and Engineering Literature: A Guide to Reference Sources**. 3rd ed. Littleton, Colo.: Libraries Unlimited, 1980. 342p.

An earlier edition of the above title. Many of the older entries are still valid as the paper sources do not change as rapidly as the new electronic tools.

7b.   Malinowsky, H. Robert, Richard A. Gray, and Dorothy A. Gray. **Science and Engineering Literature: A Guide to Reference Sources**. 2nd ed. Littleton, Colo.: Libraries Unlimited, 1976. 368p.

An earlier edition of the above title.

Bibliographies and Catalogs

8.   Smith, Roger. **Popular Physics and Astronomy: An Annotated Bibliography**. Lanham, Md.: Scarecrow Press; Pasadena, Calif.: Salem Press, 1996. 507p.

For both scholars and social critics who want to understand the recent popular physics phenomenon, and for "readers young and old, for students and armchair scientists alike, who want a thought-provoking, challenging, fun look at physics or astronomy." Includes 886 annotations with brief summaries of the content, the required mathematical level, illustrations, and indexing. Coverage includes books, anthologies, individual articles, and nonprint materials that require no more than high school algebra and calculus.

9. Yates, B. (Bryan). **How to Find Out About Physics: A Guide to Sources of Information Arranged by the Decimal Classification**. Oxford; New York: Pergamon Press, 1969. 175p. (Commonwealth and International Library. Libraries and Technical Information Division).

9a. Yates, Bryan. **How to Find Out About Physics: A Guide to Sources of Information Arranged by the Decimal Classification**. Oxford; New York: Pergamon Press, 1965. 175p.
An earlier edition of the above title.

10. Redman, L. A. **The Physics Teaching Handbook**. 3rd ed. London: Longman, 1971. 232p.

10a. Redman, L. A. **The Physics Teachers Handbook**. Lytham St. Annes, Eng.: Spectrum Books, 1966. 232p.
An earlier edition of the above title.

11. Parke, Nathan Grier. **Guide to the Literature of Mathematics and Physics Including Related Works on Engineering Science**. 2nd rev. ed. New York: Dover Publications, [1958]. 436p.
A guide to finding information for working mathematicians, applied mathematicians, physicists, and engineers. Compiled from a personal library of books. Part 1 (General Considerations) discusses how a library is organized, learning behaviors, and the research process. Part 2 (The Literature) has within subject headings short introductions, cross-references, and lists of books.

11a. Parke, Nathan Grier III. **Guide to the Literature of Mathematics and Physics Including Related Works on Engineering Science**. New York: McGraw-Hill, 1947. 205p.
An earlier edition of the above title.

History of Physics Resources

12. Brush, Stephen G. **Resources for the History of Physics: Guide to Books and Audiovisual Materials. Guide to Original Works of Historical Importance and Their Translations into Other Languages**. Hanover, N.H.: University Press of New England, 1972. 192p. $54.80. ISBN 031710599X.

In Part I, each item is coded for the intended age group, teacher, and/or library. Part II lists translations for physics students.

13. Brush, Stephen G., and Lanfranco Belloni. **The History of Modern Physics: An International Bibliography**. New York: Garland, 1983. 334p. (Bibliographies of the History of Science and Technology, vol. 4).

A critical/selective bibliography of the most important uncommon literature dealing with the history of physics; the major general history of science sources are only mentioned in the Introduction. Geophysics and astrophysics are not included, nor are materials covered in the *Isis Bibliography* (entries 15–18) or the *Literature on the History of Physics in the 20th Century* (see next entry). The entries are arranged by subdiscipline, and some contain brief descriptive annotations.

14. Heilbron, J. L., and Bruce R. Wheaton with J. G. May, Robin Rider, and David Robinson. **Literature on the History of Physics in the 20th Century**. Berkeley, Calif.: Office for History of Science and Technology, University of California, 1981. 485p. (Berkeley Papers in History of Science, vol. 5). $20.00. ISBN 0918102057.

A classic bibliography covering the history of physics. Includes an inventory of published letters to and from physicists, and an inventory of sources for the history of twentieth-century physics.

Isis Bibliographies

The Isis cumulative bibliographies (entries 15–18) are the basic source for archival bibliographies on subjects and personalities in the professional history of science literature.

15. The Isis Cumulative Bibliography, from 1976, is available on the Internet via the RLIN Eureka search engine as part of the **History of Science and Technology** database. The History of Science and Technology file describes journal articles, conference proceedings, books, book reviews, and dissertations in the history of science and technology and allied historical fields. The file comprises three bibliographies: *Isis Current Bibliography of the History of Science* (HSS) (1975–present), *Current Bibliography in the History of Technology* (Technology and Culture) (1987–present), and *Bibliografia Italiana di Storia della Scienza*. Updated annually, HST contains more than 119,000 records.

The paper versions of the Isis Bibliography are listed below (entries 16–18).

16.   Whitrow, Magda, ed. **Isis Cumulative Bibliography. A Bibliography of the History of Science from Isis Critical Bibliographies**. 1–90, 1913–1965. Volume I: (1972); Volume II: (1972); Volume III: Subjects; Volume IV: Institutions. London: Mansell with the History of Science Society, 1972.

17.   Neu, John, ed. **Isis Cumulative Bibliography, 1966–1975. A Bibliography of the History of Science, Formed from Isis Critical Bibliographies**. 91–100 indexing literature published from 1965 to 1974. Volume I: Personalities and Institutions. London: History of Science Society and Mansell, 1980. 514p. $240.00.

18.   Neu, John, ed. **Isis Cumulative Bibliography, 1976–1985**. Volume 1: Persons and Institutions. Volume 2: Subjects, Periods and Civilizations. Boston: G. K. Hall, 1989.

19.   Niels Bohr Library. **Guide to the Archival Collections in the Niels Bohr Library at the American Institute of Physics**. College Park, Md.: American Institute of Physics, 1994. 574p. (International Catalog of Sources for History of Physics and Allied Sciences, no. 7). $140.00. ISBN 1563963795.
Documentation and preservation of documents of potential significance for studying the development of physics. Interviews and oral histories with physicists, photographs, etc. Index of distributed archives. The eight chapters are arranged by format. See the website at http://www.aip.org/history/nblbro.htm (accessed May 4, 1999).

20.   Ezhela, V. V., et al. **Particle Physics: One Hundred Years of Discoveries: An Annotated Chronological Bibliography**. Woodbury, N.Y.: AIP Press, 1996. 340p. $52.00. ISBN 1563966425.
Annotated entries tracing the development of particle physics from the discovery of the electron (1897) through the discovery of the top quark (1995). Each entry includes the primary achievement, a summary of the work or excerpt, related references, reactions, reprint information, and particles studied. Author and subject indexes.

21.   Home, R. W., with Mark J. Gittins. **The History of Classical Physics: A Selected, Annotated Bibliography**. New York: Garland, 1984. 324p. (Garland Reference Library of the Humanities, vol. 420; Bibliographies of the History of Science and Technology, vol. 4).
A critical, annotated bibliography as opposed to an exhaustive bibliography, concentrating on the less popular works from 1895 to the present. Includes biographical information from obituaries after the mid-1950s, listings of anthology reprints, and translations of classic papers.

22. Stroke, H. Henry, ed. **The** *Physical Review*—**The First Hundred Years: A Selection of Seminal Papers and Commentaries**. New York: American Institute of Physics; College Park, Md.: American Physical Society, 1995. 1,200p. $99.00. ISBN 1563961881. Includes CD-ROM.

From the text: "The CD-ROM contains all the material in the book (except the photographs) as well as over 800 additional articles—a total of more than 7,500 pages."—p. xix. Includes bibliographical references and indexes. "System requirements: 386 or 486 IBM-compatible PC, VGA or SVGA monitor, hard disk drive, CD-ROM supported by Windows, 5 MB of free space, 4 MB RAM, MS-DOS 3.3 or later, Windows 3.1 or later, Microsoft DOS Extensions (MSCDEX) 2.21 or later."

A selection of 200 noteworthy articles from the first 100 years of *Physical Review* and *Physical Review Letters*, with an additional 800+ articles on the accompanying CD-ROM.

23. **Center for the History of Physics**. American Institute of Physics. http://www.aip.org/history/index.html (accessed May 4, 1999).

The American Institute of Physics' Center for the History of Physics was established "to preserve and make known the history of modern physics and allied fields including astronomy, geophysics, optics, and the like." The Center's website provides original content on the history of physics and details research efforts and facilities. Among the resources available are: full text of biannual newsletter dating from the Fall 1994 issue, information on selected publications of the Center for History of Physics and the Niels Bohr Library, and descriptions of the extensive collections in the history of physics and allied fields in the Niels Bohr Library.

24. **AIP Center for History of Physics Newsletter**. American Institute of Physics. http://www.aip.org/history/web-news.htm (accessed May 4, 1999).

The American Institute of Physics Center for the History of Physics Newsletter covers work on the history of physics and related fields. It includes news, announcements, biographies, and announcements for publications of interest. The website provides full text and illustrations from newsletters going back to the Fall of 1994. Also included is information on print subscriptions.

25. **Web Sites for the History of Science**. American Institute of Physics. http://www.aip.org/history/web-link.htm (accessed May 4, 1999).

Includes selected websites under the headings of: Sites with History of Science Links; History of Science Community; Archival and Bibliography Resources; and General History—General Physics.

See also chapter 12, "Important Works in the Development of Physics, 1600–1900," by Kristine Fowler.

Bibliometric Reference Tools

Evaluation and Administration Data from the Library

The modern library provides much more than scientific facts. Electronic tools allow researchers to evaluate the productivity and impact of their own work, the work of a department, an organization, and even specific journal titles. These new databases (e.g., University Science Indicators and Journal Citation Reports) join Science Citation Index as premier tools enabling the bibliometric analysis of scientific research.

Bibliometrics involves the use of various statistical analyses to determine patterns and relationships between and among published materials. These techniques may include calculating the raw number and growth of items in a specific field or the number of items created by particular organizations or individuals, and identifying any linkages between items, which are often determined by analyzing citation information over time. Another bibliometric technique often used to determine "value" is the creation of Impact Factors. The Institute for Scientific Information (ISI), an indexing and analysis company, compiles citation frequency data and calculates this Impact Factor using the cited reference data. An Impact Factor is the relationship between an identified domain (such as a journal or a university) and the average of a broader group (such as similar journals covering a subject discipline). Impacts are generated in comparison to other domains. The Impact Factor "relative to field" is the citation impact for a known entity (e.g., journal or university) in a particular field divided by the citation impact for the field as a whole. For example, if papers in the field of physics published at Yale have a relative impact of 1.83, the papers have been cited 83% more than physics papers produced at the average university.

26. **University Science Indicators** (USI), available as a set of floppy disks or as an online database from the Institute for Scientific Information (ISI), allows for comparisons by discipline across the top 100 U.S. research universities. Over multiple year periods, productivity and impact data can be charted in a variety of ways (e.g., data tables, pie charts, bar graphs). A sample of the possible analyses that can be produced includes examining the total number of publications, Impact Factors, total number of articles by department relative to organizational output, total number of articles by department relative to the universe of publications, Impact Factors by department relative to organizational output, and Impact Factors by department relative to the universe of publications. An example report might compare any of these categories across the physics departments from Yale, Harvard, and Cornell.

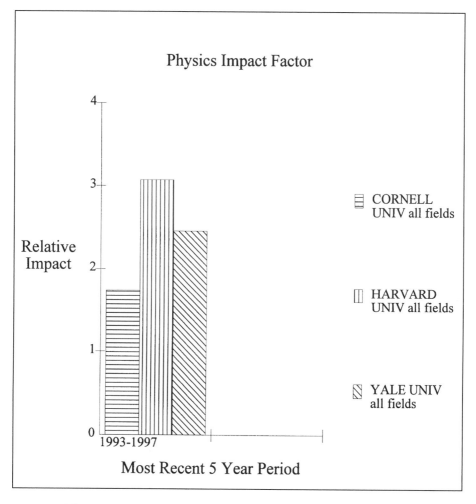

Fig. 1. University Science Indicators departmental comparison

27. **Journal Citation Reports** (JCR), also produced by ISI, provides production and Impact Factor data for hundreds of scientific journals.
Users can compare the Impact Factor of a journal in relation to other journal
titles. It is also possible to track citation patterns among specific journals.
Examples of results include reviewing the most cited journals from *Nature*,
reviewing the journals that most often cite *Nature* articles, monitoring
five-year patterns of citations to and from *Physical Review Letters*, reviewing the self-citations within any specific journal, tracking the growth of
journals over a time period, and determining a rough approximation of the
relative importance/impact of any journal through reviewing the quality
and distribution of its citations.

Science Citation Index (entry 40) allows researchers to search citing and cited references from thousands of interdisciplinary journals. Researchers can track all references to any published work since its publication by finding the number of later citations to any previously published article, and/or finding the actual references and abstracts to those citing articles. It is possible to continue this tracking approach to determine the seminal papers and the scope of new fields within a discipline. This same approach can be used to identify and evaluate all publications by a department, university, or organization. This tool can also identify related research by comparing references in articles and finding those articles with similarities in citation clusters that do not cite each other (Related Records). This discovery method can help promote new cross-disciplinary research and collaborations.

28.   Los Alamos National Laboratory (LANL) has an innovative reference tool, the **xxx.lanl.gov** e-print server, that incorporates a variety of bibliometric clustering techniques to help users find related documents. The system presents users with two options from any citation: identify later relevant articles through citations to either the e-print or the eventual published article (using the ISI data mentioned above) or find similar articles using other analysis techniques (word frequency analysis).

High Energy Physics - Experiment, abstract hep-ex/9903017

From: Victor Steiner <steiner@lepton.tau.ac.il>
Date: Thu, 11 Mar 1999 19:11:10 GMT   (49kb)

Hadron-Photon Interactions in COMPASS

Authors: Murray A. Moinester, Victor Steiner, Serguei Prakhov
Comments: 10 pages, 3 figures, 3 macros
Report-no: TAUP-2562-99

> The COMPASS experiment at CERN SPS will use hadron beams (pion, kaon and proton) and muons at 50-280 GeV/c and virtual photon targets to investigate, via Primakoff effect, important hadron properties: polarizability, chiral anomaly, radiative transitions and hybrid meson production. We present simulation studies to optimize the beam, detector setup and trigger for measuring with high statistics above topics.

Paper: <u>Source</u> (49kb), <u>PostScript</u>, or <u>Other formats</u>

(<u>N.B.</u>: delivery types and potential problems)

refers <u>to</u> , cited <u>by</u>

Links to: <u>xxx</u>, **<u>hep-ex</u>**, /<u>find</u>, /<u>abs</u> (<u>-</u>/+), /<u>9903</u>, <u>?</u> | form interface |

www-admin@xxx.lanl.gov

Fig. 2. LANL preprint options

Scientist Behaviors and Trends

A number of published works attempt to describe the working patterns and publication trends of research scientists. Below are listed a few books and journal articles that are worth reviewing.

Library Trends

29. Stankus, Tony. **Making Sense of Journals in the Physical Sciences: From Specialty Origins to Contemporary Assortment**. New York: Haworth Press, 1992. 239p. $49.95. ISBN 1560241802.

The most important reading material for any librarian responsible for creating and maintaining a physics library collection. Stankus offers short histories, criteria, analysis, and conclusions about the journal literature in physics and chemistry. He relies heavily on bibliometrics, cost factors, and anecdotal knowledge to understand and explain the patterns of physics journal publishing. Journals are compared within subject areas.

30.   Stankus, Tony, ed. **Scientific Journals: Improving Library Collections Through Analysis of Publishing Trends**. New York: Haworth Press, 1990. 206p. $39.95. ISBN 0866569057.

This book focuses on issues of importance for acquisitions, providing a theoretical basis and data for selection and deselection decisions. The book is arranged around three themes: scientist literature use and creation behavior over career changes, world publication patterns (distributions, subspecialty title generation, etc.) in the sciences, and technology and its impact on journal publication. This book provides a complete analysis of the factors at work in the paper-based science publishing arena. It should be required reading for science acquisitions librarians.

31.   Stankus, Tony, ed. **Scientific Journals: Issues in Library Selection and Management**. New York: Haworth Press, 1987. 218p. $39.95. ISBN 0866566163.

This thoughtful collection of articles raises questions that any collection development librarian in the sciences should consider. Themes cover the following areas: scholar demands and behaviors, international considerations (languages, loyalties, etc.), understanding subject fields using journal analysis, and resolutions to some journal analysis controversies (use and citation studies, quality indicators for tenure and promotion decisions, etc.). Important and interesting findings are presented in the usual no-nonsense Stankus style.

32.   Mount, Ellis, ed. **The Role of Trade Literature in Sci-Tech Libraries**. New York: Haworth Press, 1990. 135p. $29.95. ISBN 1560240385.

Selected Journal Articles

About Publishing Trends

Everest, M. J. "Comparison of the performance of SDI profiles on the INSPEC database, before and after the addition of searchable abstracts." *Journal of Information Science* 17 (1) (1991): 37–42.

"The magnitude of conference proceedings published in physics." *Special Libraries* 86 (2) (Spring 1995): 136–44.

"The relationship between price and citation data for journals in 2 subject areas." *Proceedings of the ASIS Annual Meeting* 30 (1993): 151–59.

Scientist Behavior Studies

Bayer, B., and F. G. Kilgour. "Scholarly use of referenced information in physics journals." *Journal of the American Society for Information Science* 47 (2) (February 1996): 170–72.

Youngen, Gregory K. "Citation patterns to traditional and electronic pre-prints in the published literature." *College and Research Libraries* 59 (5) (September 1998): 448–56.

33.   Walker, Richard D., and C. D. Hurt. **Scientific and Technical Literature: An Introduction to Forms of Communication**. Chicago: American Library Association, 1990. 297p. $15.00. ISBN 0838905390.

An investigation into the use of science and technology literature by scientists and engineers. Communication decisions are based on a complex mixture of information gathering and distribution needs, priority claims, and promotion and tenure concerns. In addition, new factors of technology enhancement (e.g., formats, limitations) are considered. The emphasis is on written and archival forms of communication; however, informal channels are touched on as the authors recognize the importance of considering the entire continuum of possibilities. As research fields are changing due to the narrowing of traditional disciplines and the interdisciplinary nature of new problem-oriented approaches, there is a restructuring of the *niche corpi* of literature. This book provides an excellent review of the traditional (and still core) communication methodologies for scientists. An update is desperately needed to assimilate the new Internet-based possibilities.

Chapter 2

Abstracting and Indexing Databases

Introduction

Abstracting and Indexing (A&I) tools are intended to provide search capabilities to assist researchers in the identification of relevant documents from a variety of primary (original) and secondary (review) information resources. The traditional A&I tool in physics is *Physics Abstracts*, which has provided citations to the peer-reviewed physics literature since 1898. Indexes and catalogs to book materials are covered in chapter 4. Other A&I tools cover the field of physics to varying degrees. This chapter will attempt to identify and explain the coverage and utility of these tools according to their characteristics.

Journal A&I Tool Features

In evaluating A&I tools one must determine how well the intended scope and search capabilities of a resource match the needs of the particular question. The same tool may not provide the best access for an individual in every instance. The following characteristics of A&I tools must be considered:

Scope of coverage: Each A&I tool intends to cover a portion of the literature, and it is important to understand the parameters of the domain that is indexed. Discipline-based tools intend to be subject-specific, while others attempt to be interdisciplinary. Certain tools only index materials at the professional level of expertise; some attempt to cover only popular material; and others attempt to cover all levels. Many discipline-based tools attempt to be comprehensive and cover all types of material (i.e., journals, books, conferences, and grey/unpublished materials) and all languages, but some only cover portions of the literature. Special current awareness A&I tools concentrate on currency, while others prefer to emphasize added value (abstracts and indexing) over speed. Certain tools include abstracts and will create abstracts if they are not supplied by the author. A&I tools might include special added value such as enhanced metadata (e.g., concept codes, numerical and chemical indexing) and range searching. Various indexes only cover peer-reviewed material, while others cover preprints, websites, and other information items. Some A&I tools also serve as gateways to full-text materials, either as seamless links to outside servers or as an extension of their own locally mounted materials.

Arrangement of the search options: Almost all A&I tools, be they paper-based or online, provide basic searching of author names and some form of subject access. Some will use the PACS subject schema (see this book's main introduction for the outline of this classification scheme). Many online tools will also provide powerful keyword searching capability. Online A&I tools may include subject thesauri for controlled vocabulary classification. Online tools may also provide the ability to limit results using a variety of approaches, including by language, date, publication type (e.g., journal article, conference proceeding, review article), and theoretical or experimental emphasis. They often allow the sorting of results by options such as alphabetical by author or journal title. Online tools may weight search results using a variety of techniques such as word frequency analysis and user-identified variables. Some online A&I tools can provide links between citations by cross-referencing and by citation analyses. Most online tools allow users to mark specific records for printing, saving to disk, or e-mail delivery; often they provide formatting options for customizing and integrating these results into personal database management software (see "Personal Bibliographic Database Software" section).

Unfortunately, the proliferation of proprietary search interfaces has resulted in a confusing array of search screens for users.

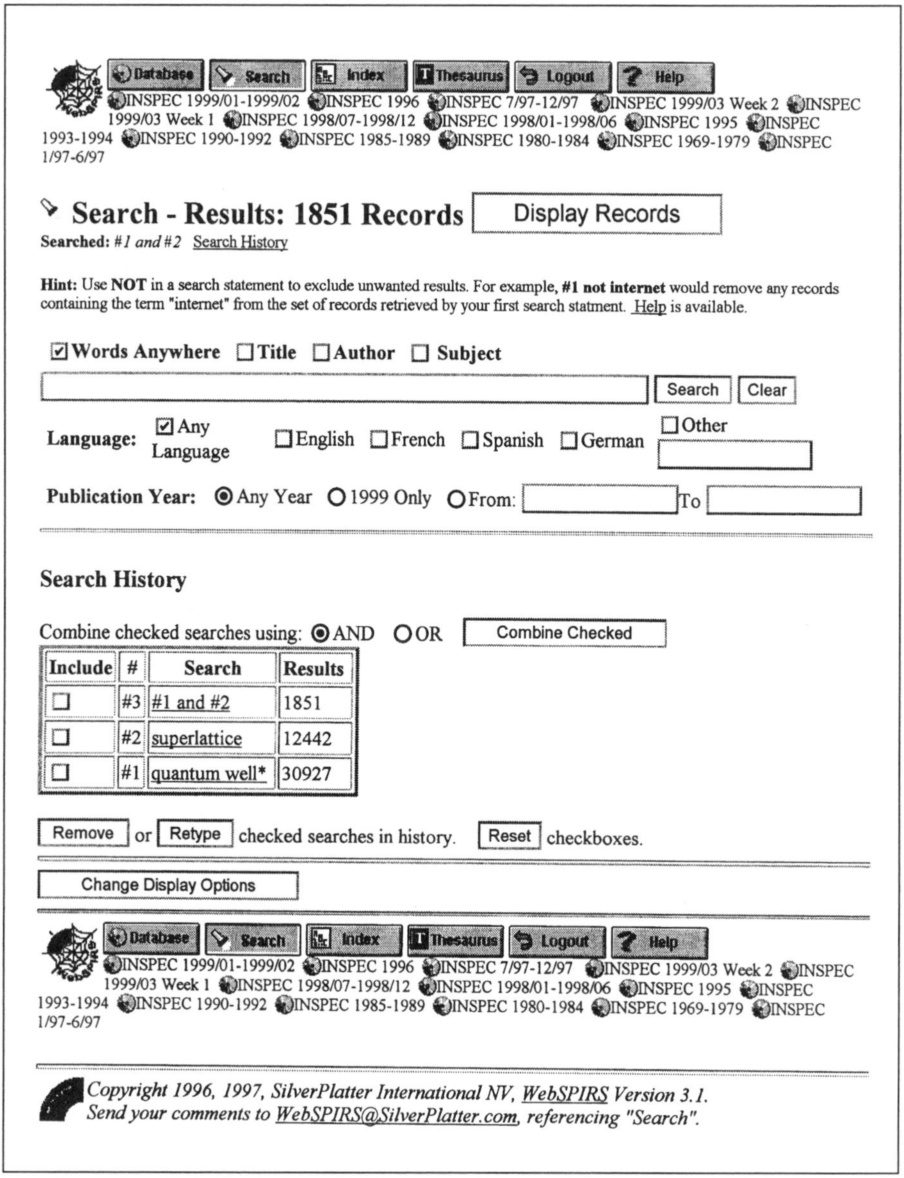
Database
Search
Index
Thesaurus
Logout
Help
INSPEC 1999/01-1999/02 INSPEC 1996 INSPEC 7/97-12/97 INSPEC 1999/03 Week 2 INSPEC 1999/03 Week 1 INSPEC 1998/07-1998/12 INSPEC 1998/01-1998/06 INSPEC 1995 INSPEC 1993-1994 INSPEC 1990-1992 INSPEC 1985-1989 INSPEC 1980-1984 INSPEC 1969-1979 INSPEC 1/97-6/97
Search - Results: 1851 Records
Display Records
Searched: #1 and #2 Search History
Hint: Use NOT in a search statement to exclude unwanted results. For example, #1 not internet would remove any records containing the term "internet" from the set of records retrieved by your first search statment. Help is available.
Words Anywhere
Title
Author
Subject
Search
Clear
Language:
Any Language
English
French
Spanish
German
Other
Publication Year:
Any Year
1999 Only
From:
To
Search History
Combine checked searches using:
AND
OR
Combine Checked
Include
#
Search
Results
#3
#1 and #2
1851
#2
superlattice
12442
#1
quantum well*
30927
Remove
or
Retype
checked searches in history.
Reset
checkboxes.
Change Display Options
Database
Search
Index
Thesaurus
Logout
Help
INSPEC 1999/01-1999/02 INSPEC 1996 INSPEC 7/97-12/97 INSPEC 1999/03 Week 2 INSPEC 1999/03 Week 1 INSPEC 1998/07-1998/12 INSPEC 1998/01-1998/06 INSPEC 1995 INSPEC 1993-1994 INSPEC 1990-1992 INSPEC 1985-1989 INSPEC 1980-1984 INSPEC 1969-1979 INSPEC 1/97-6/97
Copyright 1996, 1997, SilverPlatter International NV, WebSPIRS Version 3.1.
Send your comments to WebSPIRS@SilverPlatter.com, referencing "Search".

Fig. 3. SilverPlatter INSPEC search interface

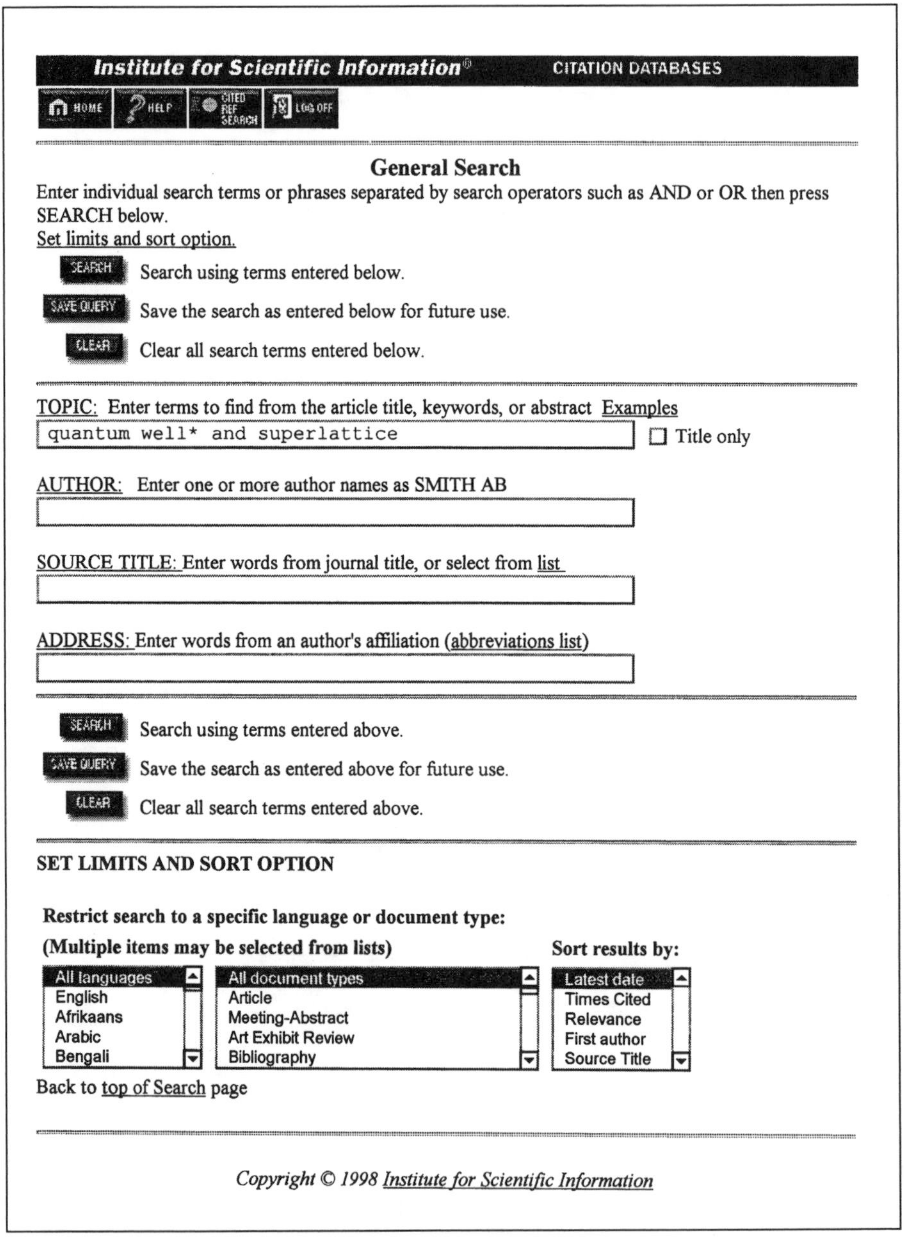

Institute for Scientific Information®   CITATION DATABASES

[HOME] [HELP] [CITED REF SEARCH] [LOG OFF]

General Search

Enter individual search terms or phrases separated by search operators such as AND or OR then press SEARCH below.
Set limits and sort option.

[SEARCH]   Search using terms entered below.

[SAVE QUERY]   Save the search as entered below for future use.

[CLEAR]   Clear all search terms entered below.

TOPIC: Enter terms to find from the article title, keywords, or abstract Examples

    quantum well* and superlattice   ☐ Title only

AUTHOR: Enter one or more author names as SMITH AB

SOURCE TITLE: Enter words from journal title, or select from list

ADDRESS: Enter words from an author's affiliation (abbreviations list)

[SEARCH]   Search using terms entered above.

[SAVE QUERY]   Save the search as entered above for future use.

[CLEAR]   Clear all search terms entered above.

SET LIMITS AND SORT OPTION

Restrict search to a specific language or document type:
(Multiple items may be selected from lists)   **Sort results by:**

All languages ▲	All document types ▲	Latest date ▲
English	Article	Times Cited
Afrikaans	Meeting-Abstract	Relevance
Arabic	Art Exhibit Review	First author
Bengali ▼	Bibliography ▼	Source Title ▼

Back to top of Search page

Fig. 4. ISI SCI search interface

O V I D **Current Contents/All Editions**
January 1998 to Present   [? Help]

Author Title Journal Search Fields Browse Contents Tools Combine Limit Basic Change Database Logoff

#	Search History	Results	Display
1	quantum well$.mp. [mp=abstract, title, author keywords, keywords plus]	2985	Display
2	superlattice.mp. [mp=abstract, title, author keywords, keywords plus]	809	Display
3	1 and 2	173	Display

● Run Saved Search   ● Save Search History   ● Delete All Searches

Enter **Keyword** or phrase:

[   ]   (Perform Search)

Limit to:
☐ Local Holdings ☐ English ☐ Articles ☐ Reviews ☐ Abstracts
☐ Latest Update
From: 1994 ▼ To: 1999 ▼

Help From A Human

Results of your search: **1 and 2**
Citations available: **173**
Citations displayed: **1-10**
☑   Citations in "Titles Display" format

☐ 1. Zimmermann S. Wixforth A. Kotthaus JP. Wegscheider W. Bichler M. A semiconductor-based photonic memory cell. [Article] *Science. 283(5406):1292-1295, 1999 Feb 26.* Table of Contents | Abstract | Complete Reference

☐ 2. Meinert G. Banyai L. Haug H. Valence band structure of a GaAs **superlattice**. [Article] *Physica Status Solidi B-Basic Research. 211(2):651-659, 1999 Feb.* Table of Contents | Abstract | Complete Reference

☐ 3. Toropov AA. Shubina TV. Sorokin SV. Lebedev AV. Kyutt RN. Ivanov SV. Karlsteen M. Willander M. Pozina GR. Bergman JP. Monemar B. Broadening of the excitonic mobility edge in a macroscopically disordered CdSe/ZnSe short-period **superlattice**. [Article] *Physical Review B-Condensed Matter. 59(4):R2510-R2513, 1999 Jan 15.* Table of Contents | Abstract | Complete Reference

☐ 4. Rashkeev SN. Limpijumnong S. Lambrecht WRL. Second-harmonic generation and birefringence

Fig. 5. Ovid Current Contents search interface

Current Awareness Tools and Techniques

Current awareness tools were originally developed to provide faster access to the new journal literature. Paper-based current awareness tools provide a competitive advantage over traditional A&I services by reproducing the tables of contents from recently released paper journals before they can be indexed and classified. In addition to fast and convenient scanning of new journals, these tools allow researchers to see what is published in journals that their organization does not receive.

Automatic Search and Delivery Service

In this age of information overload most researchers do not have the time to scan the latest journals in their immediate areas, not to mention the general science journals or materials published in journals that are somewhat peripheral to their specific field. Even the Letters sections of subject-specific journals are too numerous to be browsed by most researchers. A simple way for scholars to be alerted to new articles in their areas of interest is to create search strategies of their important concepts and have these run against the newest information added to an A&I tool. Many online tools allow researchers to store their search strategies for later use. In some cases they provide automatic searching and delivery of matching items as a current awareness service. This is traditionally referred to in the library world as Selective Dissemination of Information (SDI) or AutoAlert, and as push technology in the computer world. Those researchers without institutional support should consider individual SDI options through commercial vendors (see "Personal Current Awareness Services" section below).

Domains of Current Awareness Services

There are two major types of current awareness tools available for physicists from traditional A&I-type resources, although informal tools such as conference communications, listservs/electronic discussion groups, and e-mail correspondence serve as other efficient and effective techniques.

Peer Review–Based Tools

The first A&I tools cover those items that have made it through the traditional peer review publication process. These tools provide valuable filtering, but the materials they cover are often quite behind the leading edge when one considers the time lag in the peer review and publishing processes. Current awareness tools such as *Current Contents* (see entry 43) were developed to reduce the time lag within the A&I services by emphasizing speed of access over depth of indexing.

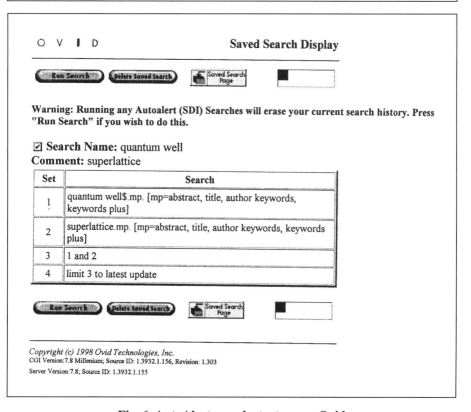

Fig. 6. AutoAlert search strategy on Ovid

Preprints and E-prints

The second set of tools provides access to prepublication materials. The SLAC SPIRES databases and the LANL preprint server are examples of these new tools that provide instant notification, and in many cases full-text distribution, of newly created physics research documents.

The Peer Review Debate

There are still debates about the validity of materials before they have passed through the peer review process, but these tools have become a major communication channel for many areas of physics in recent years. The integration of these preprints, or e-prints, into the traditional A&I services, which have only included peer reviewed material until now, is a major issue if one intends to provide a single search interface for all relevant physics material. The debate rages on, as does the issue of whether posted e-prints are still considered unpublished and are eligible for "first printing" in traditional journals. Most journals will now accept these e-prints but often require that the prepublication e-prints are removed or modified upon publication of the final documents.

Multiple Hosts and Variant Database Segments

Adding to the confusion is the fact that many of these A&I tools are available from various vendors/hosts, and each vendor provides at least one somewhat unique interface with small but often significantly different options. The actual database may be different in some cases. The currency of the information is dependent on a number of circumstances, such as whether the database is loaded locally, accessed via a consortial network, or located directly on a vendor server. Some vendors provide a variety of search engines and interfaces, limited hours of searching, alternative pricing models, and a variety of years of data depending upon the package selected.

Summary

For the present it is best to use the following complementary A&I tools in combination to provide both fast access to the literature using simple techniques and later identification of literature using more sophisticated and powerful indexing options. Unless authors begin tagging articles with better indexing at the time of creation, there will always be a time lag for classification. Automatic indexing has not proven efficient or effective, and full-text searching does not contain the context-specific information that postpublication metadata indexing provides.

Physics A&I Databases

34. **Physics Abstracts**. (Science Abstracts, Part A). London: Institution of Electrical Engineers, 1898–present.

The most comprehensive physics A&I tool in terms of number of documents, types of documents (journals, conferences, dissertations, grey literature), and indexing options. This index allows for powerful added-value searching through enhanced metadata indexing of properties such as temperatures, pressures, chemical formula, and roles of items within processes. This data allow for powerful range searching of these numerical indexes and sophisticated searching of the complex chemical indexing. The current breakdown of materials is: 77% articles (selected from 4,000 technical journals), 21% conference papers, and 2% books, chapters, dissertations, and reports.

PAPER: Divided into 10 subject areas, with six-month cumulated author, subject indexes. Title was *Science Abstracts* until 1958.

35. ONLINE DATABASE: Physics Abstracts is a portion of **INSPEC**, 1969–present.

INSPEC is the leading English-language abstracting and indexing service providing source information from the world's literature on all aspects of physics, electronics, and computing. INSPEC scans papers from approximately 4,200 journals, 1,000 conferences, and other publications, adding more than 250,000 records each year. Weekly updates.

Hosts: Ovid, SP, IoP, STN, Dialog (IoP Axiom provides enhanced personalized options).

Notes: *Physics Abstracts* can be provided in a variety of packages and on a variety of platforms. The paper copy (ISSN 0036-8091) is available for $4,230 per year as of 1999. The CD-ROM subfile of the larger INSPEC CD-ROM package, which covers 1989 to the present, is available on one disc at $5,745 per year as of 1999. The online remote access version is available as a part of the INSPEC database from a variety of hosts; it is available as either (1) a per-transaction search option or as (2) an unlimited flat-fee service for approximately $29,000 as of 1999. Another possibility is the loading of the data on a local search engine (e.g., Ovid, SilverPlatter, BASIS). There are discounts available when the Physics Abstracts portion is ordered as part of the larger INSPEC database.

35a. **List of Journals and Other Serial Sources**. London: Institution of Electrical Engineers, 1983– . Irregular.

Variant Title: INSPEC List of Journals and Other Serial Sources.

Lists titles covered by the INSPEC database, plus CODENs, abbreviations, and translation information.

36. **Referativnyi Zhurnal. Fizika**. Moscow: Institut Nauchno-Tekhnicheskoi Informatsii, 1954– .

An excellent abstracting and indexing tool covering the disciplines of physics. Slower to produce abstracts than the competition, *Physics Abstracts* (see entry 34).

37. **Physikalische Berichte** (ceased). New York: Verlag Chemie International, 1920–1978.

Superseded by Physics Briefs. PHYS was the online database.

Physics Briefs (ceased). New York: American Institute of Physics, 1979–1991.

Was a major competitor to *Physics Abstracts* until it ceased. Coverage of the European material and the grey (unpublished) literature was its strength.

38. **Current Physics Index**. American Institute of Physics. 1975– .

Provides current information about physics research published in AIP and member-society primary publications. Its quarterly issues contain approximately 9,000 abstracts of articles published in 54 primary journals, classified by subject according to AIP's Physics and Astronomy Classification Scheme.

PAPER: Monthly author and subject indexes.

39. ONLINE DATABASE: **SPIN** (Searchable Physics Information Notices), 1975– .

SPIN coverage includes all journals and proceedings published by AIP and its 10 member societies (this is the online *Current Physics Index*), as well as other American scientific journals, a total of more than 80 journals (nearly 750,000 research records). The abstracts are available online at the time the articles are published in the journal. Information provided in each SPIN entry includes article title, all authors and affiliations, bibliographic information, the author abstract, classsification codes, and index terms. SPIN is updated every two weeks, with approximately 45,000 new records added each year. SPIN coverage extends back to 1975. SPIN is a search service on the SPIN web network (free to member subscribers, available as a library subscription).

40. **Science Citation Index**. Philadelphia: Institute for Scientific Information, 1961– .

A unique and powerful tool. Interdisciplinary coverage from more than 12,000 research journals; reasonable journal coverage in most fields, but little coverage of conferences, books, and grey literature. This database provides citation values for particular papers and citation tracking, plus Related Records for unique approaches to identifying the leading edge of research fields. The database is created from *Current Contents* records plus additional titles, and therefore has good currency. There are no controlled vocabulary or hierarchical subject search capability. There are fewer abstracts than most standard A&I services for searching and display.

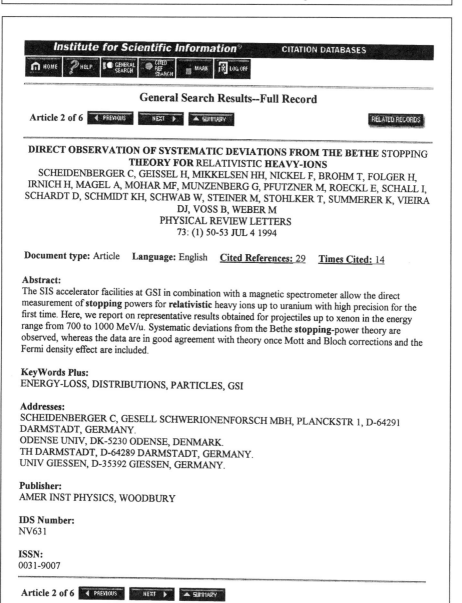

Fig. 7. SCI: Citation Tracking and Related Records Features

PAPER: Keyword in title and author searching only—no subject indexing. Cumulative indexes for 1955–1964, 1965–1969, 1970–1974, 1975–1979, 1980–1984, 1985–1989.
ONLINE DATABASE: Science Citation Index (1974–present).
Hosts: STN, Dialog, ISI website (part of Web of Science).

41. The **Web of Science** is the online version of the following three files:

Science Citation Index Expanded (SCI-EXPANDED)—1973–present

Social Sciences Citation Index (SSCI)—1973–present

Arts & Humanities Citation Index (A&HCI)—1975–present

42. **Source Publications/Science Citation Index Expanded**. Philadelphia: Institute for Scientific Information, 1998– . Annual.
Variant Title: Science Citation Index Expanded. Source Publications.
The list of publications covered by Science Citation Index. Includes the unique journal abbreviations used by ISI.

43. **Current Contents**. Philadelphia: Institute for Scientific Information, 1961– .
Reproduces the latest tables of contents from more than 10,000 major research journals. Includes keyword title and author indexes. No subject headings or controlled vocabulary are used. The most important features are the currentness of information and the ability to scan table of contents from nonsubscription titles. When enhanced with citation links these data become a part of both the *Science Citation Index* and the *Web of Science* databases. There are multiple subject sections.
PAPER: **Chemical, Physical, and Earth Sciences** section. Produced weekly.
ONLINE DATABASE: **Current Contents**
An interdisciplinary database including the latest titles, authors (some abstracts), and tables of contents from more than 10,000 major research journals. SDI capabilities on some hosts.
Hosts: ISI website, Ovid, Dialog, STN.

44. **SLAC SPIRES** (Stanford Public Information REtrieval System). http://www.slac.stanford.edu/find/spires.html (accessed May 4, 1999).
The following SLAC Library databases are currently accessible.

44a. **Books**.
SLAC Library book catalog. See also the list of books received in the last four weeks, or "clickable" subject lists, A through K and L through Z, for the BOOKS database.

44b. **HEP Preprints, E-Prints, Articles**.
HEP preprint database contains bibliographic summaries of more than 374,000 particle physics papers. Included are preprints, journal articles, technical reports, theses, etc. Searchable by author, title, report number, institution, collaboration, and more. Find citations to favorite author or article. View Postscript versions of selected preprints, read abstracts of the e-print archive papers. Earliest papers are from 1974.

44c. **Recent e-Prints**.

Useful in searching for recent high-energy physics e-prints from the Los Alamos archives, perhaps not yet covered by the HEP database. Find abstracts and viewable Postscript of articles posted today, yesterday, in the last seven days, in the week before that, or anytime. Preferred access to older e-prints is through the HEP preprint database (above).

45. **LANL** (Los Alamos National Laboratory) preprint server. http://xxx.lanl.gov (accessed May 4, 1999).

As with other preprint servers, this system provides some enhanced linkages (full-text and citation information) but also creates some difficulty for users due to alternative formats and compression algorithms.

Each section has the following options:

New—see the latest entries

Recent—see recent entries

Abs—view the abstracts

Find—search for specific terms

SDIs are also available within the following subdivisions:

Physics

Astrophysics (astro-ph)

Condensed Matter (cond-mat)

includes: Disordered Systems and Neural Networks; Materials Science; Mesoscopic Systems and Quantum Hall Effect; Soft Condensed Matter; Statistical Mechanics; Strongly Correlated Electrons; Superconductivity

General Relativity and Quantum Cosmology (gr-qc)

High Energy Physics—Experiment (hep-ex)

High Energy Physics—Lattice (hep-lat)

High Energy Physics—Phenomenology (hep-ph)

High Energy Physics—Theory (hep-th)

Mathematical Physics (math-ph)

Nuclear Experiment (nucl-ex)

Nuclear Theory (nucl-th)

physics (physics)

includes (see detailed description): Accelerator Physics; Atmospheric and Oceanic Physics; Atomic Physics; Atomic and Molecular Clusters; Biological Physics; Chemical Physics; Classical Physics; Computational Physics; Data Analysis, Statistics and Probability; Fluid Dynamics; General Physics; Geophysics; History of Physics; Instrumentation and Detectors; Medical Physics; Optics; Physics Education; Physics and Society; Plasma Physics; Popular Physics; Space Physics

Quantum Physics (quant-ph)

Mathematics

Mathematics (math)

includes (see detailed description): Algebraic Geometry; Algebraic Topology; Analysis of PDEs; Category Theory; Classical Analysis; Combinatorics; Complex Variables; Differential Geometry; Dynamical Systems; Functional Analysis; General Topology; Geometric Topology; Group Theory; History and Overview; Infinite Group Theory; K-Theory and Homology; Linear Algebra; Logic; Mathematical Physics; Metric Geometry; Number Theory; Numerical Analysis; Operator Algebras; Optimization and Control; Probability Theory; Quantum Algebra; Representation Theory; Rings and Algebras; Scientific Computation; Spectral Theory; Symplectic Geometry

Nonlinear Science

Adaptation, Noise, and Self-Organizing Systems (adap-org)

Chaotic Dynamics (chao-dyn)

Cellular Automata and Lattice Gases (comp-gas)

Nonlinear Sciences (nlin-sys)

Pattern Formation and Solitons (patt-sol)

Exactly Solvable and Integrable Systems (solv-int)

46. **SPIN Web**.
http://ojps.aip.org/spinweb/ (accessed November 10, 1999).
This site replaces the PiNet Plus Research Library network and includes the following:
SPIN (Searchable Physics Information Notices) database: (see entry 39) and

47. **Advance Abstracts**. Available to subscribers only, Advance Abstracts is composed of two individual source databases: General Physics Advance Abstracts (GPAA) and Physical Review Abstracts (PRAbs). Search both databases individually or collectively. Review abstracts of articles in AIP and Member Society journals before publication.

Browse SPIN Journal Collection allows a researcher to browse the tables of contents of AIP published and affiliated journals by issue, and to read the abstracts of included articles. Journal titles are arranged both alphabetically and by affiliation.

Tables of Contents Notification Service. This feature offers automatic advance notice of the contents of three AIP journals—not only before they are listed by other abstracting or indexing services, but before the journals even go to print. Simply select the three journals and the contents will be automatically e-mailed up to four weeks prior to publication.

Physics News Service. A gateway to the Public Information Division of the AIP.

Member Directories. A affiliated Member Society directories are searchable.

48.   **J. C. Poggendorffs biographisch-literarisches handwöorterbuch föur mathematik, astronomie, physik mit geophysik, chemie, kristallographie und verwandte wissensgebiete** . . . Leipzig: J. A. Barth, 1863–1904: Leipzig/Berlin, Verlag Chemie, g.m.b.h., 1926– . Edited by Poggendorff, J. C. (Johann Christian), 1796–1877.

Title Varies: 1.–2. bd., Biographisch-literarisches handwöorterbuch zur geschichte der exacten wissenschaften enthaltend nachweisungen öuber lebensverhöaltnisse und leistungen von mathematikern, astronomen, physikern, chemikern, mineralogen, geologen usw. aller vöolker und zeiten; 3.–4. bd., J. C. Poggendorff's biographisch-literarisches handwöorterbuch . . . bd. v– J. C.

Contents: 1. bd. A–L. 1863.—2. bd. M–Z. 1863.—3. bd. 1858–1883. 1898.—4. bd. 1883–1904. 1904.—5. bd. 1904–1922. 1926.—6. bd. 1923–1931. 1936.—7A. bd. 1932–1953. <4v.>.—7A. Suppl. bd.—7B. bd. 1953–<1994> <9v.>

The index to physics periodical literature before *Physics Abstracts*.

Related Databases

49.   **Chemical Abstracts**. American Chemical Society, 1967–present.
Chemical Abstracts is the premier chemistry database. This A&I service has a very broad scope covering far-ranging related journals and has excellent indexing options including patents. CA is the world's largest and most up-to-date collection of chemical information, with more than 15 million abstracts of journal articles, patents, and more. Sources for CA include more than 8,000 journals, patents, technical reports, books, conference proceedings, and dissertations from around the world. Updated weekly. CA is an exceptional patent database, covering 29 national patent offices and two international bodies. About 16% of the CA database, some 2 million records, are from the patent literature.

PAPER: Weekly, author, subject, chemical compound, patent indexes, cumulative indexes covering multiple year segments.

ONLINE DATABASE: **Chemical Abstracts** (1967–present).

Abstract and substructure searching are possible on some systems.

Hosts: STN (*Messenger command mode, STN on the Web interface, STN Easy interface, SciFinder, SciFinder Scholar*), after 5 p.m. Academic discount plan; Dialog; selected years are also available on CD-ROM.

50. **Chemical Abstracts Service Source Index (CASSI)**.

Columbus, Ohio: American Chemical Society, Chemical Abstracts Service.

Quinquennial (cumulative from 1907) with quarterly supplements, the fourth issue being an annual cumulation. 1969– .

Variant Title: American Chemical Society. List of periodicals abstracted by *Chemical Abstracts*.

Lists titles covered by Chemical Abstracts database; includes translation information. Arranged by bold letters (ignore other characters in alphabetical order).

51. **Engineering Index**. New York: Engineering Index, 1892– .

Engineering Index covers the engineering literature, with citations and abstracts from more than 4,500 journals, conference proceedings, technical reports, and books.

PAPER: The monthly index has an author index and is arranged alphabetically according to a subject hierarchy.

52. ONLINE DATABASE: **COMPENDEX** (1980–present).

Hosts: Ei website http://www.ei.org/ (accessed May 26, 1999) as part of the Engineering Information Village; STN, Dialog, Ovid, and SilverPlatter.

53. **Publications in Engineering: PIE: Publications Abstracted and Indexed in the . . . Engineering Information Databases**. Hoboken, N.J.: Engineering Information, 1993– . Annual.

54. **Mathematical Reviews**. Providence, R.I.: American Mathematical Society, 1940– .

The leading indexing and abstracting tool. Covers journals, conferences, and technical reports. Update frequency: paper (weekly), CD-ROM (quarterly), online (weekly).

PAPER: Mathematical Reviews and Current Mathematical Publications.

ONLINE DATABASES:

55. **MATHSCINET**—direct from the AMS website http://www.ams.org/mathscinet/ (accessed May 26, 1999); CD-ROM from SilverPlatter.

56. **Mathematical Reviews** online from Dialog and STN (MR includes *Current Index to Statistics*, which is not in the MathSciNet version).

57. **Astronomy and Astrophysics Abstracts**. Springer-Verlag.
Published for Astronomisches Rechen-Institut, Heidelberg. Prepared under the auspices of the International Astronomical Union.
Continues: Astronomischer Jahresbericht.
PAPER: v. 1– . 1969– . Semiannual.
ONLINE DATABASE: Since 1993 is searchable as a part of the **INSPEC** database.
Hosts: Dialog, SilverPlatter, Ovid, and STN.

58. **Astrophysics Data System (ADS)**. http://adswww.harvard.edu/ (accessed May 4, 1999).
The ADS is a free software service aimed at the astrophysics community. It provides access to a variety of astronomical data. The main emphasis is currently on data collected by NASA space missions, but it is being expanded to include access to data from ground-based observations. The ADS provides access to more than 190 astronomical catalogs and approximately 125,000 astronomical abstracts. It also provides direct access to the HEASARC Browse tool, NSSDC's Online Data and Information Service (NODIS), the NASA/IPAC Extragalactic Database (NED), and the powerful bibliographic and nonbibliographic SIMBAD (Set of Identifications, Measurements, and Bibliography for Astronomical Data) system.

59. **Biological Abstracts and Biological Abstracts/RRM**. Philadelphia: BIOSIS Inc. 1926– .
BIOSIS Previews is the world's most comprehensive reference database in the life sciences. It covers original research reports and reviews in biological and biomedical areas. Coverage includes traditional areas of biology, such as botany, zoology and microbiology, as well as related fields such as plant and animal science, agriculture, pharmacology, and ecology. Interdisciplinary fields such as biochemistry, biophysics, and bioengineering are also included. Close to 7,000 serials are monitored for inclusion. In addition, the database covers content summaries, books (including software from 1992 to present), and information from meetings. Content summaries include notes and letters, technical data reports, reviews, U.S. patents from 1986 to 1989, translation journals, meeting reports from 1980 to present, bibliographies, nomenclature rules, and taxonomic keys. Biological Abstracts/RRM complements Biological Abstracts by providing unique coverage of increasingly important sources of research information. These sources include international reviews, reports, and meetings, as well as books. Users have access to breakthrough research findings often not yet reported in the journal literature or covered in other secondary databases. Biological Abstracts/RRM is a unique resource for current information in

biology, medicine, agriculture, biochemistry, biomedicine, biotechnology, botany, ecology, microbiology, pharmacology, and zoology.

PAPER: Biological Abstracts (1926 to present), Biological Abstracts/RRM (1980 to present), and BioResearch Index (1969 to 1979).

60.   ONLINE DATABASE: The **BIOSIS Previews** database includes the contents of *Biological Abstracts* (1969 to present), *Biological Abstracts/RRM* (1980 to present), and *BioResearch Index* (1969 to 1979).

Hosts: Dialog, SilverPlatter, Ovid, and STN.

61.   **General Science Index**. New York: H. W. Wilson, 1984– .

Wide-ranging subject index to a limited number of basic (popular/core) English-language science journals, books, technical reports, and government reports. Book review citations are included in the back section.

PAPER: Monthly author and subject indexes.

ONLINE DATABASES:

62.   (1984–present) as part of **WILSONWEB** website http://www. hwwilson.com/default.htm (accessed May 26, 1999).

63.   **General Science Abstracts** (1984–present) is available on Dialog, SilverPlatter, and Ovid.

64.   **Applied Science and Technology Index**. New York: H. W. Wilson, 1958– .

Wide-ranging subject index to a limited number of English-language science journals in the areas of computer science, construction industry, energy, engineering, food industry, machinery, petroleum, plastics, and textiles. Book review citations are included in the back section.

PAPER: Monthly author and subject indexes.

ONLINE DATABASES:

65.   (1983–present) as part of **WILSONWEB** website http://www. hwwilson.com/default.htm (accessed May 26, 1999).

66.   **Applied Science and Technology Index** is available (1983–present) on Dialog, SilverPlatter, and Ovid.

67.   **CARL UnCover**. CARL (Colorado Alliance of Research Libraries). http://uncweb.carl.org/ (accessed May 4, 1999).

The free online CARL UnCover service covers both the popular magazine literature and the core research journal literature for many disciplines. The database includes approximately 15,000 journals from a consortium of libraries. There is an unsophisticated and therefore limited search engine. The for-fee portion of the system provides a more powerful set of options including SDI services and commercial document delivery.

68. **Dissertation Abstracts International**. Ann Arbor, Mich.: UMI.

The complete range of academic subjects appearing in dissertations accepted at accredited institutions. Dates covered: 1861 . . . (Indexing); 1980 . . . (Abstracting Dissertations); 1988 . . . (Abstracting Theses); Updated monthly; document delivery available for a fee.

PAPER: Monthly author and subject indexes.

ONLINE DATABASES: (1861–present).

Hosts: Dialog, SilverPlatter, Ovid, and STN.

69. **Index to Scientific & Technical Proceedings**. Philadelphia: ISI, 1978– .

This product provides complete bibliographic data on the world's most recently published scientific and technical conference proceedings. It covers all of the disciplines in the sciences.

PRINT: Published monthly, the print edition indexes approximately 4,800 published conference proceedings each year and more than 210,000 individual papers in all. Author/Editor Index alphabetically lists the names of all editors of proceedings and authors of proceedings papers. Permuterm Subject Index gives subject access to proceedings by listing keywords appearing in their titles and in individual paper titles. Sponsor Index alphabetically lists the sponsors of meetings. Meeting Location Index alphabetically lists the geographic location of meetings. Category Index lists approximately 200 subject categories, leading to proceedings on these subjects. Corporate Index provides access to publishing authors and their works through their corporate or academic affiliations. Contents of Books Index lists complete bibliographic information for all proceedings and papers in the issue.

CD-ROM: Published quarterly, the CD-ROM edition indexes approximately 1 million papers since 1994 from 26,000 conference proceedings. Each quarterly update adds approximately 47,000 papers from 3,500 recently published conference proceedings, providing even more coverage than the print format. A subscription includes four years of retrospective data plus quarterly cumulative updates to total five years on one disc. Networking Options/Tiers available.

MAGNETIC TAPE: ISTP Search, the magnetic tape format of the Index to Scientific & Technical Proceedings, is updated weekly. Coverage is similar to the CD-ROM format. Abstracts are included. Networking Options/Tiers available.

70. **Index to Scientific Book Contents**. Philadelphia: ISI, 1985– .

Index to Scientific Book Contents provides complete bibliographic data on the individual chapters of the world's most recently published, multiauthored scientific and technical books as well as single-authored books that are a part of a multiauthored series. It indexes approximately 42,000 chapters from 2,600 books and book series each year in disciplines of the sciences.

PRINT: The print edition is published quarterly. A subscription includes three quarterly softcover issues and an annual hardcover cumulation. Back-year annuals are available through 1985. Author/Editor Index lists the names of all editors and authors of books and chapters. Permuterm Subject Index gives subject access to reviews by listing keywords appearing in their titles. Category Index lists approximately 100 subject categories. Corporate Index provides access to publishing authors and their works through their corporate or academic affiliations. Contents of Books Index lists complete bibliographic information for all books and chapters in the issue.

71.   **Conference Papers Index**. Cambridge Scientific Abstracts, 1973– .

Conference Papers Index (CPI) provides access to records of the more than 100,000 scientific and technical papers presented at more than 1,000 major regional, national, and international meetings each year. Also included in this database are announcements of publications issued from the meetings, in addition to available preprints, reprints, abstract booklets, and proceedings volumes, including dates of availability, costs, and ordering information. Primary subject areas covered include the life sciences, chemistry, physical sciences, geosciences, and engineering.

PAPER: Conference Papers Index.

ONLINE DATABASE: 1973–present.

Host: Dialog.

72.   **Directory of Published Proceedings. Series SEMT: Science/Engineering/Medicine/Technology**. InterDok, 1965– .

Published 10 times a year, from September to June. A cumulated annual volume is also published. A cumulated index supplement is available three times per year. Indices for annual volumes are published at two- to five-year intervals.

ONLINE DATABASE: http://www.interdok.com/ (accessed May 4, 1999).

Provides article-level conference indexing, and author, organization, and location indexing.

PAPER: 1965–present.

73.   **PAIS International in Print**. 1969– .

PAIS (Public Affairs Information Service) International covers the literature of public affairs including political, economic, and social issues. It contains references to articles, books, government documents, statistical directories, research reports, conference reports, and publications of international agencies. Publications from more than 60 countries are included. Materials indexed are in English, French, German, Italian, Portuguese, and Spanish.

PAPER: Merger of PAIS bulletin and PAIS foreign language index. Quarterly updates. Issued also in an annual cumulation (1969–present).
ONLINE DATABASE: PAIS International. Coverage begins in 1974.

74.   **Government Reports Announcements & Index / NTIS**. 1968–.
NTIS (National Technical Information Service) collects and distributes technical reports produced by government contracted research, as well as a variety of other government publications.
PAPER: Government reports announcements and index. 1946–present.
ONLINE DATABASE: **NTIS** database contains references to these publications. The database provides references including basic bibliographic citation information, as well as abstracts. It can be searched by title, subject, author, and a variety of other access points. Coverage is from 1983 to present.

Aggregators Providing Full-Text Database Access

Selected subject-specific A&I databases now provide seamless access to online journals. Point-and-click access can be provided from citations to full text.
The following three services are similar in scope to UnCover (entry 67) but also serve as aggregators and gateways to online full-text journals.

75.   **EBSCOhost**. EBSCO Information Services Group. http://www. epnet.com/ (accessed May 6, 1999).
EBSCOhost offers immediate access to a variety of full-text databases that cover more than 2,000 magazines in searchable full text, more than 1,000 magazines in full image, more than 4,000 magazines abstracted and indexed, plus current citations for more than 11,000 magazines.

76.   **ProQuest**. http://www.umi.com/proquest/ (accessed May 6, 1999).
The ProQuest Research Library database contains more than 2,000 periodicals—nearly 1,000 of them in ASCII full-text or full-image formats—in a wide range of subject areas. In addition to general core title coverage, there are added subject emphases in the following areas: Arts, Business, Children, Education, General Interest, Health, Humanities, International, Law, Military, Multicultural, Psychology, Sciences, Social Sciences, and Women's Interests.

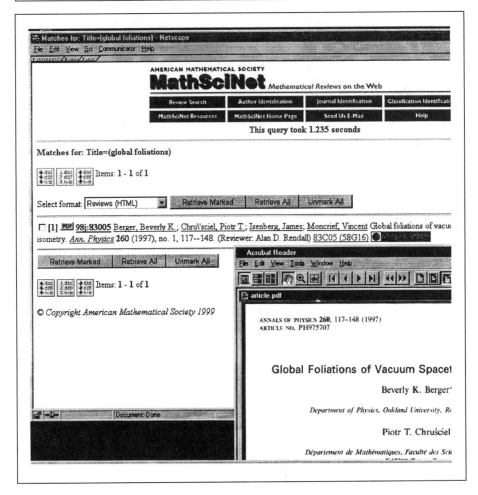

Fig. 8. Seamless access from indexes to full text

77.   **Expanded Academic ASAP**. InfoTrac. http://international. iacnet.com/products/products.html (accessed May 6, 1999).

ONLINE DATABASE: Expanded Academic ASAP offers balanced, full-text coverage of every academic concentration—from advertising and microbiology to history, political science, and art history. It also incorporates many interdisciplinary journals, national news magazines, and the *New York Times*. This comprehensive database delivers results for both the undergraduate as well as graduate researchers and faculty. Source types: academic journals and the *New York Times* (indexing only).

Search Services:
Hosts to Multiple Databases

78.   **FirstSearch**. OCLC. http://www.oclc.org/oclc/menu/fs.htm (accessed May 4, 1999).

The OCLC FirstSearch service gives library users access to more than 75 online databases and more than 3.3 million full-text articles. FirstSearch offers a variety of document delivery choices, including e-mail, interlibrary loan, fax, overnight carrier, and regular mail. Access options include a web interface, TTY interface, and Z39.50 connection. OCLC provides access to FirstSearch only through libraries. Subscriptions can be through prepaid blocks of searches or via the transactional (per search) approach. The INSPEC prepay option has been removed.

79.   **Dialog**. Dialog Corporation. http://www.dialog.com/ (accessed May 4, 1999).

This host provides access to more than 450 databases. There are many access options. Some require a monthly minimum. There are user-friendly interfaces and reduced-cost evening academic options.

DialogClassic on the Web is designed for information professionals who need high-speed access to classic Dialog and require quick response to their search queries. Searchers pointing their browsers to DialogClassic are connected to the Dialog mainframe web server, providing them direct access to the extensive content and functionality of classic Dialog.

DialogWeb provides easy access to the full content (450+ databases), power, and precision of classic Dialog through a web browser.

Dialog@CARL is an end-user interface for approximately 300 Dialog databases. The service is available on a subscription basis to academic and public libraries. Dialog@CARL is available on a per-simultaneous-connection, flat-annual-fee basis. Discounts are available for multiple connection purchases. This unique pricing scheme allows libraries to have unlimited usage of the Dialog@CARL databases. The Dialog@CARL pricing structure enables institutions to accurately budget every year for the product.

80.   **STN** (Scientific & Technical Information Network). This network is operated cooperatively by Fachinformationszentrum (FIZ) Karlsruhe, Chemical Abstracts Service (CAS), and Japan Science and Technology Corporation (JST). http://info.cas.org/stn.html (accessed May 4, 1999).

The service concentrates on science databases with more than 200 scientific, technical, business, and patent databases. They offer both the Messenger command language and the STN Easy web interface. There are reduced-cost evening academic options.

81.   **Northern Light**. Northern Light Technology LLC. http://www.
northernlight.com/ (accessed May 4, 1999).

Gateway to some 120 million web pages and a Special Collection™ of
more than 5,400 full-text sources. Covers internet non-peer review material
such as equipment, chemicals, software, reviews, biographies, etc. Results
are dynamically organized into Custom Search Folders™.

Personal Current Awareness Services

For those researchers without access to organizational current awareness services, there are a number of options. One free but complex approach is using the many free publisher websites that allow researchers to
save a set of keywords and have matching records (or tables of contents) delivered via e-mail. See their web pages for more information.

Many of the above services (e.g., Dialog, CARL UnCover, STN) allow saved strategies for a fee.

82.   **ISI Alerting Services(SM)** from the Institute for Scientific Information, producers of *Science Citation Index* (see above), has the following options:

Corporate Alert®, Discovery Agent(SM), Journal Tracker(TM), and
Personal Alert®

http://www.isinet.com/products/products.html (accessed May 4, 1999).

Chapter 3

Journals

This section identifies some traditional journal sources and progressive publishing initiatives that provide the most current information in the field of physics. In addition to simply providing a list of the resources, this section introduces the researcher to procedures and tools that evaluate the scope and quality of these serials. While standard evaluation criteria exist for paper journals, criteria for the new electronic distribution tools will undoubtedly develop over time.

History of Journal Publishing

The primary publishing tool used by physics researchers to disseminate their latest discoveries and inventions was the journal. When the lag time for editing, copy editing, and typesetting became a problem, "Letters" journals (composed of one- to three-page rapid briefs) and Rapid Communications (short report) sections became important for the quick distribution of timely information. The American Physical Society even began producing two paper publications (*Physical Review Abstracts* and *Advance Physics Abstracts*) that provided titles and abstracts accepted for publication. In the world of private communication, many manuscripts were distributed in advance of peer review and publication as paper preprints for those within the inner circle of preprint mailing lists.

With the advent of the Internet, it became very easy and inexpensive to offer (ftp) files or mount preprints on the Web for all to see. The APS produced the PiNet network, which included the electronic equivalents of *Physical Review Abstracts* and *Advance Physics Abstracts*. Electronic preprints, or e-prints, were consolidated at a few clearinghouse locations such as SLAC and LANL. Paul Ginsparg established the LANL preprint server, which not only provided a simple place to browse the latest e-prints by subdiscipline, but also allowed users to create automatic e-mail delivery systems for citations and abstracts. The library group at SLAC concentrated on converting the various formats into a few standard delivery options (e.g., TeX, PDF, HTML, Postscript, ASCII text).

Format selector for hep-ex/9903017

Set cookies: if your browser supports cookies you can configure your default format.

PostScript using Bitmapped Fonts

Select a resolution (Note: 400 and 600 dpi postscript will occasionally require new fonts to be created, and this can take a while):

Use [300 ▼] dpi Bitmapped Fonts: [Create PostScript]

PostScript using Type I Fonts

Note: you need to install additional Type I fonts for this option. Read our Type I help before proceeding.

Select a naming convention (cm=public domain, CM=bluesky):

Use [cm ▼] Type I Fonts: [Create PostScript]

PDF

Now includes fonts, and needs Acroread 3.01 or better [Create PDF]

DVI

Delivered as a **.dvi.gz** file or **.tar.gz** (including figures). [Create DVI]

For more information consult the viewing help.

Note: Please report any problems to www-admin@xxx.lanl.gov, being certain to state the archive, papernumber, explicit options you've selected and that you're using xxx.lanl.gov (we've never claimed to be mindreaders).

www-admin@xxx.lanl.gov

Fig. 9. LANL preprint display options

There are certainly concerns expressed about e-print distribution before validation through the peer review process, but there is a desire by physics researchers to adopt whatever mechanism is necessary to provide rapid access to cutting-edge research. The American Physical Society has begun to cooperate with LANL in developing their preprint server connections. They have also begun their own online-only journal, *Physical Review Special Topics—Accelerators and Beams* (PR-STAB). The Optical Society of America produces the free online journal *Optics Express*.

All traditional journal publishers are attempting to reduce the time lag in their publication processes and have mounted online versions of many of their journals. The Acoustical Society of America has collaborated with the American Institute of Physics and developed an impressive online manuscript management process used to create ARLO, *Acoustics Research Letters Online*, a new rapid-publication letters section in the Journal of the Acoustical Society of America (see http://www.asa.aip.org/arlo [accessed May 4, 1999]). Perhaps this tool will be adopted by other societies and publishers. At this time the process results in PDF and GIF files for electronic distribution, but the system can be modified for future enhanced formats (XML, SGML, etc.).

Most of these online journals are simply PDF versions of the paper journals, but a few are offering enhanced features that are possible with this new technology. Examples of possible enhancements are integrated multimedia items (e.g., simulations, Java teaching demonstrations), hyperlinks to other full-text sources, and hyperlinks to supplementary unpublished information.

Journal Bibliographies

The most common way to find journal information is to use bibliographies of journals that are housed in many libraries. These tools often provide publisher contact information, cost, ISSN (a unique international serial number), any equivalent translation titles, and a list of abstracts and indexes that cover the journal. Examples of such publisher bibliographies are:

83.   **Ulrich's International Periodicals Directory**. New York: R. R. Bowker, 1932– . Annual. 37th ed. 5 vols. $459.95.
An excellent source of journal information including contact facts, costs, and A&I services that cover the titles. Arranged by subject with the following indexes: subject, title, title changes, cessations, ISSN, refereed titles, online serials, serials on CD-ROM, and international organizations. Also includes lists of online vendors and CD-ROM producers. Includes U.S. newspapers.

84.   **The Serials Directory: An International Reference Book**. Birmingham, Ala.: EBSCO, 1986– . Annual. 5 vols. Available on CD-ROM and via EBSCOhost online service (see entry 75).
Another excellent source of journal information including contact facts, costs, and A&I services that cover the titles. Arranged by subject with similar indexes to *Ulrich's* (above), plus an index of titles that contain book reviews. Covers both U.S. and international newspapers (arranged alphabetically by country).

85. **PubList**. http://publist.com (accessed May 4, 1999).

An online bibliography of journal information. This new tool is not as complete as the paper titles listed above, but it is convenient and is growing by the day. Covers more than 150,000 publications from all around the world. It is easy to use, and it is free.

86. **Magazines for Libraries**. New York: R. R. Bowker, 1978– . Irregular.

1st–3rd ed. by Bill Katz and Berry G. Richards; 4th ed. by Bill Katz and Linda Sternberg Katz.

A selective list of journals and magazines. This bibliography lists some major serial titles for many disciplines and is a good way for beginning researchers to become familiar with some of the most important journals in a field. Due to the limited scope of coverage, it is not the right tool to use to find a promising journal for publication.

Key Publishers

The following are important publishers covering the field of physics.

Academic Press, Inc., 525 B St., Ste. 1900, San Diego, CA 92101-4495. TEL 619-231-0926. FAX 619-699-6715. URL http://www.apnet.com/

American Chemical Society, 1155 16th St., N.W., Washington, DC 20009-1749. TEL 202-332-5544; 800-333-9511. FAX 202-332-4559. E-mail service@acs.org. URL http://pubs.acs.org/

American Institute of Physics, One Physics Ellipse, College Park, MD 20740-3843. TEL 301-209-3000. URL http://www.aip.org/

American Physical Society, One Physics Ellipse, College Park, MD 20740-3844. TEL 301-209-3200. URL http://www.aps.org/

Birkhauser, P.O. Box 133, CH-4010 Basel, Switzerland. TEL 41-61-2050730. URL http://www.birkhauser.ch/

CRC Press, 2000 Corporate Blvd., N.W., Boca Raton, FL 33431. TEL 561-994-0555. FAX 561-998-9784. URL http://www.crcpress.com/

Elsevier North-Holland, P.O. Box 211, 1000 AE Amsterdam, Netherlands. TEL 31-20-4853911. FAX 31-20-4853598. URL http://www.elsevier.nl

Harwood Academic (Gordon and Breach—Harwood Academic), Poststrasse 22, 7000 Chur, Switzerland

Institute of Physics Publishing, Ltd., Dirac House, Temple Back, Bristol, BS1 6BE, England. TEL 44-117-929-7841. FAX 44-117-929-4318. E-mail custserv@ioppublishing.co.uk. URL http://www.iop.org

Kluwer Academic Publishers, Postbus 17, 3300 AA Dordrecht, Netherlands. TEL 31-78-6392392. FAX 31-78-6546474. URL http://www.wkap.nl/

Marcel Dekker, Inc., 270 Madison Ave., New York, NY 10016. TEL 212-696-9000. FAX 212-685-4540. URL http://www.dekker.com/

Plenum Press (Plenum Publishing Corp., subsidiary of Wolters Kluwer N.V.), 233 Spring St., New York, NY 10013-1578. TEL 212-620-8000; 800-221-9369. FAX 212-463-0742. E-mail info@plenum.com. URL http://www.plenum.com/

Springer (Springer-Verlag), Heidlberger Platz 3, 14197 Berlin, Germany. TEL 49-30-82787-366. FAX 49-30-82787-448. E-mail subscriptions@springer.de. URL http://link.springer.de/

Wiley (John Wiley & Sons, Inc.), 605 Third Ave., New York, NY 10158-0012. TEL 212-850-6000. FAX 212-850-6099. E-mail info@wiley.com. URL http://www.wiley.com/

World Scientific (World Scientific Publishing Co. Pte. Ltd.), Parrer Rd., P.O. Box 128, Singapore 9128, Singapore. TEL 65-3825663. FAX 65-3825919. E-mail wspsl@singnet.com/sg; saes@wspc2.demon.co.uk; wspc@wspc.com. URL http://www.worldscientific.com/

There are many university presses and other professional societies that publish in the field as well.

Evaluation of Journals

By Journal Title

It is often necessary to determine the scope and quality of existing journals. This may be done in order to determine a set of essential journals for a personal or organizational library collection, to determine where to publish, or as a tool to help in the evaluation of the research quality of a scientist's work. No amount of quantitative analysis will substitute for the careful review of the individual publications, but some of the following methods will provide data that may relate to the overall quality of specific journals. The caveats to using bibliometric analysis include the underlying effectiveness of peer review and the author patterns of self-citation and citation selection.

A common measure of quality used by many reviewers is the Impact Factor, a calculated value relating to the average number of annual citations to a journal article in a specific journal. This value is generated by the Institute for Scientific Information (ISI), the producer of *Science Citation Index* (SCI) (see entry 40). The annual Impact Factors are listed alphabetically by title, and by discipline, in the annual tool *Journal Citation Reports* (see entry 27). Keeping in mind the stated concerns about bibliometric analysis,[1] this tool can serve as a measure of the prestige and importance of particular titles. Finding titles with high Impact Factors in a number of disciplines will help researchers identify journals with interdisciplinary coverage.

ISI Impact Factors for General Physics Category

Impact Factor of Journals

Journals Grouped by Topic—in Impact Order

From the "Journal Citation Reports" published by ISI—1994

PHYSICS

14.426 REVIEWS OF MODERN PHYSICS

6.727 REPORTS ON PROGRESS IN PHYSICS

6.626 PHYSICAL REVIEW LETTERS

6.541 PHYSICS REPORTS-REVIEW SECTION OF PHYSICS LETTERS

5.824 JOURNAL OF PHYSICAL AND CHEMICAL REFERENCE DATA

3.056 PHYSICS LETTERS B

2.662 EUROPHYSICS LETTERS

2.642 PHYSICS TODAY

2.292 PHYSICAL REVIEW A

2.070 PHYSICA D

1.979 ANNALS OF PHYSICS

1.920 JOURNAL OF THE PHYSICAL SOCIETY OF JAPAN

1.792 RIVISTA DEL NUOVO CIMENTO

1.779 JOURNAL OF PHYSICS A-MATHEMATICAL NUCLEAR AND GENERAL

1.773 JOURNAL DE PHYSIQUE I

1.652 CLASSICAL AND QUANTUM GRAVITY

1.398 SOVIET PHYSICS-USPEKHI

1.377 FEW-BODY SYSTEMS

1.310 PHYSICA A

1.272 PROCEEDINGS OF THE ROYAL SOCIETY OF LONDON SERIES A-MATHEMATICAL

1.228 PHYSICS LETTERS A

1.182 PROGRESS OF THEORETICAL PHYSICS

1.147 ANNALEN DER PHYSIK

1.029 PROGRESS OF THEORETICAL PHYSICS SUPPLEMENT

0.991 PHYSICA SCRIPTA

0.917 JETP LETTERS

0.883 SOVIET PHYSICS JETP-USSR

0.800 FORTSCHRITTE DER PHYSIK-PROGRESS OF PHYSICS

0.750 CONTEMPORARY PHYSICS

0.670 GENERAL RELATIVITY AND GRAVITATION

0.657 HELVETICA PHYSICA ACTA

0.630 ZEITSCHRIFT FUR NATURFORSCHUNG SECTION A-A JOURNAL OF PHYSICAL SCIENCES

0.629 AUSTRALIAN JOURNAL OF PHYSICS

0.597 ANNALES DE L INSTITUT HENRI POINCARE-PHYSIQUE THEORIQUE

0.586 WAVE MOTION

0.569 ANNALES DE PHYSIQUE

0.550 AMERICAN JOURNAL OF PHYSICS

0.536 ACTA PHYSICA POLONICA B

0.463 NUOVO CIMENTO DELLA SOCIETA ITALIANA DI FISICA D-CONDENSED MATTER

0.411 FOUNDATIONS OF PHYSICS

0.408 CANADIAN JOURNAL OF PHYSICS

0.395 THEORETICAL AND MATHEMATICAL PHYSICS

0.346 ACTA PHYSICA POLONICA A

0.345 INTERNATIONAL JOURNAL OF THEORETICAL PHYSICS

0.345 PRAMANA-JOURNAL OF PHYSICS

0.330 CHINESE JOURNAL OF PHYSICS

0.330 CZECHOSLOVAK JOURNAL OF PHYSICS

0.306 FOUNDATIONS OF PHYSICS LETTERS

0.305 NUOVO CIMENTO DELLA SOCIETA ITALIANA DI FISICA B-GENERAL PHYSICS

0.297 INSTITUTE OF PHYSICS CONFERENCE SERIES

0.281 PHYSICS WORLD

0.261 COMMUNICATIONS IN THEORETICAL PHYSICS

0.229 INDIAN JOURNAL OF PURE & APPLIED PHYSICS

0.198 REVISTA MEXICANA DE FISICA

0.147 UKRAINSKII FIZICHESKII ZHURNAL

0.117 IZVESTIYA AKADEMII NAUK SERIYA FIZICHESKAYA

0.115 JOURNAL DE PHYSIQUE IV

0.085 PTB-MITTEILUNGEN

0.079 VESTNIK MOSKOVSKOGO UNIVERSITETA SERIYA 3 FIZIKA ASTRONOMIYA

0.039 CHINESE PHYSICS

0.039 PHYSICS ESSAYS

0 WAVES IN RANDOM MEDIA

Other available physics subdisciplines:

    PHYSICS; APPLIED
    PHYSICS; CONDENSED MATTER
    PHYSICS; FLUIDS & PLASMAS
    PHYSICS; MATHEMATICAL
    PHYSICS; NUCLEAR
    PHYSICS; PARTICLES & FIELDS
    ACOUSTICS

The online and CD-ROM *Journal Citation Reports* also include "cited by" and "cited in" information for each journal. This allows a researcher to look at both the sources of citations and the sources cited by authors in each journal. There should be a correlation between the quality of the original journal articles and the quality of the sources and follow-up research journals. The identification of common cross-discipline citation trends will also help researchers identify journals with interdisciplinary coverage.

Examples of *Science Citation Index* reports that can be generated include:

    1. Most-often-selected journals for publication by a department

    2. Most-cited journals by a department

These same reports can be generated for individuals, departments, and organizations.

Excellent scholarly analyses of the physics journal literature are published in the books by Tony Stankus (see the Bibliography section, entries 29, 30, and 31). Among many other topics, these monographs describe author trends, publication patterns and analyses, and time lags in the area of physics. These valuable books provide an interesting review of the entire journal information distribution network in physics.

By Specific Article

To help determine the quality and impact of specific journal articles, use *Science Citation Index* (SCI) (see entry 40), which includes citation counts for every article. There should be some correlation between the number of citations (removing the self-citation factor) and the impact of a work. One can also use this information to help determine the quality of the journals in which the citations appear.

Examples of *Science Citation Index* reports that can be generated include:

    1. Most-productive authors within a department

    2. Most-cited authors and articles by department

These same reports can be generated for individuals, departments, and organizations.

The use of the SCI "Related Records" feature will provide another value that will allow researchers to determine the impact and wide-ranging influence of a particular article. This value is determined by using bibliometric analysis, primarily frequency of similar citations among articles, in order to find related articles that have not cited each other. It can often locate articles in outside areas with different terminology that are not within the normal reading domain.

Local Evaluation Measures

Often libraries perform journal evaluation in order to determine core journals that are to be protected as significant cost inflation forces the cancellation of lesser-used titles. Common analysis methods involve user surveys, journal use studies, duplicate journal reviews, and cost-per-use studies. While these evaluations are not flawless, and in some cases provide contradictory information, they do provide some measures of value. Many libraries now post their highest use, highest cost, highest inflation, and first consideration cancellation journal lists on their websites. These compilations can provide valuable information, but users must be aware of the highly localized nature of these lists. In addition, these measures fail to account for the use of both personal copies and the online journals, which can be significant in the area of physics.

The online journal-use statistics that have been distributed to libraries are very skewed at this time because normal user behavior will not be represented until there are seamless links between A&I services and full-text journals. Until that time the statistics show only a small segment of the potential users and may not adequately reflect eventual usage. While it is important to review online usage statistics, many online journal publishers do not provide statistics at this time—not surprising when one considers that this ability to closely review the use of journals may have a devastating effect on the long-term viability of infrequently used commercial journals.

The following data are included as selected examples from a rough journal evaluation process. They are intended as approximations and factors in a more comprehensive review process. They are specific to Yale University and should not be considered representative of a typical library profile.

Yale Physics Department Faculty Journal Survey

Locally Held Journals with the Highest Perceived Value

Nature (London)
Science
National Academy of Sciences (Washington, D.C.). Proceedings
Scientific American
Review of Scientific Instruments
Physical Review Letters
American Scientist
Philosophical Transactions of the Royal Society of London. Series A: Mathematical and Physical Sciences
Science News
Physical Review B
Physics Letters B
Reviews of Modern Physics
Archives of Biochemistry and Biophysics
Quarterly Reviews of Biophysics
Journal of Magnetic Resonance
Advances in Biophysics (1970–)
Physics Letters A
Physical Review C: Nuclear Physics
Physical Review D: Particles and Fields
Journal of Physics: Condensed Matter
Proceedings of the Royal Society of London. Series B
Yale Scientific
Journal of Physics and Chemistry of Solids
Physics Reports
Physics Today
Journal of Physics (London). A
Nuclear Physics A
Nuclear Physics B
Journal of Physics G: Nuclear and Particle Physics

Yale Physics Journal Use Study (2 Months)

Most Used Titles

Nature (London)
Science
National Academy of Sciences (Washington, D.C.). Proceedings
Physical Review Letters
Physical Review B: Condensed Matter
Scientific American

New Scientist
Nuclear Physics B
Journal of Physical Chemistry
Biochimica et Biophysica Acta
Physics Letters B
Biochemical and Biophysical Research Communications
Journal of Chemical Physics
Physics Today
Biophysical Journal
Physical Review D: Particles and Fields
Physical Review
Physical Review A: General Physics
Science News
Physics Reports
Physical Review E
American Journal of Physics
Nuclear Physics A
Archives of Biochemistry and Biophysics
Reviews of Modern Physics
Europhysics Letters
Physical Review C: Nuclear Physics
Journal of Magnetic Resonance
American Scientist
Review of Scientific Instruments (American Institute of Physics)
Quarterly Reviews of Biophysics
Journal of Magnetic Resonance A
Nuclear Instruments and Methods in Physics Research
Annals of Physics
Journal of Physics (London). A: Mathematical and General
Communications in Mathematical Physics
Biophysical Chemistry
Proceedings of the Royal Society of London. Series B
Soviet Physics. JETP
Astrophysical Journal

Highest Efficiency Titles (Cost-Per-Use)

European Journal of Physics	$	12.81
Computers in Physics	$	11.46
Journal of Magnetic Resonance B	$	10.73
Physics World	$	9.72
APS (American Physical So.) News	$	7.78
Reviews of Modern Physics	$	7.08
Physical Review Letters	$	7.40
Physics Teacher	$	4.90
Nature (London)	$	2.84
Proceedings of the National Academy of Sciences of the United States of America	$	2.42
Science	$	1.19
Bulletin of the Atomic Scientists	$	0.94
American Scientist	$	0.83
Physics Today	$	0.68
New Scientist	$	0.56
Science News	$	0.53
Journal of Irreproducible Results	$	0.50
PC Magazine; the Independent Guide to IBM Personal Computers	$	0.49
Sciences (New York Academy of Sciences)	$	0.43
Skeptical Inquirer	$	0.36
Sky and Telescope	$	0.28
Scientific American	$	0.25
Yale Scientific	$	0.15

Most Expensive Titles (Cost-Per-Use)

* denotes no use during the test period

Nuclear Instruments and Methods in Physics Research Section A	$	1,216.33
Physica B	$	614.33
International Journal of Mass Spectrometry and Ion Processes	$	497.50
Physica D: Nonlinear Phenomena	*	
Physica C	$	449.00
Journal of Physics Condensed Matter	$	888.00
Journal of Experimental and Theoretical Physics	$	435.83
Nuclear Physics Section B	$	550.50
Quantum Electronics	$	358.33
Europhysics Letters	$	322.29
Annals of Physics	$	312.00
Physica A	$	283.58
Zeitschrift fur Physik A: Atoms and Nuclei	$	283.50

Journal of Statistical Physics	$	262.50
Physics-Doklady (Doklady Akademii nauk)	$	261.67
Journal of Modern Optics	*	
Journal of Physics D: Applied Physics	$	238.67
Astronomy Reports	$	235.00
Instruments and Experimental Techniques (Engl. transl. of: Pribory i Tekhnika Eksperimenta)	*	
Meteorology and Atmospheric Physics	$	216.33
Nuclear Physics Section A	$	213.67
JETP Letters	$	213.33
Theoretical and Mathematical Physics	$	199.17
Modern Physics Letters B	$	187.00
Physics Letters A	$	177.94
Journal of Applied Physics	$	170.42
Measurement Science and Technology	$	165.00
Inverse Problems	$	163.17
Il Nuovo Cimento della Societa Italiana di Fisica, A: Nuclei, Particles and Fields	*	
Foundations of Physics	$	152.50
Journal of the Physical Society of Japan (Nippon Butsurigakkai)	$	133.17
Communications in Mathematical Physics	$	126.28
International Journal of Theoretical Physics	$	124.17
Journal of Mathematical Physics	$	120.00
Nuclear Data Sheets (NRC)	$	115.33
Applied Optics	$	112.83
Journal of Physics B	$	110.46
Applied Physics Letters	$	109.58
Physics Reports	$	106.77
Physical Review D: Particles and Fields	$	105.56
Classical and Quantum Gravity	$	100.94
Journal of Physics G: Nuclear and Particle Physics	$	99.22
Il Nuovo Cimento della Societa Italiana di Fisica, D: Condensed Matter, Atomic, Molecular and Chemical Physics, Fluids, Plasmas, Biophysics	$	92.50
Journal of Physics (London). A: Mathematical and General	$	89.56
International Journal of Modern Physics A	$	86.25
Il Nuovo Cimento della Societa Italiana di Fisica, B: General Physics, Relativity, Astronomy and Mathematical Physics and Methods	$	79.74
Modern Physics Letters A	$	74.56
Physics Letters B	$	73.32
Letters in Mathematical Physics	$	61.58
General Relativity and Gravitation	$	60.42
International Journal of Modern Physics B	$	59.13
Foundations of Physics Letters	$	57.50

Physica Scripta

$ 54.17

Journal of Physical and Chemical Reference Data

$ 46.67

Yale Physics Journal Cost Study

Highest Cost	Price 98	97	% inflation
AIP ALL	30515	2850	7.07
Journal of Physics	24515	2249	8.97
AMERICAN CHEMICAL SOCIETY	22093	20354	8.54
Nuclear Physics. A, B	18102	17222	5.11
Nuclear Instruments and Methods in Physics Research. Section A, B	13785	13644	1.03
Physics Letters. A, B, and Physics Reports	12894	12530	2.91
APS-ALL	12015	1230	6.99
Biochimica et Biophysica Acta	10839	10528	2.95
Journal of Chromatography	9862	9414	4.76
Journal of Nuclear Materials	4848	4570	6.08
Communications in Mathematical Physics	4836	4697	2.96
European Physical Journal. C, Particles and Fields	4725		
Physics Abstracts	4030	3670	9.81
Computer Physics Communications	4004	4000	0.10
International Journal of Mass Spectrometry and Ion Processes	3477	3293	5.59
Journal of Physics and Chemistry of Solids	3202	2738	16.95
Journal of Mass Spectrometry	2850	2495	14.23
Magnetic Resonance in Chemistry	2850	2495	14.23
European Physical Journal. B, Condensed Matter	2798		
International Journal of Modern Physics A	2747	2470	11.21
Annals of Physics	2520	2100	20.00
Biochemical and Biophysical Research Communications	2495	2100	18.81
Quantum Electronics (formerly Soviet Journal of Quantum Electronics)	2415	2280	5.92

Yale Physics Journal Cost Study

Highest Inflation	Price 98	97	% inflation
Advances in Physics	1150	637	80.53
Journal of Geometry and Physics	986	739	33.42
Australian Journal of Physics	475	360	31.94
Chemistry and Physics of Lipids	1995	1611	23.84
Nature	595	495	20.20
Annals of Physics	2520	2100	20.00
Journal of Physics and Chemistry of Solids	3202	2738	16.95
Journal of Solid State Chemistry	2150	1844	16.59
La Reccherche	100	87	14.85
Journal of Mass Spectrometry	2850	2495	14.23
Magnetic Resonance in Chemistry	2850	2495	14.23
American Journal of Physics	295	260	13.46
Science	295	260	13.46
Physics Teacher	178	157	13.38
Physica Scripta	1100	975	12.82

Journals in Physics

Below are two lists that together represent the major journals in physics. The first list is composed of those titles creating a significant core physics collection. The second list is an interdisciplinary journal collection of interest to any physics researcher. These two lists are followed by lists of selected physics journals by subdiscipline, which might assist a selector in picking a smaller group of journals for a less comprehensive physics journal collection.

These lists should only serve as one in a number of tools in assisting subject selectors. Other local factors need to be considered in order to customize collections for particular user populations.

Entries below include the following publication frequency and currency information as marked:

a.–annual   bi-m.–bi-monthly   m.–monthly   irreg.–irregular
w.–weekly   q.–quarterly $–dollars   DKK–krone   F.–francs
£–pound (U.K.)   DM.–mark

Note: Only U.S. prices listed when available.

Indexing and abstracting services are abbreviated as follows:

A.S. & T. Ind.-	Applied Science & Technology Index
Biol. Abstr.-	Biological Abstracts
Chem. Abstr.-	Chemical Abstracts
Chem. Cit. Ind.-	Chemistry Citation Index
Curr. Cont.-	Current Contents
Eng. Ind.-	Engineering Index
Environ. Abstr.-	Environment Abstracts
Excerp. Med.-	Excerpta Medica
Gen. Sci. Ind.-	General Science Index
Geo. Abstr. P.G.-	Geographical Abstracts: Physical Geography
Geol. Abstr.-	Geological Abstracts
GeoRef-	Bibliography and Index of Geology (known as GeoRef)
Geotech. Abstr.-	Geotechnical Abstracts
INIS Atomind.-	I N I S Atomindex
Mat. Sci. Cit. Ind.-	Materials Science Citation Index
Met. Abstr.-	Metallurgical Abstracts (Metals Abstracts)
Meteor. & Geoastrophys. Abstr.-	Meteorological & Geoastrophysical Abstracts
Mineral. Abstr.-	Mineralogical Abstracts
Nucl. Sci. Abstr.-	Nuclear Science Abstracts
Sci. Cit. Ind.-	Science Citation Index
Sel. Water Res. Abstr.-	Selected Water Resources Abstracts
SSCI-	Social Sciences Citation Index

Significant Core Physics Journal Collection

Acoustical Physics
> American Institute of Physics, 1955– , bi-m. ISSN 1063-7710.
> $1200/yr.
> Indexed: Curr. Cont., Eng. Ind., Excerp. Med., INSPEC (1968–),
> Nucl. Sci. Abstr., Sci. Cit. Ind.

Acta Crystallographica Section A: Foundations of Crystallography
> International Union of Crystallography, 1948– , bi-m. ISSN
> 0108-7673. DKK 2600/yr.
> Indexed: Biol. Abstr., Chem. Abstr., Chem. Cit. Ind., Curr. Cont.,
> GeoRef, INSPEC (1983–), Mat. Sci. Cit. Ind., Met. Abstr., Sci. Cit. Ind.

Acta Crystallographica Section B: Structural Science
> International Union of Crystallography, 1983– , bi-m. ISSN
> 0108-7681. DKK 2600/yr.
> Indexed: Biol. Abstr., Chem. Abstr., Chem. Cit. Ind., Curr. Cont.,
> INSPEC (1983–), Mat. Sci. Cit. Ind., Met. Abstr., Sci. Cit. Ind.

Acta Crystallographica Section C: Crystal Structure Communications
> International Union of Crystallography, 1983– , bi-m. ISSN
> 0108-2701. DKK 6445/yr.
> Indexed: Chem. Abstr., Chem. Cit. Ind., Curr. Cont., INSPEC
> (1972–), Mat. Sci. Cit. Ind., Sci. Cit. Ind.

Acta Physica Polonica A-B
> IoP Jagellonian University, 1932– , m. ISSN 0587-4246 and
> 0587-4254. $228/yr. and $170/yr.
> Indexed: Chem. Abstr., Curr. Cont., INIS Atomind., INSPEC
> (1968–), Met. Abstr., Sci. Cit. Ind.

Acustica—Acta Acustica
> S. Hirzel Verlag, 1936– , bi-m. ISSN 0001-7884. DM. 840/yr.
> Indexed: Chem. Abstr., Chem. Cit. Ind., Curr. Cont., Sci. Cit. Ind.

Advances in Atomic, Molecular and Optical Physics
> Academic Press, 1965– , irreg., vol. 38, 1997. ISSN 1049-250X.
> Indexed: Chem. Abstr., Chem. Cit. Ind., INIS Atomind., INSPEC,
> Sci. Cit. Ind.

Advances in Biophysics
> Elsevier, 1968– , a. ISSN 0065-227X. $286/yr.
> Indexed: Biol. Abstr., Chem. Abstr., Curr. Excerp. Med., Sci. Cit. Ind.

Advances in Colloid and Interface Science
>   Elsevier, 1967– , m. ISSN 0001-8686. $1331/yr.
>   Indexed: Chem. Cit. Ind., Curr. Cont., Ind. Sci. Rev., INSPEC
>   (1974–1983), Mat. Sci. Cit. Ind., Photo. Abstr., Sci. Cit. Ind.

Advances in Magnetic and Optical Resonance
>   Academic Press, 1965– , irreg., vol. 20, 1997. ISSN 1057-2732.
>   Indexed: INSPEC, Sci. Cit. Ind.

Advances in Nuclear Physics
>   Plenum Press, 1968– , irreg., vol. 24, 1998. ISSN 0065-2970.
>   Indexed: INIS Atomind., INSPEC, Sci. Cit. Ind.

Advances in Physics
>   Taylor and Francis, 1952– , bi-m. ISSN 0001-8732. $1150/yr.
>   Indexed: Chem. Abstr., GeoRef, Met. Abstr., Sci. Cit. Ind.

Advances in Polymer Science
>   Springer-Verlag, 1958– , irreg., vol. 124, 1995. ISSN 0341-020X.
>   Indexed: Biol. Abstr., Chem. Abstr., Chem. Cit. Ind., INSPEC,
>   Mat. Sci. Cit. Ind., Sci. Cit. Ind.

Advances in Quantum Chemistry
>   Academic Press, 1964– , irreg., vol. 30, 1998. ISSN 0065-3276.
>   Indexed: Chem. Abstr., INSPEC, Sci. Cit. Ind.

Advances in X-Ray Analysis
>   Plenum Press, 1960– , a., vol. 39, 1998. ISSN 0069-8490.
>   Indexed: Biol. Abstr., Chem. Abstr., GeoRef, INSPEC.

American Journal of Physics
>   American Association of Physics Teachers, 1933, m. ISSN
>   0002-9505. $295/yr.
>   Indexed: A.S. & T. Ind. (1933–), Chem. Abstr., Curr. Cont., INIS
>   Atomind., INSPEC (1968–), Math. R., Met. Abstr., Sci. Cit. Ind.
>   SSCI.

American Journal of Science
>   Kline Geology Lab, Yale University, 1818– , m., (except July and
>   Aug.). ISSN 0002-9599. $90/yr.
>   Indexed: A.S. & T. Ind. (1983–), Biol. Abstr., Chem. Abstr., Chem.
>   Cit. Ind., Curr. Cont., Eng. Ind., Environ. Abstr., Excerp. Med.,
>   Gen. Sci. Ind. (1984–), Geo. Abstr. P.G., Geol. Abstr., GeoRef,
>   Geotech. Abstr., INIS Atomind., INSPEC (1972–), Met. Abstr.,
>   Mineral. Abstr., Sci. Cit. Ind., Sel. Water Res. Abstr., SSCI.

Annalen der Physik

> Bart Verlagsgesellschaft, 1790– , 8 times/yr. ISSN 0003-3804. DM. 716.
>
> Indexed: Chem. Abstr., Curr. Cont., Eng. Ind., INIS Atomind., INSPEC (1968–), Mat. Sci. Cit. Ind., Math. R., Met. Abstr., Sci. Cit. Ind.

Annales de Physique

> Les Editions de Physique, 1914– , bi-m. ISSN 0003-4169. 2950 F./yr.
>
> Indexed: Chem. Abstr., Chem. Cit. Ind., Curr. Cont., Eng. Ind., INIS Atomind., INSPEC (1968–), Met. Abstr.

Annals of Physics

> Academic Press, 1957– , 18 times/yr. ISSN 0003-4916. $2520/yr.
>
> Indexed: Chem. Abstr., Curr. Cont., Eng. Ind., INIS Atomind., INSPEC (1992–), Math. R., Met. Abstr., Sci. Cit. Ind.

Annual Review of Biophysics and Biomolecular Structure

> Annual Reviews Inc., 1972– , a. ISSN 0084-6589. $140/yr.
>
> Indexed: Biol. Abstr., Chem. Abstr., Chem. Cit. Ind., Curr. Cont., INIS Atomind., INSPEC (1968–), Nucl. Sci. Abstr., Sci. Cit. Ind.

Applied Acoustics

> Elsevier, 1968– , m. ISSN 0003-682X. $1318/yr.
>
> Indexed: Curr. Cont., Environ. Abstr., Excerp. Med., INSPEC (1969–), Sci. Cit. Ind.

Applied Optics

> Optical Society of America, 1962– , 36 times/yr. ISSN 0003-6935. $310/yr.
>
> Indexed: A.S. & T. Ind. (1983–), Chem. Abstr., Chem. Cit. Ind., Eng. Ind., Excerp. Med., Geo. Abstr. P.G., Geol. Abstr., GeoRef, INIS Atomind., INSPEC (1968–), Mat. Sci. Cit. Ind., Met. Abstr., Meteor. & Geoastrophys. Abstr., Sci. Cit. Ind., SSCI.

Applied Physics A: Materials Science and Processing

> Springer-Verlag, 1973– , m. ISSN 0947-8396. DM. 3298/yr.
>
> Indexed: Chem. Abstr., Chem. Cit. Ind., Curr. Cont., INIS Atomind., INSPEC (1968–), Mat. Sci. Cit. Ind., Met. Abstr., Sci. Cit. Ind.

Applied Physics B: Lasers and Optics

> Springer-Verlag , 1994– , m. ISSN 0946-2171 DM. 3898/yr.
>
> Indexed: Chem. Abstr., Chem. Cit. Ind., Curr. Cont., Eng. Ind., INIS Atomind., INSPEC (1973–), Mat. Sci. Cit. Ind., Met. Abstr., Sci. Cit. Ind.

Applied Physics Letters

>   American Institute of Physics, 1962– , w. ISSN 0003-6951. $1545/yr.
>   Indexed: A.S. & T. Ind. (1997–), Chem. Abstr., Chem. Cit. Ind., Curr. Cont., Eng. Ind., GeoRef, INIS Atomind., INSPEC (1968–), Mat. Sci. Cit. Ind., Met. Abstr., Sci. Cit. Ind.

Applied Scientific Research (continued by: Flow, Turbulence and Combustion)

>   Kluwer, 1966– . ISSN 1386-6184. $695/yr.
>   Indexed: Chem. Abstr., Curr. Cont., Eng. Ind., INSPEC (1968–), Met. Abstr., Sci. Cit. Ind.

Applied Spectroscopy

>   Society for Applied Spectroscopy, 1946– , 12 times/yr. ISSN 0003-7028. $310/yr.
>   Indexed: Biol. Abstr., Chem. Abstr., Chem. Cit. Ind., Curr. Cont., Eng. Ind., Excerp. Med., GeoRef, INIS Atomind., INSPEC (1968–), Mat. Sci. Cit. Ind., Met. Abstr., Sci. Cit. Ind., Sel. Water Res. Abstr., SSCI.

Applied Superconductivity

>   Elsevier, 1993– , m. ISSN 0964-1807. $1036/yr.
>   Indexed: Chem. Cit. Ind., Curr. Cont., INSPEC (1993–), Mat. Sci. Cit. Ind., Met. Abstr., Sci. Cit. Ind., SSCI.

Applied Surface Science

>   Elsevier, 1978– , 64 times/yr. ISSN 0169-4332. $4328/yr.
>   Indexed: Chem. Abstr., Chem. Cit. Ind., Curr. Cont., INIS Atomind., INSPEC (1977–), Mat. Sci. Cit. Ind., Met. Abstr., Sci. Cit. Ind.

APS News

>   American Physical Society, 1992– , m. ISSN 1058-8132. $170/yr.

Astronomical Journal

>   American Astronomical Society, 1849– , m. ISSN 0004-6256. $340.
>   Indexed: Chem. Abstr., Curr. Cont., INIS Atomind., INSPEC (1968–), Meteor. & Geoastrophys. Abstr., Sci. Cit. Ind.

Astronomy Letters (Pisma v Astronomicheskii Zhurnal)

>   American Institute of Physics, 1975– , bi-m. ISSN 1063-7737. $1050/yr.
>   Indexed: Curr. Cont., INSPEC (1975–), Sci. Cit. Ind., SSCI.

Astronomy Reports (Astronomicheskii Zhurnal)
> American Institute of Physics, 1924– , bi-m. ISSN 1063-7729. $1600/yr.
> Indexed: INSPEC (1968–), Meteor. & Geostrophys. Abstr.

Astrophysical Journal
> American Astronomical Society, 1895– , 3 times/m. ISSN 0004-637X. $1295/yr.
> Indexed: Chem. Abstr., Chem. Cit. Ind., Curr. Cont., INIS Atomind., INSPEC (1968–), Sci. Cit. Ind.

Astrophysical Journal: Letters
> American Astronomical Society, ISSN 0004-637X.

Astrophysical Journal Supplement
> American Astronomical Society, 1953– , m. ISSN 0067-0049. $220/yr.
> Indexed: Chem. Abstr., Chem. Cit. Ind., Curr. Cont., INSPEC (1968–), Sci. Cit. Ind.

Atomic Data and Nuclear Data Tables
> Academic Press, 1969– , bi-m. ISSN 0092-640X. $580/yr.
> Indexed: Chem. Abstr., Chem. Cit. Ind., Curr. Cont., Excerp. Med., INIS Atomind., INSPEC (1968–1969), Sci. Cit. Ind.

Australian Journal of Physics
> CSIRO, 1948– , bi-m. ISSN 0004-9506. $475/yr.
> Indexed: Chem. Abstr., Curr. Cont., Eng. Ind., GeoRef, INIS Atomind., INSPEC (1968–), Mat. Sci. Cit. Ind., Met. Abstr., Meteor. & Geostrophys. Abstr., Sci. Cit. Ind.

Biophysical Chemistry
> Elsevier, 1974– , 21 times/yr. ISSN 0301-4622. $2388/yr.
> Indexed: Biol. Abstr. Chem. Abstr., Chem. Cit. Ind., Curr. Cont., Excerp. Med., INIS Atomind., Sci. Cit. Ind.

Biophysical Journal
> Biophysical Society, 1960– , m. ISSN 0006-3495. $770/yr.
> Indexed: Biol. Abstr., Chem. Cit. Ind., Curr. Cont., Excerp. Med., INIS Atomind., INSPEC (1974–), Mat. Sci. Cit. Ind., Sci. Cit. Ind.

Biophysics
> Elsevier, 1957– , bi-m. ISSN 0006-3509. $2315/yr.
> Indexed: Biol. Abstr., Excerp. Med., INSPEC (1972–).

Bulletin of the American Astronomical Society
> American Astronomical Society, 1969– , q. ISSN 0002-7537. $53/yr.
> Indexed: INIS Atomind., INSPEC (1969–1991).

Bulletin of the American Physical Society
> American Physical Society, 1956– , irreg. ISSN 0002-7537. $440.
> Indexed: Biol. Abstr., Chem. Abstr.

Bulletin of the Atomic Scientists
> Educational Foundation for Nuclear Science, 1945– , bi-m. ISSN
> 0096-3402. $36/yr.
> Indexed: Biol. Abstr., Chem. Abstr., Curr. Cont., Environ. Abstr.,
> Excerp. Med., Gen. Sci. Ind. (1984–), GeoRef, INIS Atomind.,
> Met. Abstr., Nucl. Sci. Abstr., Sci. Cit. Ind., SSCI.

Bulletin of the Russian Academy of Sciences: Physics
> Allerton Press, 16 times/yr. ISSN 1062-8738. $1895/yr.
> Indexed: Chem. Cit. Ind., INSPEC (1968–), Met. Abstr.

Canadian Journal of Physics
> National Research Council of Canada, 1929– , m. ISSN 0008-4204.
> $126/yr.
> Indexed: A.S. & T. Ind. (1997–), Biol. Abstr., Chem. Abstr. Chem.
> Cit. Ind., Curr. Cont., Eng. Ind., INIS Atomind., INSPEC (1968–),
> Mat. Sci. Cit. Ind., Met. Abstr., Meteor. & Geoastrophys. Abstr.,
> Nucl. Sci. Abstr., Sci. Cit. Ind., SSCI.

CERN Courier
> European Organization for Nuclear Research, 1959– , 10 times/yr.
> ISSN 0304-288X. Free.
> Indexed: INIS Atomind, INSPEC (1981–).

Chaos
> American Institute of Physics, 1991– , q. ISSN 1054-1500. $385.
> Indexed: Curr. Cont., INSPEC (1991–), Sci. Cit. Ind.

Chemical Physics
> Elsevier, 1973– , 39 times/yr. ISSN 0301-0104. $5125/yr.
> Indexed: Chem. Abstr., Chem. Cit. Ind., Curr. Cont., INIS At-
> omind., INSPEC (1973–), Mat. Sci. Cit. Ind., Sci. Cit. Ind.

Chemical Physics Letters
> Elsevier, 1967– , 102 times/yr. ISSN 0009-2614. $8368.
> Indexed: Chem. Abstr., Chem. Cit. Ind., Curr. Cont., INIS At-
> omind., INSPEC (1968–), Mat. Sci. Cit. Ind., Sci. Cit. Ind.

Chinese Physics Letters
> Chinese Physical Society, 1984– , m. ISSN 0256-307X. $575/yr.
> Indexed: Chem. Cit. Ind., Curr. Cont., INIS Atomind., INSPEC (1984–), Mat. Sci. Cit. Ind., Sci. Cit. Ind.

Classical and Quantum Gravity
> Institute of Physics, 1984– , m. ISSN 0264-9381. $1981/yr.
> Indexed: Curr. Cont., INIS Atomind., INSPEC (1984–), Sci. Cit. Ind.

Communications in Mathematical Physics
> Springer-Verlag, 1965– , 27 times/yr. ISSN 0010-3616. DM. 8172.
> Indexed: Curr. Cont., INIS Atomind., INSPEC (1968–), Sci. Cit. Ind.

Complexity
> Wiley, 1995– , bi-m. ISSN 1076-2787. $306/yr.
> Indexed: INSPEC (1995–).

Computational Mathematics & Mathematical Physics
> Elsevier, 1962– , m. ISSN 0965-5425. $2208/yr.
> Indexed: Curr. Cont., INSPEC (1968–1995), SSCI.

Computer Physics Communications
> Elsevier, 1969– , bi-m. ISSN 0010-4655. $4004/yr.
> Indexed: Chem. Abstr., Chem. Cit. Ind., Curr. Cont., INIS Atomind., INSPEC (1969–), Mat. Sci. Cit. Ind., Sci. Cit. Ind.

Computing in Science and Engineering
> (was Computers in Physics)
> American Institute of Physics, 1987– , 6 times/yr. ISSN 0894-1866. $295/yr.
> Indexed: A.S. & T. Ind. (1997–), Curr. Cont., INIS Atomind., INSPEC (1987–).

Contemporary Physics
> Taylor and Francis, 1959– , bi-m. ISSN 0010-7514. $454/yr.
> Indexed: Chem. Abstr., Curr. Cont., Excerp. Med., Gen. Sci. Ind. (1984–), INIS Atomind., INSPEC (1968–), Met. Abstr., Sci. Cit. Ind.

Critical Reviews in Solid State and Materials Science
> CRC Press, 1970– , q. ISSN 1040-8436. $375/yr.
> Indexed: Biol. Abstr., Chem. Abstr., Chem. Cit. Ind., Curr. Cont., INIS Atomind., INSPEC (1978–), Mat. Sci. Cit. Ind., Met. Abstr., Sci. Cit. Ind.

Crystallography Reports
> American Institute of Physics, 1956– , bi-m. ISSN 1063-7745. $1500/yr.
> Indexed: Chem. Cit. Ind., GeoRef, INSPEC (1968–1992), Met. Abstr., Sci. Cit. Ind.

Doklady Physics
> American Institute of Physics, 1933– , m. ISSN 1028-3358. $1750/yr.
> Indexed: INSPEC (1968–), Met. Abstr., Mineral. Abstr.

Earth and Planetary Science Letters
> Elsevier, 1966– , 40 times/yr. ISSN 0012-821X. $2490/yr.
> Indexed: Chem. Abstr., Curr. Cont., Excerp. Med., Geo. Abstr. P.G., Geol. Abstr., GeoRef, INIS Atomind., INSPEC (1968–), Meteor. & Geoastrophys. Abstr., Mineral. Abstr., Sci. Cit. Ind.

European Biophysics Journal
> Springer-Verlag, 1984– , 8 times/yr. ISSN 0175-7571. DM. 1375/yr.
> Indexed: Chem. Cit. Ind., Curr. Cont., Excerp. Med., INIS Atomind., Sci. Cit. Ind.

European Journal of Physics
> Institute of Physics, 1980– , bi-m. ISSN 0143-0807. $505/yr.
> Indexed: Chem. Abstr., INIS Atomind., INSPEC (1980–).

European Physical Journal A—Hadrons and Nuclei
> (was Zeitschrift fur Physik A-Hadrons and Nuclei)
> Springer-Verlag, 1920– , m. ISSN 1434-6001. DM. 3135/yr.
> Indexed: Chem. Abstr., Chem. Cit. Ind., Curr. Cont., INSPEC (1986–), Mat. Sci. Cit. Ind., Sci. Cit. Ind.

European Physical Journal B—Condensed Matter Physics
> (was Zeitschrift fur Physik B-Condensed Matter)
> Springer-Verlag, 1998– , 24 times/yr. ISSN 1434-6028. DM. 4975/yr.
> Indexed: Chem. Abstr., Chem. Cit. Ind., Curr. Cont., INSPEC (1968–), Sci. Cit. Ind.

European Physical Journal C—Particles and Fields
> (was Zeitschrift fur Physik C-Particles and Fields and Journal de Physique IV)
> Springer-Verlag, 1979– , 24 times/yr. ISSN 1434-6044. DM. 9108/yr.
> Indexed: Chem. Abstr., Curr. Cont., INSPEC (1979–), Sci. Cit. Ind.

European Physical Journal D—Atomic, Molecular and Optical Physics
>   (was Journal de Physique I and Zeitschrift fiur Physik D and Nuovo
>   Cimento della Societa Italiana Di Fisica D)
>   Springer-Verlag, 1998– , 12/yr. ISSN 1434-6060. DM. 2860/yr.
>   Indexed: Chem. Cit. Ind., Curr. Cont., INSPEC (1986–), Mat. Sci.
>   Cit. Ind., Sci. Cit. Ind.

European Physical Journal—Applied Physics
>   (was Journal de Physique III)
>   Springer-Verlag, 1966– , m. ISSN 1286-0042. 6800 F./yr.
>   Indexed: Chem. Abstr., Chem. Cit. Ind., Curr. Cont., GeoRef,
>   INSPEC (1968–1996), Mat. Sci. Cit. Ind., Met. Abstr., Sci. Cit. Ind.

Europhysics Letters
>   European Physical Society, 1986– , s-m. ISSN 0295-5075. 8700 F./yr.
>   Indexed: Chem. Cit. Ind., Curr. Cont., INIS Automind., INSPEC
>   (1969–1986), Mat. Sci. Cit. Ind., Sci. Cit. Ind.

Few-Body Systems Acta Physica Austriaca New Series
>   Springer-Verlag, 1947– ; New Series, 1986– , 8 times/yr. ISSN
>   0177-7963. DM. 1146
>   Indexed: Curr. Cont., INSPEC (1968–), Met, Abstr., Sci. Cit. Ind.

Flow, Turbulence and Combustion
>   (see Applied Scientific Research)

Fortschritte der Physik = Progress of Physics
>   Akademie Verlag, 1953– , 10 times/yr. ISSN 0015-8208. $160/yr.
>   Indexed: Chem. Abstr., Curr. Cont., INIS Atomind., INSPEC
>   (1968–), Met. Abstr., Sci. Cit. Ind.

Foundations of Physics
>   Plenum, 1970– , m. ISSN 0015-9018. $1025/yr.
>   Indexed: Chem. Abstr., Curr. Cont., INIS Atomind., INSPEC
>   (1973–), Sci. Cit. Ind.

Foundations of Physics Letters
>   Plenum, 1988– , bi-m. ISSN 0894-9875. $445/yr.
>   Indexed: Curr. Cont., INSPEC (1988–), Sci. Cit. Ind.

Fractals
>   World Scientific, 1993– , q. ISSN 0218-348X. $147/yr.
>   Indexed: Curr. Cont., INSPEC (1993–).

General Relativity & Gravitation
> Plenum, 1970– , m. ISSN 0001-7701. $845/yr.
> Indexed: Curr. Cont., INSPEC (1972–), Sci. Cit. Ind.

Geochimica et Cosmochimica Acta
> Elsevier, 1950– , 24 times/yr. ISSN 0016-7037. $1530/yr.
> Indexed: Biol. Abstr., Chem. Abstr., Chem. Cit. Ind., Curr. Cont., Excerp. Med., Geo. Abstr. P.G., Geol. Abstr., GeoRef, INIS Atomind., INSPEC (1977–), Mat. Sci. Cit. Ind., Meteor. & Geoastrophys. Abstr., Mineral. Abstr.

Geophysical Research Letters
> American Geophysical Society, 1974– , s-m. ISSN 0094-8276. $780/yr.
> Indexed: Chem. Abstr., Chem. Cit. Ind., Curr. Cont., Excerp. Med., Geo. Abstr. P.G., Geol. Abstr., INIS Atomind., INSPEC (1974–), Meteor. & Geoastrophys. Abstr., Mineral Abstr., Sci. Cit. Ind.

Helvetica Physica Acta
> Birkhauser Verlag, 1926– , 6 times/yr. ISSN 0018-0238. 6985 F./yr.
> Indexed: Chem. Abstr., Curr. Cont., INIS Atomind., INSPEC (1968–), Met. Abstr., Sci. Cit. Ind.

History of Physics Newsletter
> American Institute of Physics

IEEE Journal of Quantum Electronics
> IEEE, 1965– , m. ISSN 0018-9197. $750/yr.
> Indexed: A.S. & T. Ind. (1983–), Chem. Abstr., Curr. Cont., Eng. Ind., INIS Atomind., INSPEC (1968–), Mat. Sci. Cit. Ind., Sci. Cit. Ind.

IEEE Photonics Technology Letters
> IEEE, 1989– , m. ISSN 1041-1135. $395/yr.
> Indexed: Curr. Cont., Eng. Ind., INSPEC (1989–), Mat. Sci. Cit. Ind., Sci. Cit. Ind.

IEEE Transactions on Electron Devices
> IEEE, 1952– , m. ISSN 0018-9383. $475/yr.
> Indexed: A.S. & T. Ind. (1997–), Chem. Abstr., Chem. Cit. Ind., Curr. Cont., Eng. Ind., Excerp. Med., INIS Atomind., INSPEC (1968–), Sci. Cit. Ind.

IEEE Transactions on Nuclear Science
>IEEE, 1954– , bi-m. ISSN 0018-9499. $450/yr.
>Indexed: A.S. & T. Ind., Chem. Abstr., Curr. Cont., Eng. Ind., Ex-
>cerp. Med., INIS Atomind., INSPEC (1968–), Sci. Cit. Ind.

IEEE Transactions on Plasma Science
>IEEE, 1973– , bi-m. ISSN 0093-3813. $350/yr.
>Indexed: Chem. Abstr., Curr. Cont., Eng. Ind., INIS Atomind.,
>INSPEC (1973–), Mat. Sci. Cit. Ind., Sci. Cit. Ind.

Il Nuovo Cimento Della Societa Italiana Di Fisica, A: Nuclei, Particle
>Editrice Compositori, 1855– , m. ISSN 0369-3546. $1070/yr.
>Indexed: Chem. Abstr., Curr. Cont., INSPEC (1968–), Sci. Cit. Ind.

Il Nuovo Cimento Della Societa Italiana Di Fisica, B: General Physics
>Editrice Compositori, 1855– , m. ISSN 0369-3554. $745/yr.
>Indexed: Chem. Abstr., Curr. Cont., INSPEC (1968–), Sci. Cit. Ind.

Il Nuovo Cimento Della Societa Italiana Di Fisica, C: Geophysics
>Editrice Compositori, 1978– , bi-m. ISSN 0390-5551. $378/yr.
>Indexed: Chem. Abstr., Curr. Cont., INSPEC (1978–), Meteor. &
>Geastrophys. Abstr.

Il Nuovo Cimento Della Societa Italiana Di Fisica, D: Condensed
>(now in European Physical Journal B and D)

Industrial Physicist
>American Institute of Physics, 1995– , q. ISSN 1082-1848. $48/yr.

Infrared Physics and Technology
>Elsevier, 1961– , 6 times/yr. ISSN 1350-4495. $1032/yr.
>Indexed: Chem. Abstr., Chem. Cit. Ind., Curr. Cont., INIS At-
>omind., INSPEC (1968–1996), Mat. Sci. Cit. Ind., Met. Abstr., Sci.
>Cit. Ind.

Instruments and Experimental Techniques (Probory I Tekhnika Eksperimenta)
>Consultants Bureau, 1956– , bi-m. ISSN 0020-4412. $1755/yr.
>Indexed: Curr. Cont., Eng. Ind., INIS Atomind., INSPEC (1968–),
>Mat. Sci. Cit. Ind., Met. Abstr., Sci. Cit. Ind.

International Journal of Mass Spectrometry and Ion Processes
>Elsevier, 1968– , 27 times/yr. ISSN 0168-1176. $3153/yr.
>Indexed: Chem. Abstr., Chem. Cit. Ind., Curr. Cont., Excerp. Med.,
>INSPEC (1968–1983), Sci. Cit. Ind.

International Journal of Modern Physics A: High Energy Physics
>   World Scientific, 1986– , 32 times/yr. ISSN 0217-751X. $2398/yr.
>   Indexed: Curr. Cont., INIS Atomind., INSPEC (1987–), Sci. Cit.
>   Ind.

International Journal of Modern Physics B: Condensed Matter Physics
>   World Scientific, 1987– , 32 times/yr. ISSN 0217-9792. $1774/yr.
>   Indexed: Chem. Cit. Ind., Curr. Cont., INSPEC (1987–), Mat. Sci.
>   Cit. Ind., Sci. Cit. Ind.

International Journal of Modern Physics C: Physics and Computers
>   World Scientific, 1990– , bi-m. ISSN 0129-1831. $481/yr.
>   Indexed: Chem. Cit. Ind., Curr. Cont., INSPEC (1990–1996), Sci.
>   Cit. Ind.

International Journal of Modern Physics D: Gravitation, Astrophysics and
Cosmology
>   World Scientific, 1992– , 6 times/yr. ISSN 0218-2718. $298/yr.
>   Indexed: Curr. Cont., INSPEC (1992–), Sci. Cit. Ind.

International Journal of Modern Physics E: Nuclear Physics
>   World Scientific, 1992– , q. ISSN 0218-3013. $260/yr.
>   Indexed: Curr. Cont., INSPEC (1992–).

International Journal of Non-Linear Mechanics
>   Elsevier, 1966– , bi-m. ISSN 0020-7462. $1258/yr.
>   Indexed: Curr. Cont., Eng. Ind., INSPEC (1968–), Mat. Sci. Cit.
>   Ind., Met. Abstr., Sci. Cit. Ind.

International Journal of Solids and Structures
>   Elsevier, 1965– , 36 times/yr. ISSN 0020-7683. $4546/yr.
>   Indexed: Chem. Abstr., Curr. Cont., Eng. Ind., Geotech. Abstr.,
>   INSPEC (1968–), Mat. Sci. Cit. Ind., Met. Abstr., Sci. Cit. Ind.

International Journal of Theoretical Physics
>   Plenum, 1968– , m. ISSN 0020-7748. $855/yr.
>   Indexed: Chem. Abstr., Curr. Cont., INIS Atomind., INSPEC
>   (1969–), Sci. Cit. Ind.

Inverse Problems
>   Institute of Physics, 1985– , bi-m. ISSN 0266-5611. $1072/yr.
>   Indexed: Curr. Cont., INSPEC (1985–), Sci. Cit. Ind.

Japanese Journal of Applied Physics Part 1: Regular Papers

Japanese Journal of Applied Physics, 1962– , m. ISSN 0021-4922.
Indexed: Chem. Abstr., Curr. Cont., Eng. Ind., GeoRef, INIS Atomind., INSPEC (1968–1996), Mat. Sci. Cit. Ind., Met. Abstr., Sci. Cit. Ind.

Japanese Journal of Applied Physics Part 2: Letters

Japanese Journal of Applied Physics, 1962– , m. ISSN 0021-4922.
Indexed: Chem. Abstr., Curr. Cont., Eng. Ind., GeoRef, INIS Atomind., INSPEC (1968–1996), Mat. Sci. Cit. Ind., Met. Abstr., Sci. Cit. Ind.

Japanese Journal of Applied Physics Supplement

Japanese Journal of Applied Physics, 1962– , m. ISSN 0021-4922.
Indexed: Chem. Abstr., Curr. Cont., Eng. Ind., GeoRef, INIS Atomind., INSPEC (1968–1996), Mat. Sci. Cit. Ind., Met. Abstr., Sci. Cit. Ind.

JETP Letters

American Institute of Physics, 1965– , s-m. ISSN 0021-3640. $1500/yr.
Indexed: Chem. Cit. Ind., Curr. Cont., INIS Atomind., INSPEC (1968–), Mat. Sci. Cit. Ind., Met. Abstr., Sci Cit. Ind.

Journal de Physique I

(now European Physical Journal D)

Journal de Physique II

(now in European Physical Journal D)

Journal de Physique III

(now European Physical Journal—Applied Physics)

Journal de Physique IV

(now European Physical Journal C)

Journal of Algorithms

Academic Press, 1980– , 8 times/yr. ISSN 0196-6774. $425/yr.
Indexed: Curr. Cont., INSPEC (1981–), Sci. Cit. Ind.

Journal of Applied Geophysics

Elsevier, 1963– , 8 times/yr. ISSN 0926-9851. $668/yr.
Indexed: Chem. Abstr., Curr. Cont., Eng. Ind., Excerp. Med., Geo. Abstr. P.G., Geol. Abstr., GeoRef, Geotech. Abstr., INIS Atomind., INSPEC (1971–1991), Sci. Cit. Ind.

Journal of Applied Physics

American Institute of Physics, 1931– , s-m. ISSN 0021-8979. $2400/yr.
Indexed: A.S. & T. Ind. (1983–), Chem. Abstr., Chem. Cit. Ind., Curr. Cont., INSPEC (1968–), Mat. Sci. Cit. Ind., Met. Abstr., Sci. Cit. Ind.

Journal of Atmospheric and Solar-Terrestrial Physics

Elsevier, 1950– , 18 times/yr. ISSN 1364-6826. $2270/yr.
Indexed: Chem. Abstr., Curr. Cont., Geo. Abstr. P.G., GeoRef, INIS Atomind., INSPEC (1968–1997), Meteor. & Geoastrophys. Abstr., Sci. Cit. Ind.

Journal of Chemical Physics

American Institute of Physics, 1931– , w. ISSN 0021-9606. $3480/yr.
Indexed: Chem. Abstr., Chem Cit. Ind., Curr. Cont., Eng. Ind., INIS Atomind., INSPEC (1968–), Mat. Sci. Cit. Ind., Met. Abstr., Sci. Cit. Ind.

Journal of Computational Physics

Academic Press, 1966– , 18 times/yr. ISSN 0021-9991. $2328/yr.
Indexed: Chem. Abstr., Chem. Cit. Ind., Curr. Cont., Excerp. Med., GeoRef, INIS Atomind., INSPEC (1968–), Mat. Sci. Cit. Ind., Sci. Cit. Ind.

Journal of Crystal Growth

Elsevier, 1967– , 52 times/yr. ISSN 0022-0248. $7545/yr.
Indexed: Chem. Abstr., Chem. Cit. Ind., Curr. Cont., GeoRef, INSPEC (1968–), Met. Abstr., Mineral. Abstr., Sci. Cit. Ind.

Journal of Electron Microscopy

Oxford University Press, 1953– , 6 times/yr. ISSN 0022-0744. $295/yr.
Indexed: Biol. Abstr., Chem. Abstr., Chem. Cit. Ind., Curr. Cont., Excerp. Med., INIS Atomind., INSPEC (1968–1997), Mat. Sci. Cit. Ind., Met. Abstr., Sci. Cit. Ind.

Journal of Electron Spectroscopy and Related Phenomena

Elsevier, 1972– , 24 times/yr. ISSN 0368-2048. $2562/yr.
Indexed: Chem. Abstr., Chem. Cit. Ind., Curr. Cont., INIS Atomind., INSPEC (1972–), Mat. Sci. Cit. Ind., Met. Abstr., Sci. Cit. Ind.

Journal of Experimental and Theoretical Physics
>   American Institute of Physics, 1955– , m. ISSN 1063-7761.
> $3065/yr.
>   Indexed: Eng. Ind., INSPEC (1968–), Met. Abstr., Sci. Cit. Ind.

Journal of Geometry and Physics
>   Elsevier, 1984–1987, resumed vol. 8, 1991, 16 times/yr. ISSN
>   0393-0440. $978/yr.
>   Indexed: Curr. Cont., INSPEC (1984–1992).

Journal of Geophysical Research A-E
>   American Geophysical Society, 1896– , m. ISSN 0148-0227.
> $2790/yr.
>   Indexed: Environ. Abstr., Geo. Abstr. P.G., Geol. Abstr., INIS At-
>   omind., INSPEC (1968–), Meteor. & Geoastrophys. Abstr., Min-
>   eral. Abstr.

Journal of Low Temperature Physics
>   Plenum, 1969– , 24 times/yr. ISSN 0022-2291. $1175/yr.
>   Indexed: Chem. Abstr., Curr. Cont., Eng. Ind., INIS Atomind.,
>   INSPEC (1969–), Mat. Sci. Cit. Ind., Met. Abstr., Sci. Cit. Ind.

Journal of Luminescence
>   Elsevier, 1970– , 20 times/yr. ISSN 0022-2313. $1841/yr.
>   Indexed: Chem. Abstr., Chem. Cit. Ind., Curr. Cont., Eng. Ind.,
>   GeoRef, INIS Atomind., INSPEC (1970–), Mat. Sci. Cit. Ind., Sci.
>   Cit. Ind.

Journal of Magnetic Resonance
>   Academic Press, 1969– , m. ISSN 1090-7807. $1990/yr.
>   Indexed: Chem. Abstr., Chem. Cit. Ind., Curr. Cont., INIS At-
>   omind., INSPEC (1970; 1992–1997), Sci. Cit. Ind.
>   (was Journal of Magnetic Resonance: Series A and Series B)

Journal of Magnetism and Magnetic Materials
>   Elsevier, 1976– , 45 times/yr. ISSN 0304-8853. $5326/yr.
>   Indexed: Chem. Abstr., Chem. Cit. Ind., Curr. Cont., GeoRef, INIS
>   Atomind., INSPEC (1975–), Mat. Sci. Cit. Ind., Met. Abstr., Sci.
>   Cit. Ind.

Journal of Mass Spectrometry
>   Wiley, 1968– , m. ISSN 1076-5174. $2850/yr.
>   Indexed: Chem. Abstr., Chem. Cit. Ind., Curr. Cont., Excerp. Med.,
>   Sci. Cit. Ind.

Journal of Materials Research

> Materials Research Society, 1986– , m. ISSN 0884-2914. $683/yr.
> Indexed: Chem. Abstr., Chem Cit. Ind., Curr. Cont., INIS Atomind., INSPEC (1986–), Mat. Sci. Cit. Ind., Met. Abstr., Sci. Cit. Ind.

Journal of Mathematical Physics

> American Institute of Physics, 1960– , m. ISSN 0022-2488. $1680/yr.
> Indexed: Chem. Abstr., Chem. Cit. Ind., Curr. Cont., Eng. Ind., INIS Atomind., INSPEC (1968–), Sci. Cit. Ind.

Journal of Micromechanics and Microengineering

> Institute of Physics, 1991– , q. ISSN 0960-1317. $444/yr.
> Indexed: Curr. Cont., INSPEC (1991–), Met. Abstr.

Journal of Modern Optics

> Taylor and Francis, 1954– , m. ISSN 0950-0340. $1664/yr.
> Indexed: Chem. Abstr., Curr. Cont., Excerp. Med., INSPEC (1968–1987), Sci. Cit. Ind.
> (was Optica Acta)

Journal of Non-Crystalline Solids

> Elsevier, 1969– , 54 times/yr. ISSN 0022-3093. $5514/yr.
> Indexed: Chem. Abstr., Chem. Cit. Ind., Curr. Cont., INIS Atomind., INSPEC (1968–), Mat. Sci. Cit. Ind., Met. Abstr., Sci. Cit. Ind.

Journal of Nonlinear Optical Physics and Materials

> World Scientific, 1992– , q. ISSN 0218-1991. $440/yr.
> Indexed: Curr. Cont., INSPEC (1992–1995).

Journal of Nuclear Materials

> Elsevier, 1959– , 36 times/yr. ISSN 0022-3115. $4797/yr.
> Indexed: Chem. Abstr., Chem. Cit. Ind., Curr. Cont., Eng. Ind., INIS Atomind., INSPEC (1968–), Mat. Sci. Cit. Ind., Met. Abstr., Sci. Cit. Ind.

Journal of Nuclear Science and Technology

> Atomic Energy Society of Japan, 1964– , m. ISSN 0022-3131. $150/yr.
> Indexed: Chem. Abstr., Chem. Cit. Ind., Curr. Cont., Eviron. Abstr., Excerp. Med., INIS Atomind., INSPEC (1968–), Mat. Sci. Cit. Ind., Met. Abstr., Sci. Cit. Ind.

Journal of Optical Technology (Opticheskii Zhurnal)
>   Optical Society of America, 1966– , m. ISSN 1070-9762. $1635/yr.
>   Indexed: Curr. Cont., Eng. Ind., INSPEC (1968–1993), Mat. Sci.
>   Cit. Ind.

Journal of Physical and Chemical Reference Data
>   National Institute for Science and Technology, 1972– , 6 times/yr.
>   ISSN 0047-2689. $665/yr.
>   Indexed: A.S. & T. Ind. (1983–1990), Chem. Abstr., Chem. Cit.
>   Ind., Curr. Cont., INIS Atomind., INSPEC (1973–), Met. Abstr.,
>   Nucl. Sci. Abstr.

Journal of Physical Chemistry Section A
>   American Chemical Society, 1896– , w. ISSN 1089-5639. $430/yr.
>   Indexed: A.S. & T. Ind. (1983–1996), Chem. Abstr., Chem. Cit.
>   Ind., Curr. Cont., Eng. Ind., INIS Atomind., INSPEC (1968–1997),
>   Mat. Sci. Cit. Ind., Met. Abstr., Sci. Cit. Ind.

Journal of Physical Chemistry Section B
>   American Chemical Society, 1896– , w. ISSN 1089-5647. $215/yr.
>   Indexed: Chem. Cit. Ind., Curr. Cont., INSPEC (1968–1997), Sci.
>   Cit. Ind.

Journal of Physics and Chemistry of Solids
>   Elsevier, 1956– , m. ISSN 0022-3697. $3419/yr.
>   Indexed: Chem. Abstr., Chem. Cit. Ind., Curr. Cont., GeoRef, INIS
>   Atomind., INSPEC (1968–), Mat. Sci. Cit. Ind., Met. Abstr., Sci.
>   Cit. Ind., SSCI.

Journal of Physics A: Mathematical and General
>   Institute of Physics, 1968– , s-m. ISSN 0305-4470. $3516/yr.
>   Indexed: Chem. Abstr., Chem. Cit. Ind., Curr. Cont., Eng. Ind.,
>   INIS Atomind., INSPEC (1968–), Mat. Sci. Cit. Ind., Met. Abstr.,
>   Sci. Cit. Ind., SSCI.

Journal of Physics B: Atomic, Molecular and Optical Physics
>   Institute of Physics, 1968– , s-m. ISSN 0953-4075. $2891/yr.
>   Indexed: Chem. Abstr., Chem. Cit. Ind., Curr. Cont., Eng. Ind.,
>   INIS Atomind., INSPEC (1968–), Met. Abstr., Sci. Cit. Ind.

Journal of Physics: Condensed Matter
>   Institute of Physics, 1968– , w. ISSN 0953-8984. $5682/yr.
>   Indexed: Chem. Abstr., Chem. Cit. Ind., Curr. Cont., Eng. Ind.,
>   GeoRef, INIS Atomind., INSPEC (1968–), Mat. Sci. Cit. Ind., Met.
>   Abstr., Sci. Cit. Ind.

Journal of Physics D: Applied Physics
> Institute of Physics, 1968– , s-m. ISSN 0022-3727. $1907/yr.
> Indexed: A.S. & T. Ind. (1983–), Chem. Abstr., Chem. Cit. Ind.,
> Curr. Cont., Eng. Ind., GeoRef, INIS Atomind., INSPEC (1968–),
> Mat. Sci. Cit. Ind., Met. Abstr., Sci. Cit. Ind.

Journal of Physics G: Nuclear and Particle Physics
> Institute of Physics, 1975– , m. ISSN 0954-3889. $1948/yr.
> Indexed: Chem. Abstr., Curr. Cont., INIS Atomind., INSPEC
> (1975–), Sci. Cit. Ind.

Journal of Plasma Physics
> Cambridge University Press, 1967– , 10 times/yr. ISSN 0022-3778.
> $714/yr.
> Indexed: Chem. Abstr., Curr. Cont., INIS Atomind., INSPEC
> (1968–), Sci. Cit. Ind.

Journal of Research of the National Institute of Standards and Technology
> (was National Bureau of Standards)
> NIST, 1928– , bi-m. ISSN 1044-677X. $28/yr.
> Indexed: A.S. & T. Ind. (1983–), Chem. Abstr., Chem. Cit. Ind.,
> Curr. Cont., Eng. Ind., INIS Atomind., INSPEC (1968–1977;
> 1988–), Met. Abstr., Sci. Cit. Ind.

Journal of Rheology
> Society of Rheology, 1957– , bi-m. ISSN 0148-6055. $375/yr.
> Indexed: Chem. Abstr., Chem. Cit. Ind., Curr. Cont., Eng. Ind.,
> INIS Atomind., INSPEC (1971–), Mat. Sci. Cit. Ind., Sci. Cit. Ind.

Journal of Solid State Chemistry
> Academic Press, 1969– , 16 times/yr. ISSN 0022-4596. $2150/yr.
> Indexed: Chem. Abstr., Chem. Cit. Ind., Curr. Cont., Eng. Ind.,
> GeoRef, INIS Atomind., INSPEC (1971–), Mat. Sci. Cit. Ind., Met.
> Abstr., Sci. Cit. Ind.

Journal of Sound and Vibration
> Academic Press, 1964– , 50 times/yr. ISSN 0022-460X.
> Indexed: Biol. Abstr., Curr. Cont., Eng. Ind., Excerp. Med., INIS
> Atomind., INSPEC (1968–), Mat. Sci. Cit. Ind., Sci. Cit. Ind.

Journal of Statistical Physics
> Plenum, 1969– , 24 times/yr. ISSN 0022-4715. $1725/yr.
> Indexed: Chem. Cit. Ind., Curr. Cont., Eng. Ind., INIS Atomind.,
> INSPEC (1969–), Nucl. Sci. Abstr., Sci. Cit. Ind., SSCI.

Journal of Supercritical Fluids
> Elsevier, 1988– , 6 times/yr. ISSN 0896-8446. $656/yr.
> Indexed: Chem. Abstr., Chem. Cit. Ind., Curr. Cont., Excerp. Med.

Journal of the Acoustical Society of America
> Acoustical Society of America, 1929– , m. ISSN 0001-4966. $1020/yr.
> Indexed: A.S. & T. Ind., Biol. Abstr., Chem. Abstr., Chem. Cit. Ind., Curr. Cont., Eng. Ind., Environ. Abstr., Excerp. Med., Geo. Abstr. P.G., Geol. Abstr., INIS Atomind., INSPEC (1968–), Meteor. & Geoastrophys. Abstr., Sci. Cit. Ind., SSCI.

Journal of the American Chemical Society
> American Chemical Society, 1879– , w. ISSN 0002-7863. $2042/yr.
> Indexed: A.S. & T. Ind. (1983–), Biol. Abstr., Chem. Abstr., Chem. Cit. Ind., Curr. Cont., Eng. Ind., Excerp. Med., Gen. Sci. Ind. (1984–), INIS Atomind., INSPEC (1968–), Mat. Sci. Cit. Ind., Met. Abstr., Sci. Cit. Ind.

Journal of the American Society for Mass Spectrometry
> Elsevier, 1990– , m. ISSN 1044-0305. $420/yr.
> Indexed: Chem. Abstr., Chem. Cit. Ind., Curr. Cont., Environ. Abstr., Excerp. Med. (1996–), INSPEC (1990–), Sci. Cit. Ind.

Journal of the Atmospheric Sciences
> American Meteorological Society, 1944– , s-m. ISSN 0022-4928. $475/yr.
> Indexed: A.S. & T. Ind., Chem. Abstr., Curr. Cont., Excerp. Med., Gen. Sci. Ind. (1984–), Geo. Abstr. P.G., GeoRef, INIS Atomind., INSPEC (1968–), Meteor. & Geoastrophys. Abstr., Sci. Cit. Ind.

Journal of the Mechanics and Physics of Solids
> Elsevier, 1952– , m. ISSN 0022-5096. $2423/yr.
> Indexed: A.S. & T. Ind. (1991–), Chem. Abstr., Chem. Cit. Ind., Curr. Cont., Eng. Ind., Geotech. Abstr., INIS Atomind., INSPEC (1968–), Mat. Sci. Cit. Ind., Met. Abstr., Sci. Cit. Ind.

Journal of the Optical Society of America A
> Optical Society of America, 1917– , 12 times/yr. ISSN 0740-3232. $917/yr.
> Indexed: A.S. & T. Ind. (1983–1993), Chem. Abstr., Curr. Cont., Eng. Ind., GeoRef, INIS Atomind., INSPEC (1968–), Met. Abstr. Meteor. & Geastrophys. Abstr., Sci. Cit. Ind., SSCI.

Journal of the Optical Society of America B
> Optical Society of America, 1917– , 12 times/yr. ISSN 0740-3224. $917/yr.
> Indexed: A.S. & T. Abstr. (1984–), Biol. Abstr., Chem. Abstr. Chem. Cit. Ind., Curr. Cont., Eng. Ind., GeoRef, INIS Atomind., INSPEC (1968–), Met. Abstr., Meteor. & Geoastrophys. Abstr., Sci. Cit. Ind.

Journal of the Physical Society of Japan
> Physical Society of Japan, 1946– , m. ISSN 0031-9015. 89400 yen/yr.
> Indexed: Chem. Abstr., Chem. Cit. Ind., Curr. Cont., GeoRef, INIS Atomind., INSPEC (1986–1972), Met. Abstr., Sci. Cit. Ind.

Journal of Vacuum Science and Technology. Part A. Vacuum, Surfaces and Films
> American Vacuum Society, 1964– , 6 times/yr. ISSN 0734-2101. $727/yr.
> Indexed: Chem. Abstr., Chem. Cit. Ind., Curr. Cont., Eng. Ind., INIS Atomind., INSPEC (1968–), Mat. Sci. Cit. Ind., Met. Abstr., Sci. Cit. Ind.

Journal of Vacuum Science and Technology. Part B. Microelectronics and Nanometer Structures
> American Vacuum Society, 1964–, 6 times/yr. ISSN 1071-1023. $727/yr.
> Indexed: Chem. Cit. Ind., Curr. Cont., INIS Atomind., INSPEC (1968–), Mat. Sci. Cit. Ind., Sci. Cit. Ind.

Laser & Particle Beams: Pulse Power & High Energy Densities
> Cambridge University Press, 1983–, q. ISSN 0263-0346. $450/yr.
> Indexed: Chem. Abstr., Curr. Cont., INIS Atomind., INSPEC (1983–), Sci. Cit. Ind.

Letters in Mathematical Physics
> Kluwer, 1975– , 16 times/yr. ISSN 0377-9017. $1000/yr.
> Indexed: Astron. & Astrophys. Abstr., Chem. Abstr., Curr. Cont., INIS Atomind., INSPEC (1975–), Sci. Cit. Ind.

Los Alamos Science (Los Alamos Series in Basic and Applied Sciences)
> Los Alamos National Laboratory, 1979– , irreg., no. 13, 1994.

Low Temperature Physics (Fizika Nizkikh Temperatur)
> American Institute of Physics, 1975–, m. ISSN 1063-777X. $260/yr.
> Indexed: Chem. Abstr., Chem. Cit. Ind., Curr. Cont., INIS Atomind., INSPEC (1975–), Mat. Sci. Cit. Ind., Sci. Cit. Ind.

Materials Chemistry and Physics
>   Elsevier, 1976– , 15 times/yr. ISSN 0254-0584. $1904/yr.
>   Indexed: Chem. Abstr., Chem. Cit. Ind., Curr. Cont., INSPEC (1983–), Mat. Sci. Cit. Ind., Met. Abstr., Sci. Cit. Ind.

Materials Letters
>   Elsevier, 1982– , 30 times/yr. ISSN 0167-577X. $1482/yr.
>   Indexed: Chem. Abstr., Chem. Cit. Ind., Curr. Cont., INIS Atomind., INSPEC (1982–), Mat. Sci. Cit. Ind., Met. Abstr., Sci. Cit. Ind.

Materials Research Bulletin
>   Elsevier, 1966– , 15 times/yr. ISSN 0025-5408. $1628/yr.
>   Indexed: Chem. Abstr., Chem. Cit. Ind., Curr. Cont., Eng. Ind., GeoRef, INIS Atomind., INSPEC (1968–), Mat. Sci. Cit. Ind., Sci. Cit. Ind.

Materials Science and Engineering B: Solid-State Materials for Advanced Technology
>   Elsevier, 1988– , 27 times/yr. ISSN 0921-5107. $2757/yr.
>   Indexed: Chem. Cit. Ind., Curr. Cont., INSPEC (1968–), Mat. Sci. Cit. Ind., Met. Abstr., Sci. Cit. Ind.

Measurement Science and Technology
>   Institute of Physics, 1968– , m. ISSN 0957-0233. $1064/yr.
>   Indexed: A.S. & T. Ind. (1983–), Biol. Abstr., Chem. Abstr., Chem. Cit. Ind., Curr. Cont., Eng. Ind., Excerp. Med., GeoRef, INIS Atomind., INSPEC (1968–), Mat. Sci. Cit. Ind., Met. Abstr., Sci. Cit. Ind.

Mechanics of Materials
>   Elsevier, 1982– , m. ISSN 0167-6636. $1187/yr.
>   Indexed: Chem. Cit. Ind., Curr. Cont., Geotech. Abstr., INSPEC (1982–), Mat. Sci. Cit. Ind., Met. Abstr.

Medical Engineering and Physics
>   Elsevier, 1979– , 10 times/yr. ISSN 1350-4533. $1084/yr.
>   Indexed: Biol. Abstr., Chem. Abstr., Curr. Cont., Excerp. Med., INSPEC (1979–), Sci. Cit. Ind., SSCI.

Meteorology and Atmospheric Physics
>   Springer-Verlag, 1949– , 12 times/yr. ISSN 0177-7971. DM. 1740/yr.
>   Indexed: Curr. Cont., Geo. Abstr. Geol. Abstr., INIS Atomind., INSPEC (1984–), Meteor. & Geoastrophys. Abstr., Sci. Cit. Ind.

Modelling & Simulation in Materials Science and Engineering
>   Institute of Physics, 1992– , q. ISSN 0965-0393. $437/yr.
>   Indexed: Curr. Cont., INSPEC (1992–), Mat. Sci. Cit. Ind., Met.
>   Abstr., Sci. Cit. Ind.

Modern Physics Letters A
>   World Scientific, 1986– , 40 times/yr. ISSN 0217-7323. $1544/yr.
>   Indexed: Curr. Cont., INSPEC (1987–), Sci. Cit. Ind.

Modern Physics Letters B
>   World Scientific, 1987– , 30 times/yr. ISSN 0217-9849. $1290/yr.
>   Indexed: Curr. Cont., INSPEC (1987–), Mat. Sci. Cit. Ind., Sci. Cit.
>   Ind.

Molecular Physics
>   Taylor and Francis, 1958– , 18 times/yr. ISSN 0026-8976.
> $2395/yr.
>   Indexed: Chem. Abstr., Chem. Cit. Ind., Curr. Cont., INSPEC
>   (1968–), Mat. Sci. Cit. Ind., Sci. Cit. Ind.

Nanostructured Materials
>   Elsevier, 1992– , 8 times/yr. ISSN 0965-9773. $785/yr.
>   Indexed: Chem. Cit. Ind., Curr. Cont., INSPEC (1992), Mat. Sci.
>   Cit. Ind., Met. Abstr.

Nanotechnology
>   Institute of Physics, 1990– , q. ISSN 0957-4484. $436/yr.
>   Indexed: Curr. Cont., INSPEC (1990–), Mat. Sci. Cit. Ind., Met.
>   Abstr., Sci. Cit. Ind.

Network: Computation in Neural Systems
>   Institute of Physics, 1990– , q. ISSN 0954-898X. $350/yr.
>   Indexed: Curr. Cont., INSPEC (1990–), Sci. Cit. Ind.

Nonlinearity
>   Institute of Physics, 1988– , bi-m. ISSN 0951-7715.
>   Indexed: Curr. Cont., INSPEC (1988–), Sci. Cit., Ind.

Nuclear Data Sheets
>   Academic Press, 1966– , m. ISSN 0090-3752. $790/yr.
>   Indexed: Chem. Abstr., Excerp. Med., INSPEC (1974–).

Nuclear Instruments and Methods in Physics Research Section A: Accelerators, Spectrometers, Dectors and Associated Equipment
> Elsevier, 1957– , 54 times/yr. ISSN 0168-9002. $8361/yr.
> Indexed: Chem. Abstr., Chem. Cit. Ind., Curr. Cont., Eng. Ind., Excerp. Med., GeoRef, INSPEC (1968–), Mat. Sci. Cit. Ind., Nucl. Sci. Abstr., Sci. Cit. Ind.

Nuclear Instruments and Methods in Physics Research Section B: Beam Interactions with Materials and Atoms
> Elsevier, 1957– , 52 times/yr. ISSN 0168-583X. $6409/yr.
> Indexed: Chem. Cit. Ind., Curr. Cont., INSPEC (1968–), Mat. Sci. Cit. Ind., Met. Abstr., Sci. Cit. Ind., SSCI.

Nuclear Physics Section A
> Elsevier, 1956– , 68 times/yr. ISSN 0375-9474. $7234/yr.
> Indexed: Chem. Abstr., Curr. Cont., INSPEC (1968–), Met. Abstr., Sci. Cit. Ind.

Nuclear Physics Section B
> Elsevier, 1956– , 84 times/yr. ISSN 0550-3213. $11267/yr.
> Indexed: Chem. Abstr., Curr. Cont., INSPEC (1968–), Sci. Cit. Ind.

Nuclear Physics Proceedings Supplement
> Elsevier, 1987– , 33 times/yr. ISSN 0920-5632. $2315/yr.
> Indexed: Curr. Cont., INSPEC (1987–), Sci. Cit. Ind.

Nuclear Safety
> Oak Ridge National Laboratory, 1959– , bi-a. ISSN 0029-5604. $14/yr.
> Indexed: A.S. & T. Ind. (1991–), Biol. Abstr., Chem. Abstr., Curr. Cont., Eng. Ind., Environ. Abstr., Excerp. Med., INSPEC (1968–), Met. Abstr., Sci. Cit. Ind.

Nuclear Science & Engineering
> American Nuclear Society, 1956– , m. (3 vols./yr.). ISSN 0029-5639. $585/yr.
> Indexed: Biol. Abstr., Chem. Abstr., Curr. Cont., Eng. Ind., Environ. Abstr., Excerp. Med., INSPEC (1968–), Met. Abstr., Sci. Cit. Ind.

Nuclear Technology
> American Nuclear Society, 1965– , m. ISSN 0029-5450. $595/yr.
> Indexed: A.S. & T. Ind. (1983–), Biol. Abstr., Chem. Abstr., Curr. Cont., Eng. Ind., Environ. Abstr., INSPEC (1968–), Mat. Sci. Cit. Ind., Met. Abstr., Sci. Cit. Ind., SSCI.

Optics and Laser Technology
> Elsevier, 1968– , 8 times/yr. ISSN 0030-3992. $855/yr.
> Indexed: Chem. Abstr., Curr. Cont., Eng. Ind., Excerp. Med.,
> INSPEC (1969–), Sci. Cit. Ind.

Optics and Photonics News
> Optical Society of America, 1975– , m. ISSN 1047-6938. $99/yr.
> Indexed: INSPEC (1990–1994).

Optics & Spectroscopy
> Interperiodica, 1959– , m. ISSN 0030-400X. $1897/yr.
> Indexed: Chem. Cit. Ind., Curr. Cont., Eng. Ind., INSPEC (1968–),
> Met. Abstr., Sci. Cit. Ind.

Optics and Spectroscopy (Optika I Spektroskopiya)
> Optical Society of America, 1956– , 12 times/yr. ISSN 0030-400X.
> $1970/yr.

Optics Communications
> Elsevier, 1969– , 84 times/yr. ISSN 0030-4018. $4293/yr.
> Indexed: Chem. Abstr., Chem. Cit. Ind., Curr. Cont., Eng. Ind.,
> INSPEC (1969–), Mat. Sci. Cit. Ind., Sci. Cit. Ind.

Optics Express (online only)
> Optical Society of America, 1997– , ISSN 1094-4087.

Optics Letters
> Optical Society of America, 1977– , ISSN 0146-9592.

Philosophical Magazine A: Physics of Condensed Matter: Structure, Defects and Mechanical Properties
> Taylor and Francis, 1978– , 12 times/yr. ISSN 0141-8610.

Philosophical Magazine B: Physics of Condensed Matter: Statistical Mechanics, Electronic, Optical and Magnetic Properties
> Taylor and Francis, 1995– , 12 times/yr. ISSN 0141-8637.
> (Price for both A and B is $1795/yr.)

Philosophical Magazine Letters
> Taylor and Francis, 1987– , m. ISSN 0950-0839. $440/yr.
> Indexed: Chem. Cit. Ind., Curr. Cont., INSPEC (1987–), Mat. Sci.
> Cit. Ind., Met. Abstr., Sci. Cit. Ind.

Physica A—Statistical and Theoretical Physics

> Elsevier, 1934– , 56 times/yr. ISSN 0378-4371. $4068/yr.
> Indexed: Chem. Abstr., Chem. Cit. Ind., Curr. Cont., INSPEC (19680–), Met. Abstr., Sci. Cit. Ind., SSCI.

Physica B—Physics of Condensed Matter

> Elsevier, 1934– , 64 times/yr. ISSN 0921-4526. $4324/yr.
> Indexed: Chem. Cit. Ind., Curr. Cont., Eng. Ind., INSPEC (1975–), Mat. Sci. Cit. Ind., Met. Abstr., Sci. Cit. Ind.

Physica C—Superconductivity

> Elsevier, 1934– , 76 times/yr. ISSN 0921-4534. $5724/yr.
> Indexed: Chem. Cit. Ind., Curr. Cont., Eng. Ind., INSPEC (1975–), Mat. Sci. Cit. Ind., Met. Abstr., Sci. Cit. Ind., SSCI.

Physica D—Nonlinear Phenomena

> Elsevier, 1980– , 52 times/yr. ISSN 0167-2789. $3778/yr.
> Indexed: Chem. Cit. Ind., Curr. Cont., Eng. Ind., INSPEC (1975–), Mat. Sci. Cit. Ind., Met. Abstr., Sci. Cit. Ind., SSCI.

Physica E: Low-Dimensional Systems and Nanostructures

> Elsevier, 1999– , 8 times/yr. ISSN 1386-9477. $608/yr.
> Indexed: Curr. Cont., Eng. Ind., INSPEC, Mat. Sci. Cit. Ind., Met. Abstr.

Physica Scripta

> Royal Swedish Academy of Sciences, 1970– , m. ISSN 0031-8949. $1100/yr.
> Indexed: Chem. Abstr., Chem. Cit. Ind., Curr. Cont., GeoRef, INSPEC (1968–), Mat. Sci. Cit. Ind., Met. Abstr., Sci. Cit. Ind.

Physica Status Solidi. A: Applied Research

> Akadmie Verlag, 1970– , 12 times/yr. ISSN 0031-8965. $2495/yr.
> Indexed: Chem. Abstr., Chem. Cit. Ind., Curr. Cont., GeoRef, INSPEC (1970–), Mat. Sci. Cit. Ind., Met. Abstr., Sci. Cit. Ind.

Physica Status Solidi. B: Basic Research

> Akadmie Verlag, 1961– , 12 times/yr. ISSN 0370-1972. $2495/yr.
> Indexed: Chem. Abstr., Chem. Cit. Ind., Curr. Cont., Eng. Ind., INSPEC (1968–), Mat. Sci. Cit. Ind., Met. Abstr., Sci. Cit. Ind.

Physical Review A (Atomic, Molecular and Optical Physics)

> American Physical Society, 1893– , m. ISSN 1050-2947. $1530/yr.
> Indexed: Chem. Abstr., Chem. Cit. Ind., Curr. Cont., Eng. Ind., INSPEC (1968–1992), Mat. Sci. Cit. Ind., Sci. Cit. Ind.

Physical Review B (Condensed Matter and Materials Physics)
>American Physical Society, 1893– , 48 times/yr. ISSN 1063-1829.
$4420/yr.
>Indexed: Chem. Abstr., Chem. Cit. Ind., Curr. Cont., Eng. Ind.,
GeoRef, INSPEC (1970–1979), Mat. Sci. Cit. Ind., Met. Abstr., Sci.
Cit. Ind.

Physical Review C (Nuclear Physics)
>American Physical Society, 1970– , m. ISSN 0556-2813. $1240/yr.
>Indexed: Chem. Abstr., Curr. Cont., Eng. Ind., INSPEC (1979–),
Met. Abstr., Nucl. Sci. Abstr., Sci. Cit. Ind.

Physical Review D (Particles, Fields, Gravitation, and Cosmology)
>American Physical Society, 1970– , m. ISSN 0556-2821. $1240/yr.
>Indexed: Chem. Abstr., Curr. Cont., Eng. Ind., INSPEC (1991–),
Met. Abstr., Nucl. Sci. Abstr., Sci. Cit. Ind.

Physical Review E (Statistical Physics, Plasmas, Fluids, and Related Interdisciplinary Topics)
>American Physical Society, 1993– , m. ISSN 1063-651X. $1360/yr.
>Indexed: Chem. Cit. Ind., Curr. Cont., INSPEC (1993–), Mat. Sci.
Cit. Ind., Sci. Cit. Ind., SSCI.

Physical Review Focus (online only)
>American Physical Society, focus.aps.org

Physical Review Letters
>American Physical Society, 1958– , w. ISSN 0031-9007. $2110/yr.
>Indexed: Chem. Abstr., Chem. Cit. Ind., Curr. Cont., Eng. Ind.,
INSPEC (1968–), Mat. Sci. Cit. Ind., Met. Abstr., Sci. Cit. Ind.

Physical Review Special Topics—Accelerators and Beams (online only)
>American Physical Society, 1998– , q. ISSN 1098-4402.

Physics Education
>Institute of Physics, 1966– , bi-m. ISSN 0031-9120. $252/yr.
>Indexed: Chem. Abstr., INSPEC (1968–).

Physics Letters A
>Elsevier, 1962– , 84 times/yr. ISSN 0375-9601. $3501/yr.
>Indexed: Chem. Abstr., Chem. Cit. Ind., Curr. Cont., INSPEC
(1968–), Mat. Sci. Cit. Ind., Met. Abstr., Sci. Cit. Ind.

Physics Letters B

    Elsevier, 1962– , 108 times/yr. ISSN 0370-2693. $7056/yr.
Indexed: Chem. Abstr., Chem. Cit. Ind., Curr. Cont., INSPEC (1968–), Sci. Cit. Ind.

Physics of Atomic Nuclei (Yadernaya Fizika)

    American Institute of Physics, 1965– , 108 times/yr. ISSN 1063-7788. $2900/yr.
Indexed: Curr. Cont., INSPEC (1968–1992; 1994–), Mat. Sci. Cit. Ind., Sci. Cit. Ind.

Physics of Fluids

    (was Physics of Fluids and Plasmas)
American Institute of Physics, 1958– , m. ISSN 1070-6631. $1440/yr.
Indexed: Chem. Cit. Ind., Curr. Cont., Geol. Abstr., INSPEC (1989–1994), Mat. Sci. Cit. Ind., Sci. Cit. Ind.

Physics of Particles and Nuclei (Fizika Elementanykh Chastits I Atomnogo Yadra)

    American Institute of Physics, 1972– , bi-m. ISSN 1063-7796. $1710/yr.
Indexed: Curr. Cont., INSPEC (1972–1993).

Physics of Plasmas

    (was Physics of Fluids and Plasmas)
American Institute of Physics, 1958– , m. ISSN 1070-664X. $1700/yr.
Indexed: Curr. Cont., INSPEC (1994–), Mat. Sci. Cit. Ind, Sci. Cit. Ind.

Physics of the Earth and Planetary Interiors

    Elsevier, 1967– , 28 times/yr. ISSN 0031-9201. $1785/yr.
Indexed: Chem. Abstr., Curr. Cont., Geol. Abstr., GeoRef, INSPEC (1967–), Mat. Sci. Cit. Ind., Sci. Cit. Ind.

Physics of the Solid State (Fizika Tverdogo Tela/St. Petersburg)

    American Institute of Physics, 1959– , m. ISSN 1063-7834. $3200/yr.
Indexed: Eng. Ind., INSPEC (1968–), Met. Abstr., Sci. Cit. Ind.

Physics Reports

    Elsevier, 1971– , 96 times/yr. ISSN 0370-1573. $4002/yr.
Indexed: Chem. Abstr., Chem. Cit. Ind., Curr. Cont., INSPEC (1971–1978), Sci. Cit. Ind.

Physics Teacher

American Association of Physics Teachers, 1963– , 9 times/yr. ISSN 0031-921X. $178/yr.
Indexed: Chem. Abstr., Curr. Cont., Gen. Sci. Ind. (1984–), INSPEC (1973–1989).

Physics Today

American Institute of Physics, 1948– , m. ISSN 0031-9228. $165/yr.
Indexed: A.S. & T. Ind. (1983–), Chem. Abstr., Curr. Cont., Gen. Sci. Ind. (1984–), Geol. Abstr., GeoRef, INSPEC (1968–), Mat. Sci. Cit. Ind., Sci. Cit. Ind., SSCI.

Physics World

Institute of Physics, 1950– , m. ISSN 0953-8585.
Indexed: Chem. Abstr., Curr. Cont., Excerp. Med., INSPEC (1973–), Mat. Sci. Cit. Ind., Met. Abstr., SSCI.

Physics-Uspekhi (English translation of Uspekhi Fizicheskikh Nauk)

Turpion, 1918– , m. ISSN 1063-7869. $1440/yr.
(was Soviet Physics-Uspekhi until 1993)
Indexed: Curr. Cont., GeoRef, INSPEC (1968–), Met. Abstr.

Physics-Uspekhi

Uspekhi Fizicheskikh Nauk, Leninksi, 1918– , m. ISSN 0042-1294. $283/yr.

Pis'ma v Zhurnal Eksperimental'noi I Teoreticheskoi Fiziki

(English translation in JETP Letters)
Akademiya Nauk SSSR, Leninski, 1969– , 24 times/yr. ISSN 0370-274X. $322/yr.

Pis'ma v Zhurnal Tekhnicheskoi Fizika

(English translation in Technical Physics Letters)
Izdatel'stvo Nauka, Leningrad, 1975– , 24 times/yr. ISSN 0320-0108. $242/yr.

Plasma Physics and Controlled Fusion

Institute of Physics, 1959– , m. ISSN 0741-3335. $1724/yr.
Indexed: A.S. & T. Ind. (1983–1990), Chem. Abstr., Chem. Cit. Ind., Curr. Cont., Eng. Ind., INSPEC (1984–), Mat. Sci. Cit. Ind., Sci. Cit. Ind.

Plasma Physics Reports (Fizika Plazmy)
> American Institute of Physics, 1975– , m. ISSN 1063-780X. $2050/yr.
> Indexed: Curr. Cont., INSPEC (1975–), Sci. Cit. Ind.

Plasma Sources Science and Technology
> Institute of Physics, 1992– , q. ISSN 0963-0252. $396/yr.
> Indexed: Curr. Cont., INSPEC (1992–), Met. Abstr.

Progress in Biophysics and Molecular Biology
> Elsevier, 1950– , 8 times/yr. ISSN 0079-6107. $1326/yr.
> Indexed: Biol. Abstr., Chem. Abstr., Chem. Cit. Ind., Curr. Cont., Excerp. Med., INSPEC (1975–), Sci. Cit. Ind.

Progress in Materials Science
> Elsevier, 1949– , 5 times/yr. ISSN 0079-6425. $839/yr.
> Indexed: Chem. Abstr., Curr. Cont., Eng. Ind., GeoRef, INSPEC (1968–), Mat. Sci. Cit. Ind., Met. Abstr., Sci. Cit. Ind.

Progress in Nuclear Magnetic Resonance Spectroscopy
> Elsevier, 1966– , 8 times/yr. ISSN 0079-6565. $812/yr.
> Indexed: Chem. Abstr., Chem. Cit. Ind., INSPEC (1995–), Met. Abstr., Sci. Cit. Ind.

Progress in Particle and Nuclear Physics
> Elsevier, 1977– , s-a. ISSN 0146-6410. $1020/yr.
> Indexed: Chem. Abstr., INSPEC (1978–), Sci. Cit. Ind.

Progress in Solid State Chemistry
> Elsevier, 1964– , q. ISSN 0079-6786. $575/yr.
> Indexed: Chem. Abstr., Chem. Cit. Ind., INSPEC (1975–), Mat. Sci. Cit. Ind., Met. Abstr., Sci. Cit. Ind.

Progress in Surface Science
> Elsevier, 1971– , 24 times/yr. ISSN 0079-6816. $1307/yr.
> Indexed: Chem. Abstr., Chem. Cit. Ind., Curr. Cont., INSPEC (1972–), Mat. Sci. Cit. Ind., Met. Abstr., Sci. Cit. Ind.

Progress of Theoretical Physics
> Yukawa Institute for Theoretical Physics/Physical Society of Japan, 1946– , m. ISSN 0033-068X. 75000 yen/yr.
> Indexed: Chem. Abstr., Chem. Cit. Ind., Curr. Cont., GeoRef, INSPEC (1968–), Met. Abstr., Sci. Cit. Ind.

Progress of Theoretical Physics, Supplement
> Yukawa Institute for Theoretical Physics/Physical Society of Japan, 1955– , irreg. (approx. 4 times/yr.) ISSN 0375-9687.
> Indexed: Chem. Cit. Ind., Curr. Cont., INSPEC (1968–), Sci. Cit. Ind.

Pure and Applied Optics: Journal of the European Optical Society A
> Institute of Physics, 1992– , bi-m. ISSN 0963-9659. $426/yr.
> Indexed: Curr. Cont., INSPEC (1992–), Sci. Cit. Ind.

Quantum and Semiclassical Optics: Journal of the European Optical Society B
> Institute of Physics, 1989– , bi-m. ISSN 1355-5111. $476/yr.
> Indexed: Curr. Cont., INSPEC (1989–1994).

Quantum Electronics [Kvantovaia Elektronika]
> Turpion, 1971– , m. ISSN 1063-7818. $2585/yr.
> Indexed: Curr. Cont., Eng. Ind., INSPEC (1971–1992), Mat. Sci. Cit. Ind., Nucl. Sci. Abstr., Sci. Cit. Ind.

Radiation Physics and Chemistry
> Elsevier, 1969– , 18 times/yr. ISSN 0969-806X. $1476/yr.
> Indexed: Chem. Abstr., Chem. Cit. Ind., Curr. Cont., Excerp. Med., INSPEC (1977–1991), Mat. Sci. Cit. Ind., Met. Abstr.

Radiation Research
> Radiation Research Society, 1954– , m. ISSN 0033-7587. $595/yr.
> Indexed: Biol. Abstr., Chem. Abstr., Chem. Cit. Ind., Curr. Cont., Excerp. Med., INSPEC (1968–), Sci. Cit. Ind.

Reports on Mathematical Physics
> Elsevier, 1975– , bi-m. ISSN 0034-4877. $899/yr.
> Indexed: INSPEC (1970–).

Reports on Progress in Physics
> Institute of Physics, 1934– , m. ISSN 0034-4885. $1496/yr.
> Indexed: Chem. Abstr., Chem. Cit. Ind., Curr. Cont., GeoRef, INSPEC (1968–), Met. Abstr., Sci. Cit. Ind.

Review of Scientific Instruments
> American Institute of Physics, 1930– , m. ISSN 0034-6748. $1125/yr.
> Indexed: A.S. & T. Ind. (1983–), Biol. Abstr., Chem. Abstr., Chem. Cit. Ind., Curr. Cont., Excerp. Med., GeoRef, INSPEC (1968–), Meteor. & Geoastrophys. Abstr., Sci. Cit. Ind.

Reviews in Mathematical Physics

> World Scientific, 1989– , 8 times/yr. ISSN 0129-055X. $589/yr.
> Indexed: Curr. Cont., INSPEC (1989–), Sci. Cit. Ind.

Reviews of Geophysics

> American Geophysical Union, 1963– , q. ISSN 8755-1209. $255/yr.
> Indexed: Chem. Abstr., Curr. Cont., Environ. Abstr., Excerp. Med.,
> INSPEC (1968–1984), Meteor. & Geoastrophys. Abstr., Sci. Cit.
> Ind.

Reviews of Modern Physics

> American Physical Society, 1929– , q. ISSN 0034-6861. $385/yr.
> Indexed: A.S. & T. Ind. (1997–), Biol. Abstr., Chem. Abstr., Curr.
> Cont., Excerp. Med., Gen. Sci. Ind. (1997–), GeoRef, INSPEC
> (1968–), Met. Abstr., Sci. Cit. Ind.

Semiconductor Science and Technology

> Institute of Physics, 1986– , m. ISSN 0268-1242. $1565/yr.
> Indexed: A.S. & T. Ind. (1991–), Chem. Cit. Ind., Curr. Cont.,
> INSPEC (1986–), Mat. Sci. Cit. Ind., Met. Abstr., Sci. Cit. Ind.

Semiconductors (Fizika I Tekhnika Poluprovodnikov)

> American Institute of Physics, 1967– , m. ISSN 1063-7826.
> $2920/yr.
> Indexed: Curr. Cont., Eng. Ind., INSPEC (1968–1992), Mat. Sci.
> Cit. Ind., Met. Abstr., Sci. Cit. Ind.

Sky & Telescope

> Sky Publishing Corp., 1941– , m. ISSN 0037-6604. $37.95/yr.
> Indexed: Astron. & Astrophys. Abstr., Curr. Cont., Gen. Sci. Ind.
> (1984–), GeoRef, INSPEC (1970–).

Smart Materials and Structures

> Institute of Physics, 1992– , q. ISSN 0964-1726. $437/yr.
> Indexed: INSPEC (1992–), Mat. Sci. Cit. Ind., Met. Abstr.

Solid State Communications

> Elsevier, 1963– , 48 times/yr. ISSN 0038-1098. $3080/yr.
> Indexed: Chem. Abstr., Chem. Cit. Ind., Curr. Cont., Eng. Ind.,
> GeoRef, INSPEC (1968–), Mat. Sci. Cit. Ind., Met. Abstr.

Solid State Ionics

> Elsevier, 1980– , 40 times/yr. ISSN 0167-2738. $2947/yr.
> Indexed: Chem. Abstr., Chem. Cit. Ind., Curr. Cont., INSPEC
> (1980–), Mat. Sci. Cit. Ind., Met. Abstr., Sci. Cit. Ind., SSCI.

Solid State Nuclear Magnetic Resonance
> Elsevier, 1992– , 8 times/yr. ISSN 0926-2040. $802/yr.
> Indexed: Chem. Abstr., Chem. Cit. Ind., Curr. Cont., Eng. Ind., INSPEC (1992–), Met. Abstr., Sci. Cit. Ind.

Spectrochimica Acta Part B: Atomic Spectroscopy
> Elsevier, 1939– , 14 times/yr. ISSN 0584-8547. $2345/yr.
> Indexed: Biol. Abstr., Chem. Abstr., Chem. Cit. Ind., Curr. Cont., Excerp. Med., INSPEC (1968–), Mat. Sci. Cit. Ind., Met. Abstr., Sci. Cit. Ind.

Superconductor Science and Technology
> Institute of Physics, 1988– , m. ISSN 0953-2048. $733/yr.
> Indexed: Chem. Cit. Ind., Curr. Cont., INSPEC (1988–), Mat. Sci. Cit. Ind., Met. Abstr., Sci. Cit. Ind.

Superlattices and Microstructures
> Academic Press, 1985– , m. ISSN 0749-6036.
> Indexed: Curr. Cont., INSPEC (1985–), Mat. Sci. Cit. Ind., Met. Abstr., Sci. Cit. Ind.

Surface Science (and Letters)
> Elsevier, 1964– , 78 times/yr. ISSN 0039-6028. $9234/yr.
> Indexed: Chem. Abstr., Chem. Cit. Ind., Curr. Cont., INSPEC (1968–), Mat. Sci. Cit. Ind., Met. Abstr., Sci. Cit. Ind., SSCI.

Surface Science Reports
> Elsevier, 1981– , 32 times/yr. ISSN 0167-5729. $1036/yr.
> Indexed: Chem. Abstr., Chem. Cit. Ind., Curr. Cont., INSPEC (1981–), Mat. Sci. Cit. Ind., Met. Abstr., Sci. Cit. Ind.

Surface Science Spectra
> American Vacuum Society, 1991– , q. ISSN 1055-5269. $987/yr.
> Indexed: INSPEC (1992–).

Synthetic Metals
> Elsevier, 1979– , 24 times/yr. ISSN 0379-6779. $3215/yr.
> Indexed: Chem. Abstr., Chem. Cit. Ind., Curr. Cont., INSPEC (1979–), Mat. Sci. Cit. Ind., Met. Abstr., Sci. Cit. Ind.

Technical Physics (Zhurnal Tekhnicheskoi Fiziki)
> American Institute of Physics, 1956– , m. ISSN 1063-7842. $2800/yr.
> Indexed: Curr. Cont., Eng. Ind., INSPEC (1968–), Met. Abstr., Sci. Cit. Ind.

Technical Physics Letters (Pisma v Zhurnal Tekhnicheskoi Fiziki)
> American Institute of Physics, 1975– , m. ISSN 1063-7850. $1685/yr.
> Indexed: Curr. Cont., INSPEC (1975–), Met. Abstr., Sci. Cit. Ind.

Theoretical and Mathematical Physics (Teoreticheskaya I Matematicheskaya Fizika)
> Consultants Bureau, 1969– , m. ISSN 0040-5779. $1515/yr.
> Indexed: Curr. Cont., INSPEC (1972–), Sci. Cit. Ind.

Thin Solid Films
> Elsevier, 1968– , 44 times/yr. ISSN 0040-6090. $7742/yr.
> Indexed: Chem. Abstr., Chem. Cit. Ind., Curr. Cont., Eng. Ind., Mat. Sci. Cit. Ind., Met. Abstr., Sci. Cit. Ind.

Transactions of the American Nuclear Society (American Nuclear Society Transactions)
> American Nuclear Society, 1958– , 2 times/yr. ISSN 0003-018X. $450/yr.
> Indexed: Biol. Abstr., Chem. Abstr., Curr. Cont., Eng. Ind., INSPEC (1968–), Met. Abstr.

Transactions of the ASME: Journal of Vibration and Acoustics
> American Society of Mechanical Engineers, 1978– , q. ISSN 1048-9002. $1850/yr.
> Indexed: Curr. Cont., Eng. Ind., Environ. Abstr., Excerp. Med., INSPEC (1978–), Mat. Sci. Cit. Ind., Met. Abstr.

Ultrasonics
> Elsevier, 1963– , 11 times/yr. ISSN 1350-4177. $776/yr.
> Indexed: A.S. & T. Ind. (1983–), Biol. Abstr., Chem. Abstr., Curr. Cont., Excerp. Med., INSPEC (1968–), Sci. Cit. Ind.

Waves in Random Media
> Institute of Physics, 1991– , q. ISSN 0959-7171. $429/yr.
> Indexed: Curr. Cont., INSPEC (1991–).

Zeitschrift fur Physikalische Chemie
> R. Oldenbourg Verlag, 1887– , 10 times/yr. ISSN 0044-3336. DM. 1568/yr.
> Indexed: A.S. & T. Ind., Biol. Abstr., Chem. Abstr., Chem. Cit. Ind., Curr. Cont., GeoRef, INSPEC (1968–1991), Mat. Sci. Cit. Ind., Met. Abstr., Sci. Cit. Ind.

Zeitschrift fur Physik: A, Hadrons and Nuclei
(now European Physical Journal A)

Zeitschrift fur Physik: B, Condensed Matter
(now European Physical Journal B)

Zeitschrift fur Physik: C, Particles and Fields
(now European Physical Journal C)

Zeitschrift fur Physik: D, Atomic
(now European Physical Journal D)

Interdisciplinary Journals Covering Physics

AAAS Report: Research and Development
American Association for the Advancement of Science, 1976– , a.
ISSN 1041-8857. $18.95/yr.

American Scientist
Sigma Xi, Scientific Research Society, 1913– , bi-m. ISSN
0003-0996. $50/yr.
Indexed: A.S. & T. Ind. (1983–), Biol. Abstr., Chem. Abstr., Curr.
Cont., Eng. Ind., Environ. Abstr., Excerp. Med., Gen. Sci. Ind.
(1984–), Geol. Abstr., INIS Atomind., INSPEC (1970–), Met.
Abstr., Sci. Cit. Ind., SSCI.

Annals of Improbable Research: AIR
Annals of Improbable Research, 1995– , 6 times/yr. ISSN
1079-5146. $23/yr.

Annals of Science
Taylor & Francis, 1936– , q. ISSN 0003-3790. $540/yr.
Indexed: Biol. Abstr., Chem. Abstr., Curr. Cont., INSPEC
(1972–1994), Sci. Cit. Ind., SSCI.

Archive for History of Exact Sciences
Springer-Verlag, 1960– , 6 times/yr. ISSN 0003-9519. DM. 1148/yr.
Indexed: Curr. Cont., Sci. Cit. Ind., SSCI.

Archives des Sciences (Geneve) and Supplement (Archives des Sciences et
Compte Rendu des Seances de la Societe de Physique et d'Histoire Na-
turelle de Geneve)
Societe de Physique et d'Histoire Naturelle de Geneve, 1846– , 3
times/yr. ISSN 0252-9289.
Indexed: Biol. Abstr., Chem. Abstr., Curr. Cont., INSPEC (1968–).

Bulletin de la Societe Royale des Sciences de Liege. Comptes Rendus de l'Academie des Sciences. Serie II. Fascicule B, Mecanique, Physique, Astronomie
> (Variant Title: Mechanics, Physics, Astronomy)
> Paris, France: Publications Elsevier, 1998– .

Doklady Akademii Nauk (Doklady Rossiiskaya Akademiya Nauk)
> MAIK Nauka, 1933– , 36 times/yr. ISSN 0869-5652. $855/yr.
> Indexed: Biol. Abstr., Chem. Abstr., Geol. Abstr., GeoRef, Geotech. Abstr., INIS Atomind., INSPEC (1968–1992), Met. Abstr., Meteor. & Geoastrohpys. Abstr., Sci. Cit. Ind.

Endeavour
> Elsevier, 1942– , q. ISSN 0160-9327. $216/yr.
> Indexed: Biol. Abstr., Chem. Abstr., Curr. Cont., Eng. Ind., Excerp. Med., Gen. Sci. Ind. (1984–), Geo. Abstr., Geol. Abstr., INSPEC (1968–1994), Met. Abstr., Meteor. & Geoastrophys. Abstr., Sci. Cit. Ind.

Ghana Journal of Science
> National Science and Technology Press, 1961– , s-a. ISSN 0016-9544. $20/yr.
> Indexed: Biol. Abstr., Chem. Abstr., INIS Atomind.

History of Science
> Science History Publications, 1962– , 4 times/yr. ISSN 0073-2753. $146/yr.
> Indexed: Curr. Cont., Sci. Cit. Ind., SSCI.

Interdisciplinary Science Reviews
> Institute of Materials, 1976– , q. ISSN 0308-0188. $406/yr.
> Indexed: Chem. Abstr., Chem. Cit. Ind., Curr. Cont., INSPEC (1976–1991), Met. Abstr., SSCI.

ISIS: Journal of the History of Science Society
> University of Chicago Press, 1912– , q. ISSN 0021-1753. $170/yr.
> Indexed: Biol. Abstr., Chem. Abstr., Curr. Cont., Eng. Ind., Gen. Sci. Ind. (1984–), INSPEC (1968–1990), Sci. Cit. Ind., SSCI.

Issues in Science and Technology
> Wiley, 1984– , q. ISSN 0748-5492. $75/yr.
> Indexed: Curr. Cont., Environ. Abstr., Gen. Sci. Ind. (1992–), INIS Atomind., Met. Abstr., Sci. Cit. Ind., SSCI.

Journal of College Science Teaching
>National Science Teachers Association, 1971– , 6 times/yr. ISSN 0047-231X. $56/yr.
>Indexed: Biol. Abstr., Chem. Abstr., INSPEC.

Journal of Irreproducible Results
>Dr. George H. Scherr, 1955– , bi-m. ISSN 1016-1058. $32/yr.
>Indexed: Biol. Abstr., Curr. Cont.

Nature
>Macmillan, 1869– , w. ISSN 0028-0836. $159/yr.
>Indexed: Biol. Abstr., Chem. Abstr., Chem. Cit. Ind., Eng. Ind., Eviron. Abstr., Gen. Sci. Ind. (1984–), Geo. Abstr. P.G., Geol. Abstr., GeoRef, INSPEC (1968–), Mat. Sci. Cit. Ind., Met. Abstr., Meteor. & Geoastrophys. Abstr., Sel. Water Res. Abstr., SSCI.

Naturwissenschaften, Die
>Springer-Verlag, 1913– , m. ISSN 0028-1042. DM. 620/yr.
>Indexed: Biol. Abstr., Chem. Abstr., Chem. Cit. Ind., Curr. Cont., Excerp. Med., Geol. Abstr., INSPEC (1968–1992), Sci. Cit. Ind., Sel. Water Res. Abstr., SSCI.

Ohio Journal of Science
>Ohio Academy of Science, 1901– , 5 times/yr. ISSN 0030-0950. $50/yr.
>Indexed: Biol. Abstr., Chem. Abstr., Curr. Cont., Environ. Abstr., Geo. Abstr. P.G., Geol. Abstr., Sci. Cit. Ind., Sel. Water Res. Abstr., SSCI.

Osiris
>University of Chicago Press, 1936– , a. ISSN 0369-7827. $25/yr. for paper; $39/yr. for cloth.
>Indexed: Curr. Cont., Sci. Cit. Ind., SSCI.

Philosophical Transactions. Mathematical, Physical, and Engineering Sciences
>Royal Society, 1996– , m. ISSN 1364-503X. L 655/yr. Vol. 354, no. 1704 (Jan. 15, 1996–) .
>Indexed: Biol. Abstr., Chem. Cit. Ind., Curr. Cont., Eng. Ind., Environ. Abstr., Geo. Abstr. P.G., Geol. Abstr., GeoRef, INSPEC (1968–), Met. Abstr, Sci. Cit. Ind.

Popular Science

>   Times Mirror Magazines, 1872– , m. ISSN 0161-7370. $17.94/yr.
>   Indexed: Environ. Abstr., Gen. Sci. Ind. (1992–), GeoRef.

Proceedings of the National Academy of Sciences (USA)

>   National Academy of Sciences of the United States of America,
>   1915– , bi-w. ISSN 0027-8424. $685/yr.
>   Indexed: Biol. Abstr., Chem. Abstr., Chem. Cit. Ind., Curr. Cont.,
>   Excerp. Med., Gen. Sci. Ind. (1992–), Geol. Abstr., INSPEC
>   (1968–1985), Mat. Sci. Cit. Ind., SSCI.

Proceedings of the Royal Society of London

>   Series A: Mathematical and Physical Sciences
>   Royal Society of London, 1832– , m. ISSN 1364-5021. $851/yr.
>   Indexed: Chem. Abstr., Chem. Cit. Ind., Curr. Cont., Eng. Ind., Ex-
>   cerp. Med., Geol. Abstr., GeoRef, INSPEC (1968–), Met. Abstr.,
>   Mineral. Abstr., Sci. Cit. Ind.

Public Understanding of Science

>   IoP, 1992– , q. ISSN 0963-6625. $185/yr.
>   Indexed: Curr. Cont., SSCI.

Recherche, La

>   Societe d'Editions Scientifiques, 1970– , m. ISSN 0029-5671. 432
>   F./yr.
>   Indexed: Biol. Abstr., Chem. Abstr., Curr. Cont., Excerp. Med.,
>   Geol. Abstr., INSPEC (1968–), Met. Abstr., Sci. Cit. Ind., SSCI.

Review of Scientific Instruments

>   American Institute of Physics, 1930– , m. ISSN 0034-6748.
> $1125/yr.
>   Indexed: A.S. & T. Ind. (1983–), Biol. Abstr., Chem. Abstr., Chem.
>   Cit. Ind., Curr. Cont., Excerp. Med., GeoRef, INSPEC (1968–),
>   Meteor. & Geoastrophys. Abstr., Sci. Cit. Ind.

Science

>   American Association for the Advancement of Science, 1880– , w.
>   4 vols./yr. ISSN 0036-8075. $260/yr.
>   Indexed: A.S. & T. Ind. (1983–), Biol. Abstr., Chem. Abstr., Chem.
>   Cit. Ind., Curr. Cont., Environ. Abstr., Excerp. Med., Gen. Sci. Ind.
>   (1984–), Geol. Abstr., Geotech. Abstr., INSPEC (1968–), Met.
>   Abstr., Meteor. & Geoastrophys. Abstr., Sci. Cit. Ind., Sel. Water
>   Res. Abstr.

Science and Technology Libraries
> Haworth, 1980– , q. ISSN 0194-262X. $160/yr.
> Indexed: Biol. Abstr., Chem. Abstr., Eng. Ind., Excerp. Med.,
> INSPEC (1982–).

Science in China. Series A, Mathematics, Physics, Astronomy
> Harwood Academic, 1952–, 12 times/yr. ISSN 1006-9283. $838/yr.
> Indexed: Chem. Cit. Ind., Curr. Cont., INSPEC (1984–), Sci. Cit.
> Ind., SSCI.

Science News
> Science Service, 1921– , w. ISSN 0036-8423. $49.50/yr.
> Indexed: Chem. Abstr., Eng. Ind., Gen. Sci. Ind. (1984), Met. Abstr.

Science Progress
> Science Reviews, 1894– , q. ISSN 0036-8504. $200/yr.
> Indexed: Biol. Abstr., Chem. Abstr., Curr. Cont., Geo. Abstr. P.G.,
> Geol. Abstr., INSPEC (1968–), Sci. Cit. Ind.

Science Technology and Human Values
> Sage Publications, 1972– , q. ISSN 0162-2439. $220/yr.
> Imdexed: Curr. Cont., SSCI.

Sciences
> New York Academy of Sciences, 1961– , bi-m. ISSN 0036-861X.
> $21/yr.
> Indexed: Biol. Abstr., Curr. Cont., Gen. Sci. Ind. (1984–), SSCI.

Scientific American
> Scientific American, 1845– , m. ISSN 0036-8733. $34.97/yr.
> Indexed: A.S. & T. Ind., Biol. Abstr., Curr. Cont., Eng. Ind., Ex-
> cerp. Med. (until 1994), Gen. Sci. Ind. (1984–), Geo. Abstr. P.G.,
> INSPEC (1968–), Meteor. & Geoastrophys. Abstr., Sci. Cit. Ind.,
> SSCI.

Scientific Computing World
> IoP, 1994–, bi-m. ISSN 1356-7853. Free to some; £ 282/yr. (U.K.)
> Indexed: INSPEC (1994–).

Scientific Meetings
> Scientific Meetings Publications, 1957– , q. ISSN 0487-8965.
> $75/yr.

Skeptical Inquirer

>Committee for the Scientific Investigation of Claims of the Paranormal, 1976– , bi-m. ISSN 0194-6730. $32.50/yr.

South African Journal of Science

>Foundation for Education, Science and Technology, 1903– , m. ISSN 0038-2353. $125/yr.
>Indexed: Biol. Abstr., Chem. Abstr., Chem. Cit. Ind., Curr. Cont., Excerp. Med., Geo. Abstr. P.G., Geol. Abstr., Geotech. Abstr., INSPEC (1968–1977), Met. Abstr., Meteor. & Geoastrophys. Abstr., Sci. Cit. Ind., Sel. Water Res. Abstr., SSCI.

Southern California Academy of Sciences Bulletin

>Southern California Academy of Sciences, 1902– , 3 times/yr. ISSN 0038-3872. $30/yr.
>Indexed: Biol. Abstr.

Technology Review

>MIT, 1899– , 6 times/yr. ISSN 0040-1692. $19.95/yr.
>Indexed: A.S. & T. Ind. (1983–1997), Biol. Abstr., Chem. Abstr., Curr. Cont., Eng. Ind., Environ. Abstr., Excerp. Med., Gen. Sci. Ind. (1992–), Geol. Abstr., Sci. Cit. Ind., SSCI.

University of Kansas Science Bulletin (University of Kansas Museum of Natural History Scientific Papers)

>University of Kansas, 1996– , irreg., approx. 5 times/yr. ISSN 1094-0482.
>Indexed: Biol. Abstr., Chem. Abstr., GeoRef.

Yale Scientific Magazine

>Yale Scientific Publications, 1958– , 4 times/yr. ISSN 0091-0287. $12/yr.

Selected Physics Journals by Subdiscipline

Below are objective lists of selected titles in subdisciplines of physics. They were compiled based upon a combination of Yale faculty surveys, Yale use studies, and ISI citation Impact Factors. They are not arranged in a strict order of importance, but other than the first category, which is alphabetical, the remaining lists are arranged in an objective ranked order with the top half representing the most important titles for a serious physics collection. The entire listing starting from the top to the bottom would represent a fairly strong core collection of journals. There is a small amount of overlap due to the interdisciplinary nature of some of the journal titles. Important journals in these areas for nonphysics researchers (e.g., biologists, medical practitioners) are not included.

General Physics, Reviews, and Overview Materials

The (t) symbol identifies those titles of primary interest to educators.

Advances in Atomic Molecular and Optical Physics
Advances in Nuclear Physics
Advances in Physics
American Journal of Physics (t)
Annalen der Physik
Annales de Physique
Annals of Physics
Annual Review of Fluid Mechanics
Annual Review of Nuclear and Particle Science
Bulletin of the American Physical Society
Contemporary Physics
Critical Reviews in Solid State and Materials Sciences
European Journal of Physics (t)
Fortschritte der Physik—Progress of Physics
Materials Science & Engineering R—Reports
Physics Education (t)
Physics Teacher (t)
Physics Reports
Physics World
Progress in Optics
Progress in Particle and Nuclear Physics
Progress in Surface Science
Progress of Theoretical Physics
Progress of Theoretical Physics Supplement
Quarterly Reviews of Biophysics
Reports on Mathematical Physics
Reports on Progress in Physics
Reviews of Modern Physics
Rivista del Nuovo Cimento

General Physics, Interdisciplinary Materials

American Scientist

Atomic Data and Nuclear Data Tables

Journal of Physical and Chemical Reference Data

Nature

New Scientist

Nuclear Data Sheets

Philosophical Magazine Letters

Philosophical Transactions of the Royal Society of London. Series A: Mathematical and Physical Sciences

Proceedings of the National Academy of Sciences (Washington, D.C.)

Proceedings of the Royal Society of London. Series A: Mathematical and Physical Sciences

Science

Science News

Scientific American

General Physics

Physical Review Letters

Europhysics Letters

Physics Letters B

Physics Today

Reviews of Modern Physics

Physica D

Journal of the Physical Society of Japan

Journal of Physics A—Mathematical Nuclear and General

European Physical Journal D

(was Journal de Physique I and Zeitschrift fur Physik D and Nuovo Cimento della Societa Italiana di Fisica D)

Proceedings of the Royal Society of London. Series A—Mathematical and Physical Sciences

Philosophical Magazine Letters

Measurement Science and Technology

Physica Scripta

JETP Letters

JETP

Classical and Quantum Gravity

Physics—Uspekhi
  (was Soviet Physics—Uspekhi)

Canadian Journal of Physics

Foundations of Physics

Theoretical and Mathematical Physics

Doklady Physics

Few-Body Systems

Physica A

Physics Letters A

Astrophysical Journal

Astrophysical Journal Letters

Astrophysical Journal Suppplement

Computing in Science and Engineering

General Relativity and Gravitation

Helvetica Physica Acta

Zeitschrift Fur Naturforschung Section A—A Journal of Physical Sciences

Australian Journal of Physics

Annales de L'Institut Henri Poincare—Physique Theorique

Foundations of Physics Letters

Communications in Theoretical Physics

Journal of Statistical Physics

Wave Motion

Acta Physica Polonica A

Acta Physica Polonica B

International Journal of Theoretical Physics

European Physical Journal C—Particles and Fields
  (was Zeitschrift fur Physik C—Particles and Fields and Journal de
  Physique IV)

International Journal of Modern Physics C: Physics and Computers

International Journal of Modern Physics D: Gravitation, Astrophysics
and Cosmology

Pramana—Journal of Physics

Bulletin of the Russian Academy of Sciences. Physics

Chinese Journal of Physics

Czechoslovak Journal of Physics

Indian Journal of Pure & Applied Physics

Revista Mexicana de Fisica
Ukrainskii Fizicheskii Zhurnal
Izvestiya Akademii Nauk Seriya Fizicheskaya
Chinese Physics Letters

Acoustics

Journal of the Acoustical Society of America
Journal of Sound and Vibration
Ultrasound in Medicine and Biology
Physical Acoustics
Acustica
Ultrasonics
Wave Motion
Acoustical Physics
  (was Soviet Physics Acoustics)

Journal of the Audio Engineering Society
Journal of Vibration, Acoustics, Stress and Reliability
Applied Acoustics
Noise Control Engineering Journal
Acoustical Physics

Applied Physics

Applied Physics Letters
Journal of Applied Physics
Physical Review B—Condensed Matter and Materials Physics
Solid State Communications
Journal of Physics—Condensed Matter
Japanese Journal of Applied Physics
Applied Physics A—Materials Science and Processing
Physica C—Superconductivity
Philosophical Magazine A—Physics of Condensed Matter, Defects and Mechanical Properties
Philosophical Magazine B—Physics of Condensed Matter, Structural Electronic, Optical, and Magnetic Properties
Journal of Materials Research
MRS (Materials Research Society) Bulletin

Langmuir (American Chemical Society)

Surface Science

Thin Solid Films

Applied Surface Science

European Physical Journal—Applied Physics
   (was Journal de Physique III)

Journal of Vacuum Science & Technology A—Vacuum Surfaces and Films

Journal of Vacuum Science & Technology B

Critical Reviews in Solid State and Materials Sciences

Progress in Surface Science

Applied Physics B—Lasers and Optics

Journal of Physics D—Applied Physics

Journal of Physical Chemistry

Solid-State Electronics

Superconductor Science & Technology

Quantum Optics

Plasma Chemistry and Plasma Processing

Journal of Superconductivity

Journal of Low Temperature Physics

Review of Scientific Instruments

IEEE Transactions on Electron Devices

IEEE Journal of Quantum Electronics

IEEE Photonics Technology Letters

Topics in Applied Physics

International Journal of Thermophysics

Applied Superconductivity

Metrologia

International Journal of Modern Physics B

Cryogenics

Laser and Particle Beams

Pisma V Zhurnal Tekhnicheskoi Fiziki

Zhurnal Tekhnicheskoi Fiziki

High Temperature

Modern Physics Letters B

Atomic, Molecular, and Chemical Physics

Physical Review A
Journal of Physics B—Atomic Molecular and Optical Physics
European Physical Journal D
  (was Journal de Physique II and Zeitschrift fur Physik D)

Journal of Chemical Physics
Journal of Magnetic Resonance
Chemical Physics Letters
Atomic Data and Nuclear Data Tables
Physica Scripta
Advances in Atomic Molecular and Optical Physics
International Journal of Mass Spectrometry and Ion Processes
Molecular Physics
Chemical Physics
Journal of the Chemical Society—Faraday Transactions
Physics Letters A
Journal of Magnetic Resonance
Journal of Molecular Spectroscopy
Hyperfine Interactions
Nuovo Cimento della Societa Italiana di Fisica D
  (now European Physical Journal D)

Physics of Atomic Nuclei

Condensed Matter

Physical Review B—Condensed Matter and Materials Physics
Semiconductors and Semimetals
European Physical Journal B
  (was Zeitschrift fur Physik B—Condensed Matter)

Journal of the Mechanics and Physics of Solids
Journal of Physics—Condensed Matter
Superconductor Science & Technology
Philosophical Magazine Letters
Physics Letters A
Solid State Communications
Thin Solid Films

Semiconductor Science and Technology

Journal of Superconductivity

Journal of Physics and Chemistry of Solids

Synthetic Metals

Surface Science

Applied Surface Science

Physica B

Solid State Ionics

Journal of Magnetism and Magnetic Materials

Applied Superconductivity

International Journal of Modern Physics B

Superlattices and Microstructures

Solid-State Electronics

Physica Status Solidi A—Applied Research

Physica Status Solidi B—Basic Research

Nuovo Cimento della Societa Italiana di Fisica B—General Physics

Hyperfine Interactions

Radiation Effects and Defects in Solids

Fizika I Tekhnika Poluprovodnikov. English.
   (was Soviet Physics Semiconductors)

Phase Transitions

Ferroelectrics—Letters

Fizika Tverdogo Tela

Semiconductors

Physica A—Superconductivity and Its Applications

Modern Physics Letters B

Journal of Physical Chemistry B—Condensed Matter, Materials, Surfaces, Interfaces, and Biophysical

Fluids and Plasmas

Physics of Fluids and Plasmas
   (was Physics of Fluids B—Plasma Physics and Physics of Fluids A—Fluid Dynamics)

Plasma Physics and Controlled Fusion

Journal of Plasma Physics

Nuclear Fusion

Physical Review E
Journal of Fluid Mechanics
Plasma Chemistry and Plasma Physics
IEEE Transactions on Plasma Science
International Journal for Numerical Methods in Fluids
Experimental Thermal and Fluid Science
Contributions to Plasma Physics

Mathematical Physics

Communications in Mathematical Physics
Physica D
Foundations of Physics
Foundations of Physics Letters
Physical Review E
Computer Physics Communications
General Relativity and Gravitation
Progress of Theoretical Physics
Classical and Quantum Gravity
Journal of Statistical Physics
Nonlinearity
International Journal of Theoretical Physics
Modern Physics Letters A
Journal of Computational Physics
Letters in Mathematical Physics
Inverse Problems
Journal of Mathematical Physics
International Journal of Modern Physics B
Theoretical and Mathematical Physics
Computational Mathematics and Mathematical Physics
Chaos
Journal of Physics A—Mathematical and General
Journal of Geometry and Physics

Nuclear Physics

Nuclear Physics A
Nuclear Physics B

Physical Review C—Nuclear Physics

Nuclear Fusion

European Physical Journal A—Hadrons and Nuclei
   (was Zeitschrift fur Physik A—Hadrons and Nuclei)

Annual Review of Nuclear and Particle Science

International Journal of Modern Physics A

Journal of Physics G—Nuclear and Particle Physics

Atomic Data and Nuclear Data Tables

Modern Physics Letters A

Nuclear Instruments & Methods in Physics Research B—Beam Interactions with Materials and Atoms

Physics of Atomic Nuclei
   (was Soviet Journal of Nuclear Physics)

Hyperfine Interactions

Physics of Atomic Nuclei

Nuovo Cimento della Societa Italiana di Fisica A—Nuclei, Particles and Fields

International Journal of Modern Physics E: Nuclear Physics

Optics

Optics Letters

Journal of the Optical Society of America—B

Journal of the Optical Society of America—A

Applied Optics

Optics Communications

Journal of Modern Optics

Optik

Particles and Fields

Physical Review Letters

Europhysics Letters

Nuclear Physics B

Physics Letters B

Physical Review D

Accelerators, Spectrometers, Detectors, and Associated Equipment

Modern Physics Letters A

Journal of Physics G—Nuclear and Particle Physics

Nuovo Cimento della Societa Italiana di Fisica A—Nuclei, Particles and Fields

Physics of Atomic Nuclei

E-Print Servers

The proliferation of self-publication, either before or during peer review, has created a confusing situation for readers, authors, publishers, and indexing/abstracting services. The highly dynamic nature of the manuscripts and the distribution tools has created a more democratic and effective network, but has also created additional options that require sophisticated and costly computer equipment and either additional user navigation skills or the development of better network-wide search tools.

The principle e-print servers at this time are located at the Los Alamos National Laboratory and the Stanford Linear Accelerator Center, with mirror sites located worldwide. The American Physical Society has also developed a preprint server, as have many other publishers and organizations.

LANL. http://xxx.lanl.gov/ (accessed May 4, 1999) (see entries 28, 45).

SLAC. http://www.slac.stanford.edu/find/spires.html (accessed May 4, 1999) (see entry 44).

87.   APS. http://publish.aps.org/eprint/ (accessed May 4, 1999).

Some Statistics and Comments on E-Prints

The following are random comments about e-print use that were sent on the PAMnet electronic discussion list and might prove interesting for an overall perspective of the current acceptance and infiltration of electronic e-prints into user behaviors.

From Louise Addis, librarian at SLAC:

"During the first three months of 1999, the SLAC SPIRES-HEP database collected bibliographic information for 3,989 e-prints (dated 1 Jan 99—9 Apr 99) of which 1,269 were from astro-ph. . . . If past experience is any guide, 80% of these e-print/preprints will eventually be published in refereed journals or conference proceedings."

From Michael Kurtz, ADS:

"The astro-ph preprints contain only a small fraction of what is published in astronomy; one cannot currently use the xxx archives to find articles. The statistics are:
1998 articles in astro-ph: 4,747

1998 articles in ADS: 23,537
Only one in five articles in astronomy appears in astro-ph.

"The number of articles and abstracts accessed through astro-ph is about the same as the number accessed through the electronic journals, and is about a third the number accessed through ADS (200,000/month).
ADS use (US server only) we see the following access of 1998 ApJ articles:
Abstracts: 9231 (via ADS)
HTML: 3654 (via UCP)
PDF: 4949 (via UCP)
The HTML initial screen is very similar to the Abstract screen in content. It is likely that a number of users prefer it to read the abstract."

From Arthur Smith, American Physical Society (apsmith@aps.org):
"And yet we have seen submissions to Phys Rev D increase, and subscriptions to PRD have hardly budged over the past seven years of xxx operation. The reason, I believe, is that the community understands that a journal does many things besides the 'obvious' communication function that xxx has pretty much taken over. And those things must be valued. What I believe has happened is that xxx has inserted itself as a new 'institutional layer' in the fabric of at least some fields, in between the traditional means of informal communication (conferences and seminars, theses, private communications, old-style preprints) and the formal communication/criticism function that was once reserved for journals. I don't think this is a bad thing, but I think it means both will be with us for a long time to come. See http://ridge.aps.org/APSMITH/ALPSP/talk.html for some recent thoughts on this, if you want more details."

Endnotes

1. See Eugene Garfield's *Essays of an Information Scientist*; in particular, the following essays:

"Can researchers bank on citation analysis?," vol. 11, pp. 354–56; no. 44, Oct 31, 1988.

"Uses and misuse of citation frequency," vol. 8, pp. 403–9; no. 43, Oct 28, 1985.

"Evaluating research: Do bibliometric indicators provide the best measures?," vol. 12, p. 93; no. 15 April 10, 1989.

Jean King. "A review of bibliometric and other science indicators and their role in research evaluation," vol. 12, pp. 95–100, 1989. An abridged version of the article published in the *Journal of Information Science* 13 (5): 261–76.

Chapter 4

Books

This chapter discusses important books in physics. There is an annotated list of selected reference books (e.g., dictionaries, encyclopedias, handbooks, directories), a list of important monographic series, a list of major physics book publishers, tools to help readers identify recently released books, book review sources, and a description of how libraries acquire books. In addition, this chapter introduces researchers to sophisticated book searching techniques and powerful databases that cover numerous library catalogs. Brief mention will be made of the latest experiments in online books.

Key Publishers

The following are important book publishers covering the field of physics:

Academic Press, 525 B St., Ste. 1900, San Diego, CA 92101-4495. TEL 619-231-0926. FAX 619-699-6715. URL http://www.apnet.com/

American Chemical Society, 1155 16th St., N.W., Washington, DC 20009-1749. TEL 202-332-5544; 800-333-9511. FAX 202-332-4559. E-mail service@acs.org. URL http://pubs.acs.org/

American Institute of Physics, One Physics Ellipse, College Park, MD 20740-3843. TEL 301-209-3000. URL http://www.aip.org/

American Physical Society, One Physics Ellipse, College Park, MD 20740-3844. TEL 301-209-3200. URL http://www.aps.org/

Birkhauser, P.O. Box 133, CH-4010 Basel, Switzerland. TEL 41-61-2050730. URL http://www.birkhauser.ch/

CRC Press, 2000 Corporate Blvd., N.W., Boca Raton, FL 33431. TEL 561-994-0555. FAX 561-998-9784. URL http://www.crcpress.com/

Elsevier North-Holland, P.O. Box 211, 1000 AE Amsterdam, Netherlands. TEL 31-20-4853911. FAX 31-20-4853598. URL http://www.elsevier.nl

Harwood Academic (Gordon and Breach—Harwood Academic), Poststrasse 22, 7000 Chur, Switzerland

Institute of Physics Publishing, Dirac House, Temple Back, Bristol, BS1 6BE, England. TEL 44-117-929-7841. FAX 44-117-929-4318. E-mail custserv@ioppublishing.co.uk. URL http://www.iop.org

Kluwer Academic Publishers, Postbus 17, 3300 AA Dordrecht, Netherlands. TEL 31-78-6392392. FAX 31-78-6546474. URL http://www.wkap.nl/

Marcel Dekker, 270 Madison Ave., New York, NY 10016. TEL 212-696-9000. FAX 212-685-4540. URL http://www.dekker.com/

Plenum Press (Plenum Publishing Corp., subsidiary of Wolters Kluwer N.V.), 233 Spring St., New York, NY 10013-1578. TEL 212-620-8000; 800-221-9369. FAX 212-463-0742. E-mail info@plenum.com. URL http://www.plenum.com/

Prentice-Hall, One Lake Street, Upper Saddle River, NJ 07458. TEL 800-643-5506. FAX 1-800-835-5327. E-mail corpsales@prenhall.com. URL http://www.prenhall.com/

Springer (Springer-Verlag), Heidlberger Platz 3, 14197 Berlin. TEL 49-30-82787-366. FAX 49-30-82787-448. E-mail subscriptions@springer.de. URL http://link.springer.de/

Wiley (John Wiley & Sons), 605 Third Ave., New York, NY 10158-0012. TEL 212-850-6000. FAX 212-850-6099. E-mail info@wiley.com. URL http://www.wiley.com/

World Scientific (World Scientific Publishing), Parrer Rd., P.O. Box 128, Singapore 9128, Singapore. TEL 65-3825663. FAX 65-3825919. E-mail wspsl@singnet.com/sg; saes@wspc2.demon.co.uk; wspc@wspc.com. URL http://www.worldscientific.com/

There are many university presses and other professional societies that publish in the field as well.

Many publishers produce and distribute catalogs to scholars using mailing lists. In addition, many large publishers now have websites with on-line book catalogs and ordering capabilities. One good gateway to these online catalogs is the AcqWeb Directory of Publishers and Vendors: http://www.library.vanderbilt.edu/law/acqs/pubr.html (accessed June 18, 1999).

Types/Uses of Sources

There are a number of types of books, and each type of book can have multiple uses. For example, an encyclopedia can be used for short descriptions of topics, as a source of citations to primary works, or for finding images. It is not unusual for librarians to find that books are often used for many purposes that were never intended by the authors at the time of creation. This alternative perspective is part of what makes the librarian an important variable in the information-seeking process. However, for many researchers there are common uses for types of books.

> *Fact books*: dictionaries, almanacs, encyclopedias, handbooks, methods manuals. This type of book provides quick facts and has comprehensive indexes and table of contents to help in precise navigation.

> *Contact information*: directories, associations, biographical sources. This type of book provides information about individuals, groups, and companies. They often have controlled vocabulary subject arrangements to co-locate similar entries.

> *Reading sources*: texts, textbooks. This type of book provides information and/or entertainment through reading material either cover-to-cover or by chapter.

> *Verification sources*: local library catalogs, the Library of Congress library catalog, *Books in Print* (see entry 88), RLIN (see entry 185), OCLC WorldCat (see entry 184). This type of tool provides bibliographic information to confirm the publication information for books.

Ordering Books

Individual researchers can order books through bookstores, online via web services such as Amazon.com, or directly through the publishers. Available books can be identified using tools such as the following.

88.   **Books in Print**. New Providence, N.J.: R. R. Bowker. Annual.
This tool lists the availability and price of hardcover and paperback editions of books from major publishers in the United States. The books are arranged by author and title, and by subject in the *Books in Print Subject Guide*. There is also a volume containing publisher contact information. It is available in paper and as a for-fee online database. Most libraries have this tool, as well as the complementary *Forthcoming Books*. This tool is also available on CD-ROM and from a variety of online services.

89.   **Bowker/Whitaker Global Books in Print on Disc**. New Providence, N.J.: R. R. Bowker, CD-ROM.

Includes: *Books in Print*; *Subject Guide to Books in Print*; *Books in Print Supplement*; *Forthcoming Books in Print*; *Paperbound Books in Print*; *Children's Books in Print*; *Subject Guide to Children's Books in Print*; *Bowker's Canadian Books in Print*; *Publishers, Distributors and Wholesalers of the United States*; *Whitaker's Books in Print*; *International Books in Print*; *Australian Books in Print*; and *New Zealand Books in Print*.

Online Bookstores

There are many online bookstores that provide federated searching and ordering across a number of publishers. A few of the most important of these services are listed below.

90.   Amazon.com: http://www.amazon.com (accessed May 6, 1999).

91.   Barnes and Noble: http://www.barnesandnoble.com (accessed May 6, 1999).

92.   Borders: http://www.borders.com (accessed May 6, 1999).

Out-of-Print Dealers

93.   Out-of-print titles can be ordered through out-of-print dealers. Searching and ordering can be accomplished across a number of dealers using the online clearinghouse at URL http://www.bookfinder.com (accessed May 6, 1999).

Library Approval Plans and Firm Orders

Libraries do purchase individual books from publishers, but they generally use vendors and receive a discount on each item. These vendors often create "approval plans" that either deliver books or book order forms based upon a library collection profile. In this way libraries are automatically aware of the latest books from the major publishers. The identification of unusual and esoteric books is still accomplished by subject librarians reviewing publisher catalogs and fliers. Purchases made using this labor-intensive technique are often called firm orders. The identification of these difficult-to-locate materials is where the libraries depend upon the expertise and liaison activities of the physics researchers and teachers.

Library Acquisition Lists

94. **Resources in Physics**. Many libraries publish their acquisition lists on paper and on the Web. Reviewing these lists is a great way to discover the latest items deemed valuable by libraries. A listing of online acquisition lists is located within the "Resources in Physics" page on the website for the Physics-Astronomy-Mathematics Division of the Special Libraries Association at http://www.sla.org/division/dpam/phys.html (accessed May 6, 1999).

Selected Bibliography

Below are listed some representative physics reference titles in a variety of categories. This list is selective and is not intended to be complete. Included are selected core materials and some newer materials not represented in earlier bibliographies (see Bibliographies section). It would be worthwhile to consult a librarian for additional suggestions. In addition to these paper reference sources, consider the many online tools that are becoming available (see the Online Tools section).

Dictionaries/Encyclopedias

95. **Encyclopedia of Physics**. 2nd ed. Lerner, Rita, and George L. Trigg, eds. New York: VCH, 1990. 1,408p. $95.00. ISBN 0895737523.
Concise definitions in alphabetical order. Articles contain charts, tables, and figures; cross-references; and further readings with categories (elementary, intermediate, advanced).

96. **Encyclopedia of Physics**. 3rd ed. Besancon, R. M., ed. New York: Van Nostrand Reinhold, 1985. ISBN 0442257783.
There are three levels of coverage. The main divisions are intended for beginners; subdivisions are for more knowledgeable readers; and finer divisions are for those with a solid background in both physics and mathematics.

97. **Macmillan Encyclopedia of Physics**. John S. Rigden, editor in chief. New York: Simon & Schuster/Macmillan, 1996. 4 v. 1,470p. $400.00. ISBN 0028973593.
This somewhat less technical encyclopedia has brief alphabetic entries with cross-references, a reader's guide for teaching organization, a glossary of short concept definitions, biographies, history, general overviews of disciplines, and an index. Excellent for beginners in the field.

98. **Encyclopedia of Applied Physics**. Trigg, George L., Eduardo S. Vera, and Walter Greulich, eds. New York: VCH, 1991- . 23+ vols. ISBN 1560810580.

Concise and comprehensive information on physics applications. More technical than a general-purpose encyclopedia but less detailed and extensive than a textbook. Written for professionals (physicists, engineers, computer scientists). Covers areas of physics that have already found technical applications and those that promise to be industrially applicable in the future. Some nonphysics areas (e.g., astronomy, geology, biology, medicine). Alphabetical entries with cross-references. Cumulative indexes every third volume. The final volume will be an index to the entire set.

99. **McGraw-Hill Dictionary of Physics**. 2nd ed. Sybil P. Parker, editor in chief. New York: McGraw-Hill, 1997. 656p. $16.95. ISBN 0070524297.

This subset of the *McGraw-Hill Dictionary of Scientific and Technical Terms*, 5th ed., covers physics and related fields. Entries labeled within 15 subdisciplines.

100. **Facts on File Dictionary of Physics**. 3rd ed. Daintith, John, and John Clark, eds. New York: Facts on File, 1999. 250p. $68. 40.; $17.95p. ISBN 0816039119; 39127pa.

A brief student dictionary with a limited number of figures and tables. Contains appendixes for symbols and basic conversion factors.

101. **McGraw-Hill Dictionary of Physics and Mathematics**. Lapedas, D. N., ed. New York: McGraw-Hill, 1978. o.p. ISBN 0070454809.

These entries cover physics, mathematics, and related disciplines such as statistics, astronomy, electronics, and geophysics; each is assigned to a subdiscipline. Materials were created specially for this volume, and much was taken from *McGraw-Hill Dictionary of Physics* (1978). This tool was designed for a wide audience: high school and college students, librarians, teachers, engineers, researchers, and the general public. Contains approximately 700 illustrations, cross-references, and appendixes on the International System of Units, conversion tables, properties of elements, elementary particles, planets and stars, diagrams of crystal lattices, and mathematical and special constants.

102. **Encyclopedia of Physical Science and Technology**. 2nd ed. San Diego, Calif.: Academic Press, 1992. 18 vols. ISBN 0122269306.

Comprehensive coverage of the physical sciences written by leading experts. General and in-depth reviews of areas in approximately 20 pages. Subject and relational (groupings of related articles) indexes.

103. **Encyclopaedic Dictionary of Physics**. New York: Macmillan, 1961–1964 (9 vols. + 5 supplements). Also known as *Thewlis' Encyclopedia*.

Articles are written at the graduate level, and the index is comprehensive. Volume 9 is a multilingual dictionary (English, French, German, Spanish, Russian, and Japanese).

104. **Handbuch der Physik**. 2nd ed. (Encyclopedia of Physics). Flugge, S., ed. Berlin: Springer, 1955–1988. 55 vols.

Intended as a systematic encyclopedic treatise on all areas of physics. German, English, and French are used, with the subject indexes in each volume serving as multilingual dictionaries. Vol. 55 is a subject index for the entire set.

105. Gribbin, John. **Q Is for Quantum: An Encyclopedia of Particle Physics**. New York: Free Press, 1998. 560p. $35.00. ISBN 068485578X.

An easy-to-read dictionary of nuclear physics, with many biographical entries and a timeline containing scientists, key dates in physical science, and important world events within a scientific context.

106. **Concise Encyclopedia of Solid State Physics**. Lerner, R. G., and G. L. Trigg, eds. Reading, Mass.: Addison-Wesley, 1983. 300p. $55.95. ISBN 020114204X.

107. Jerrard, H. G., and D. B. McNeill. **A Dictionary of Scientific Units**. 6th ed. London: Chapman and Hall, 1992. 244p. $19.95. ISBN 0412467208.

An excellent source of conversion factors, with an explanation of the international SI measurement system.

108. **Encyclopedia of Acoustics**. Crocker, Malcolm J., ed. New York: John Wiley, 1997– . $475.00. ISBN 0471804657.

V. 1: General linear acoustics, nonlinear acoustics and cavitation, aeroacoustics and atmospheric sound, underwater sound. V. 3: Architectural acoustics, acoustical signal processing, physiological acoustics, psychological acoustics. V. 4: Speech communication, music and musical acoustics, bioacoustics, animal bioacoustics, acoustical measurements and instrumentation, transducers, index.

Comprehensive treatment of acoustics by a selection of specialists results in thorough coverage of all areas, understandable to general readers, at the advanced level. Excellent cross-references show relationships between the 18 wide-ranging subject areas. Intended for acoustics researchers in all fields.

109.   Emiliani, Cesare. **The Scientific Companion: Exploring the Physical World with Facts, Figures, and Formulas**. 2nd ed. New York: John Wiley, 1995. 384p. $19.95. ISBN 0471133248.

Intention is to enable the reader to reach a personal appreciation of the awesome beauty and wondrous workings of the system of which we are a part, and draw from it both comfort and guidance. A simplistic introduction to scientific concepts and the historical development of scientific thoughts, this book will be popular with interested laypersons and beginning scientists.

Handbooks

110.   **CRC Handbook of Chemistry and Physics**. Cleveland, Ohio: Chemical Rubber Publishing and Boca Raton, Fla.: CRC Press, 1913– . Annual.

The authority for chemical and physical information for students or laboratory scientists in search of quick data. It includes a wealth of mathematical information and good sections on chemical nomenclature and structures. Beilstein references and Chemical Abstract Service registry numbers are also included. Excellent glossary.

111.   **American Institute of Physics Handbook**. 3rd ed. New York: McGraw-Hill, 1972.

Another authoratative source of physical data and graphs, with an excellent index. Dated but still of great value.

112.   **Physics Vade Mecum: AIP 50th Anniversary**. Herbert L. Anderson, editor in chief. New York: American Institute of Physics, 1981. 330p.

Intended as a pocket book to provide "the essence of concepts and numerical data contained primarily in archival journals." Designed for ready reference, the 22 subject categories contain information, formulas, numerical data, definitions, and references. The General Section contains fundamental constants, SI units, conversion factors, magnitudes, basic mathematical and physics formulas, formulas used in practical physics applications, and a list of physics data centers. Contains illustrations, charts, and tables.

113.   **Handbook of Physics**. 2nd ed. Condon, Edward Uhler, and Hugh Odishaw, eds. New York: McGraw-Hill, 1967.

A one-volume compendium of "what every physicist should know." Each section was written by a specialist in the field.

114. **The Practicing Scientist's Handbook: A Guide for Physical and Terrestrial Scientists and Engineers**. Moses, Alfred J. New York: Van Nostrand Reinhold, 1978. 1,292p.

Applications-oriented tool providing a comprehensive source of materials property data to practicing physicists, chemists, engineers, and designers. Includes safety concerns, but does not include a great deal of theory and mathematical data.

115. **Tables of Physical & Chemical Constants**. 16th ed. Essex, Eng.: Longman, 1995. 611p. ISBN 0582226295.

Intended to provide physical and chemical data required for everyday laboratory purposes.

115a. **Tables of Physical & Chemical Constants and Some Mathematical Functions**. 15th ed. London: Longman, 1986. ISBN 0582463548.

Arranged in three sections: physics, chemistry, and mathematical functions.

116. **Handbook of Optics**. 2nd ed. Optical Society of America. Michael Bass, editor in chief. New York: McGraw-Hill, 1994. $199.00. ISBN 0079118070.

General-purpose desktop reference covering both basic and applied topics but not applications of optics. Seventeen parts with cross-references among 83 chapters. Volume I has tutorial articles on underlying concepts of optics, and Volume II covers specific devices, instruments, and techniques.

116a. **Handbook of Optics**. Optical Society of America. Driscoll, Walter G., ed. New York: McGraw-Hill, 1978. ISBN 0070477108.

Earlier edition of the above.

117. **Handbook of Optical Constants of Solids I–III**. Palik, Edward, D., ed. San Diego: Academic Press, 1998. 3 vols. (and Volume 5: **Subject Index and Contributor Index**). ISBN 0125444206.

Collection of references and tabulations for the refractive index (n) and extinction coefficient (k) for a large number of materials of technological and physics interest over a wide spectral range. Along with short summaries, tables, and figures, a critique is provided for each material. These critiques cover the experimental techniques, reasons for choices of numbers used in the table, the most important literature references, and some idea of the accuracy and precision.

118. **Handbook of Optical Constants of Solids**. Ghosh, Gorachand, ed. San Diego: Academic Press, 1998. Volume IV of the **Handbook of Optical Constants of Solids**.

A reference handbook for the refractive index (n), thermo-optic coefficients, and their applications.

119. Shackelford, James F., William Alexander, and Jun S. Park. **CRC Practical Handbook of Materials Selection**. Boca Raton, Fla.: CRC Press, 1995. ISBN 0849337097.

Includes a simple (keyword in context) KWIC index.

A companion to the *CRC Materials Science and Engineering Handbook*, this volume provides an introduction to key professional societies, educational institutions, and employment opportunities in materials science; easy-to-find materials properties; and data sets in a Selection-Format in which materials can be compared by property value.

120. **Handbook of Vacuum Science and Technology**. Hoffman, Dorothy M., Bawa Singh, and John H. Thomas, III, eds. San Diego, Calif.: Academic Press, 1998. 835p. $150.00. ISBN 0123520657.

This title offers a practical overview for the practitioner of vacuum technology. It updates and expands *Vacuum Physics and Technology*, Weissler, G. L., and R. W. Carlson, eds. (Academic Press, 1979). It does not duplicate the basic material included in the earlier work. The coverage includes modern pump technologies, methods of monitoring, components, and applications of high-vacuum and ultra-high-vacuum in commercial products.

121. Tuma, Jan J. **Handbook of Physical Calculations**. New York: McGraw-Hill, 1983. ISBN 0070654395.

Intended as a study guide for students, with many examples of applications.

122. Alenitsyn, Alexander G., Eugene I. Butikov, and Alexander S. Kondratyev. Kratkiòi fiziko-matematicheskiòi spravochnik. **Concise Handbook of Mathematics and Physics**. Boca Raton, Fla.: CRC Press; Moscow: Nauka Publishers, 1997. 528p. $49.95. ISBN 0849377455.

Systematics (vs. alphabetic) arrangement plus many examples, problems, and solutions. An overview and study guide. The thin index makes this item most appropriate for knowledgeable users.

123. **Handbook of Physical Quantities**. Grigoriev, Igor S., and Evgenii Z. Meilikhov, eds. Editor of the English edition, A. A. Radzis. Boca Raton, Fla.: CRC Press, 1997. 1,792p. $130.00. ISBN 0849328616.

Intended for specialists (students, postgraduates, engineers, and scientists) who need specific numerical information in their everyday work and research. Contains summaries of principles that apply, lists of units, and references for each area for nonspecialists. The material is presented in charts and figures when possible.

124.   **Handbook of Conducting Polymers**. Skotheim, Terje A., Ronald L. Elsenbaumer, and John R. Reynolds, eds. 2nd ed., rev. and expanded. New York: M. Dekker, 1998. 1,112p. $195.00. ISBN 0824700503.

This collection of chapters written by experts provides an update on fundamental progress and applications. Section headings are: theory and transport, synthesis, processing, properties, and applications of conducting polymers.

Data Tables/Books

125.   **Landolt-Börnstein Numerical Data and Functional Relationships in Science and Technology. New Series**. Berlin: Springer-Verlag, 1961– . ISBN 0387521283.

The world's most complete collection of information (in tabular format) concerning the fundamental properties of physics, chemistry, astronomy, geophysics, and technology. In German.

125a.   **Landolt-Börnstein Zahlenwerte und Funktionen aus Physik, Chemie, Astronomie, Geophysik, Technik**. Berlin: Springer-Verlag, 1950.

Earlier version of previous title (above).

126.   **Thermophysical Properties of Matter**. Touloukian, Y. S., ed. New York: IFI/Plenum, 1970. 14 vols. (TPRC Data Series). ISBN 0306670208.

Thermal conductivity (vols. 1–3), specific heat (4–6), thermal radiative properties (7–9), thermal diffusivity (10), viscosity (11), thermal expansion (12–13), and index (14).

127.   **NIST-JANAF Thermochemical Tables**. 4th ed. Washington, D.C.: American Chemical Society; New York: American Institute of Physics for the National Institute of Standards and Technology, 1998. (Journal of Physical and Chemical Reference Data monograph, no. 9.) ISBN 1563968312.

Covers approximately 1,800 inorganic and organic substances containing only one or two carbon atoms. Properties include heat capacity, entropy, Gibbs energy function, enthalpy, enthalpy of formation, Gibbs energy of formation, and the logarithm of the equilibrium constant for formation of each compound from the elements in their standard reference states.

127a.   **JANAF Thermochemical Tables**. 3rd ed. Washington, D.C.: American Chemical Society; New York: American Institute of Physics for the National Bureau of Standards, 1986.

Earlier version of previous title (above).

128. **International Critical Tables of Numerical Data, Physics, Chemistry and Technology**. National Research Council. New York: McGraw-Hill, 1926–1933.

A critical compilation of data from 1910–1923. Still a useful source of information.

129. **Smithsonian Physical Tables**. 9th rev. ed. Washington, D.C.: Smithsonian Institution Press, 1954.

Although dated, this is still a useful compilation of chemical and physical tables.

130. **Absorption Spectra in the Ultraviolet and Visible Region**. New York: Academic Press. 1959– .

Author, subject, and formula indexes. Includes diagrams and tables.

131. **Aldrich Library of Infrared Spectra**. Edition III. Pouchert, C. J., ed. Milwaukee, Wis.: Aldrich Chemical, 1981.

Contains 10,000 spectra arranged in order of increasing complexity. Alphabetical and Molecular Formula indexes.

132. **M.I.T. Wavelength Tables**. Cambridge, Mass.: MIT Press, 1969. 816p. $95.00/vol. ISBN 0262080028 (v. 1); ISBN 0262160870 (v. 2).

More than 100,000 spectrum lines most strongly emitted by the atomic elements under normal conditions of excitation between 10,000 A. and 2000 A. Volume 1 includes tables of wavelengths; Volume 2 is arranged as wavelengths by element. Used for analysis of materials and identifying impurities; one of the first compilations created using the new computing capabilities.

133. **Desk Book of Infrared Spectra**. 2nd ed. Craver, Clara D., ed. Coblentz Society, 1977.

A selection of high-quality spectra for principal compound classes. Includes a beginner's bibliography and a short section on the interpretation of IR spectra.

134. **Nuclear Level Schemes A = 45 through A = 257, from Nuclear Data Sheets**. Nuclear Data Group. New York: Academic Press, 1973. ISBN 0123556503.

A ready-reference book to nuclear structures for A = 45 and above.

135. **CINDA**. Vienna: International Atomic Energy Agency.

Computer index of neutron data. CINDA-A. "An index to the literature on microscopic neutron data." Cumulative vols. issued from time to time with title: CINDA-A.

Kept up-to-date between vols.: by supplements. "Published on behalf of: USA National Nuclear Data Center, USSR Nuclear Data Center. NEA Data Bank, IAEA Nuclear Data Section."

Contains factual (measurements, calculations, evaluations) and bibliographic information on neutron data, arranged by element and mass number.

136.   Watson, P. R., M. A. Van Hove, and K. Hermann. **Atlas of Surface Structures: Based on the NIST Surface Structure. Database (SSD)**. Washington, D.C.: American Chemical Society; Woodbury, N.Y.: American Institute of Physics, for the National Institute of Standards and Technology, 1994– . (Journal of physical and chemical reference data. Monograph, no. 5). ISBN 1563964147.

This supplement to the journal provides atomic scale structures of surfaces from listings of crystallographic studies on almost 600 surface structures in the NIST Surface Structure Database. Includes high-quality computer-generated views of the surfaces and explanatory text, references, and methods.

137.   **Table of Isotopes**. 8th ed. Firestone, Richard B., and Coral M. Baglin, eds. 1998 update with CD-ROM. New York: Wiley, 1998. 140p. $175.00. ISBN 0471246999. (System requirements for accompanying computer disc: Windows 95, NT, or 3.1; Macintosh; UNIX; OS/2 Warp; DOS. Uses Adobe Acrobat Reader software.)

Nuclear structure and decay data for more than 3,100 isotopes and isomers with $1<=A<=272$. Partial reprints from Nuclear Physics A ($A<=44$) and Nuclear Data Sheets ($45<=A<=266$). Data is also available from Evaluated Nuclear Structure Data File (ENSDF). Other data elements include nuclear mass and Q-value data, neutron cross-section data, spontaneous fission probabilities, nuclear moment data, fission isomers, and superdeformed nuclear band structure. Mass chain decay reaction level schemes are replaced by high-spin nuclear band drawings. Organized by mass number (A) and subordered by atomic number (Z). Contains all isotopes and isomers of each mass.

138.   **International Tables for Crystallography**. Hahn, Theo, ed. Dordrecht, Holland, and Boston: International Union of Crystallography by D. Reidel Publishing, 1983– . $140.00. ISBN 9027714452.

Directories

139. **Graduate Programs: Physics, Astronomy, and Related Fields**. New York: American Institute of Physics. Annual. $45.00. ISSN 0147-1821.

Variant Titles: Graduate Programs in Physics, Astronomy, and Related Fields.

Provides the information for North American institutions by state, by institution, and by highest degree granted, with geographic charts for doctoral programs identifying theoretical, experimental, or both emphases, and geographic charts for master's programs identifying terminal degree or toward Ph.D. tracks.

140. **Directory of Physics, Astronomy and Geophysics Staff**. New York: American Institute of Physics. Biennial ed. 1997. ISSN 0361-2228.

Alphabetical listing by department, providing address, phone, fax, and faculty listing. Geographical listing. Sections for corporations, small companies, consulting firms, private practices, government agencies, government laboratories, federally funded research and development centers, and other research institutes. Listing of professional societies. Individual staff entries provide address, phone, and e-mail.

141. **Research Centers Directory**. 24th ed. Detroit: Gale, 1998. 2 vols. $530.00. ISBN 0787621951.

A listing of major laboratories, research institutes, and universities in the United States and Canada, excluding federally funded centers, which are covered in the *Government Research Directory* (see next entry). Entries include contact information, descriptions of organization and research areas, research budget, resources, publications, meetings, scholarships, awards, and library holdings.

142. **Government Research Directory**. 12th ed. Detroit: Gale, 1999. (Was *Government Research Centers Directory*).

A listing of federally funded major laboratories, research institutes, and universities in the United States and Canada. Entries include contact information, descriptions of organization and research areas, research budget, resources, publications, meetings, scholarships, awards, and library holdings.

143. **International Research Centers Directory**. 11th ed. Detroit: Gale, 1999.

A listing of major laboratories, research institutes, and universities, excluding the United States and Canada. Entries include contact information, descriptions of organization and research areas, research budget, resources, publications, meetings, scholarships, awards, and library holdings.

144. **Commonwealth of Independent States: 1996–1997 Directory of Physics and Astronomy Staff**. Shkuratov, S. I., and E. F. Talantsev. In cooperation with the Physical and Astronomical Society. [Ekaterinburg]: Pub. Co. of the Urals Division of the Russian Academy of Sciences, 1996. ISBN 5769105534.

Variant Titles: 1996–1997 Directory of Physics and Astronomy Staff; Directory of Physics and Astronomy Staff.

Entries include brief personal information (department address, phone, fax, e-mail) for approximately 5,151 professional scientists from more than 15 former republics of the Soviet Union. Listing of personnel by institution (geographic); members (Academicians) of the National Academies of Sciences; corresponding members; and an alphabetic list of research organizations and academic institutions.

145. **American Men and Women of Science: Physical and Biological Sciences, 1998–1999**. 20th ed. New York: R. R. Bowker, 1998. 8 vols. 8,500p. $900.00. ISBN 0835237486.

Compact entries contain name, occupation, career, education, honors and awards, memberships, research and publications, mailing address, fax, and e-mail. Includes a geographic index.

146. **Who's Who in Science and Engineering, 1998–1999**. 4th ed. New Providence, N.J.: Marquis Who's Who, 1997. $259.95. ISSN 1063-5599.

Biographies of approximately 26,000 scientists, doctors, and engineers. The majority are from the United States. Entries contain the following information: name, occupation, birthdate and place, parents, family, education, professional certifications, career, awards, memberships, political affiliation, religion, achievements (patents), and home and office addresses.

147. **Who's Who in Science in Europe: A Biographical Guide to Science, Technology, Agriculture, and Medicine**. 9th ed. New York: Stockton, 1995. 2 vols. ISBN 1561591327.

Entries contain the following information: name, occupation, birthdate, professional and research interests, education, memberships, book publications, telephone and fax, and office address. Arranged in alphabetical order by surname, with an index by country/subject.

See the many online directories that can be identified using Physics Gateway sources (see Online Tools section).

Key Monographic Series

Many book series are considered monographic sets; some have regular publication patterns, and others have irregular production cycles. Some serials are numbered sets (e.g., Lecture Notes in Physics, vol. 123), while others are simply grouped within a general series title (e.g., *Physics of Atoms and Molecules*). Depending on library policy, these items may be shelved together or as separates according to their subjects. Many are purchased on "standing orders," which means they are received automatically upon publication; specific titles are not reviewed individually. These titles can best be found using keyword searches on library catalogs. Below is a list of several important physics book series.

148. **Advances in Atomic, Molecular, and Optical Physics**. New York: Academic Press. Annual. $125.00. ISSN 1049-250X.

149. **Advances in Imaging and Electron Physics**. San Diego, Calif.: Academic Press. Irregular. $130.00. ISSN 1076-5670.

150. **Advances in Magnetic Resonance**. New York: Academic Press. $120.00. ISSN 0065-2873. Extent: v. 1–14; 1965–1990.
Succeeding entry: Advances in Magnetic and Optical Resonance.

151. **Advances in Nuclear Physics**. New York: Plenum Press. Annual (irregular). $90–$95. ISSN 0065-2970.

152. **AIP Conference Proceedings**. New York: American Institute of Physics, 1970– . ISSN 0094-243X.

153. **Annals of the Israel Physical Society**. Bristol, Eng.: Institute of Physics and Jerusalem, Israel Physical Society. ISSN 0309-8710.

154. **Annual Review of Astronomy and Astrophysics**. Palo Alto, Calif. Annual Reviews. $70.00. ISSN 0066-4146.

155. **Annual Review of Nuclear and Particle Science**. Palo Alto, Calif. Annual Reviews. $140.00. ISSN 0163-8998.
Preceding entry: Annual Review of Nuclear Science.

156. **Astrophysics and Space Science Library**. Dordrecht, Boston: Kluwer Academic Publishers. Irregular.

157. **Experimental Methods in the Physical Sciences**. San Diego, Calif.: Academic Press. Irregular. Approx. $100. ISSN 1079-4042.

158. **Handbook on the Physics and Chemistry of Rare Earths**. Karl A. Gschneidner, Jr. and LeRoy Eyring, eds. Amsterdam, N.Y.: North-Holland; distr. New York: Elsevier North-Holland, 1978– . $297.00. ISBN 0444850228.

159. **Institute of Physics Publishing Conference Series**. Bristol, Eng. and Philadelphia: Institute of Physics. ISSN 0305-2346.

160. **International Conference on the Physics of Electronic and Atomic Collisions**. Amsterdam, N.Y.: North-Holland. Annual.

161. **International Review of Nuclear Physics**. Singapore and Philadelphia: World Scientific.

162. **Lecture Notes in Physics**. Berlin and New York: Springer-Verlag. Irregular. ISSN 0075-8450.

163. **NATO Advanced Science Institutes Series. Series B, Physics**. New York: Plenum Press.

164. **Physics of Atoms and Molecules**. New York: Plenum Press. ISSN 0891-4524.

165. **Physics of Solids and Liquids**. New York: Plenum Press. ISSN 1066-372X.

166. **Progress in Low Temperature Physics**. Amsterdam, North-Holland and New York: Interscience Publishers. Irregular. $244.00. ISSN 0079-6417.

167. **Progress in Optics**. Amsterdam, N.Y.: North-Holland. Annual. $155.00. ISSN 0079-6638.

168. **Progress in Particle and Nuclear Physics**. Oxford and New York: Pergamon Press, 1978– . ISSN 0146-6410.
Preceding entry: Progress in Nuclear Physics.

169. **Progress in Physics**. Boston: Birkhäuser, 1980– . ISSN 0736-7422.

170. **Reviews of Plasma Physics**. New York: Consultants Bureau. $125.00. ISSN 0080-2050.

171. **Semiconductors and Semimetals**. New York: Academic Press. ISSN 0080-8784.

172. **Solid State Physics: Advances in Research and Applications**. New York: Academic Press. ISSN 0081-1947.

173. **Solid State Physics: Advances in Research and Applications. Supplement**. New York: Academic Press. ISSN 0081-1955.

174. **Soviet Scientific Reviews. Section A: Physics Reviews**. Chur, Switzerland, and New York: Harwood Academic Publishers. ISSN 0143-0394.
    Variant Titles: Physics Reviews.

175. **Springer Series in Computational Physics**. New York: Springer-Verlag. ISSN 0172-5726.

176. **Springer Series in Electronics and Photonics**. Berlin and New York: Springer-Verlag. ISSN 0931-7260.

177. **Springer Series in Solid-State Sciences**. Heidelberg and New York: Springer-Verlag. ISSN 0171-1873.

178. **Subnuclear Series**. New York: Plenum Press. ISSN 8756-4475.

179. **Superconducting Devices and Their Applications: Proceedings of the Xth International Conference SQUID 'XX (Session on Superconducting Devices)**. Berlin and New York: Springer-Verlag. $98.00.

180. **Topics in Applied Physics**. Berlin and New York: Springer-Verlag. ISSN 0303-4216.

Zahlenwerte und Funktionen aus Naturwissenschaften und Technik. neue Serie Gesamtherausgabe. K. H. Hellwege, ed. Berlin: Springer-Verlag, 1961– .
    Variant Titles: Numerical Data and Functional Relationships in Science and Technology. Landolt-Börnstein (see entries 125, 125a).

Book Reviews

Book reviews can be found in a number of discipline-specific journals and library review sources. Key science journals that contain book reviews are *Physics Today, American Scientist, Science, Nature, American Journal of Physics, Scientific American, The Physics Teacher, Contemporary Physics, Bulletin of the Atomic Scientists*, and *New Scientist*. Library journals that contain book reviews include *Choice* and *Booklist*.

Indexes that identify general book reviews include the following.

181. **Book Review Digest**. Bronx, N.Y.: H. W. Wilson.
Book Review Digest is a bibliographic database that cites and provides excerpts of reviews of current English-language fiction and nonfiction books for children and adults. An abstract of each book is also provided. Periodical coverage includes approximately 100 leading magazines from the United States, Canada, and Great Britain.

182. **Book Review Index**. Detroit: Gale.
Reviews indexed are primarily in the fields of general fiction and nonfiction, humanities, social sciences, librarianship, and bibliography. Includes children's and young adult books. Covers United States, Canadian, and British newspapers and journals.

183. **General Science Abstracts**. (See entries 61, 63.)
General Science Abstracts includes book reviews for popular science material.

INSPEC. (See entry 35.)
The INSPEC database includes some book reviews, but is not a primary source for this type of material. It includes the best technical reviews.

Library Catalog Searching

One excellent way to identify books by subject, or to locate or verify a known item, is to search library catalogs. Physicists can search either individual library catalogs or groups of catalogs. Individual catalogs are often available on the Internet and can be found using a listing in the Web such as URL http://sunsite.berkeley.edu/Libweb (accessed May 6, 1999).

Book Indexing/Consortial Gateways

In terms of indexes to books, there is no one catalog. Users will need to check local library catalogs, publisher sales lists (e.g., Amazon.com, *Books in Print*), and possibly union lists of multiple library catalogs such as RLIN and Worldcat (see entries 185, 184). For current awareness information on newly released books, it may be useful to review selected library web book acquisition lists such as the ones listed on the Special Libraries Association Physics-Astronomy-Mathematics Division website at http://www.sla.org/division/dpam/pamtop.html (accessed May 6, 1999). Most book catalogs only index authors, editors, titles, and subjects. Chapter-level indexing is only offered by a few commercial products at this time, and only for a very select group of books (see below). Chapter-level and table of contents book information has just started to be loaded into the most innovative library catalogs.

Innovative "broadcast" technology allows users to search multiple library catalogs simultaneously using the Z39.50 protocol. This technology is not widely distributed at this time; however, the newer online catalogs are beginning to incorporate it.

In addition, some libraries provide free searching of fee-based consortial gateways. Two major gateways are:

184.   The OCLC FirstSearch **WorldCat** database, which covers many public and research libraries at URL http://www.oclc.org/oclc/menu/colpro.htm (accessed May 6, 1999).

185.   The Eureka search system interface into the Research Libraries Group's **RLIN Bibliographic Database**, which includes research libraries and special libraries in RLG member institutions, plus more than 100 additional law, technical, and corporate libraries, available at URL http://www.rlg.org/eureka.html (accessed May 6, 1999).

Advanced Search Techniques

Regardless of the library catalog(s) selected, there are certain techniques that can make searches more productive and powerful. While simple author and title searching techniques provide results, much better results can be obtained using advanced techniques such as truncation, keywords as phrases or in Boolean combinations, and Library of Congress (LC) subject headings.

Examples of advanced search techniques

Truncation

Use the root of a term plus the appropriate truncation symbol for the local system.

example: atom? will pick up atom, atoms, atomic, etc.

Keywords

Use keywords instead of exact title searches to increase results.

AND OR nesting

Use AND and OR nested operators for better coverage.

example: (atomic and spectroscop?) and (table or tables)

This will pick up items with the title "Atomic and molecular spectroscopy."

NEAR and adjacency operators

Use NEAR command for wider coverage than the adjacency operator.

example: atomic near3 spectroscopy

This will find the terms atomic and spectroscopy within three words in any order (e.g., atomic spectrometry and spectroscopy).

Note: Some catalogs assume adjacency, while others automatically default to AND.

Subject headings and hyperlinks

Use official subject headings to scan hierarchies of subject breakdowns.

Many online catalogs have hyperlinks to subject headings from all matching records.

Start with keyword searches and look for the appropriate subject headings.

There are two major subject hierarchies: LC (Library of Congress) and Dewey.

(See the "Introduction" section for each general classification schema.)

No researcher can deny the wonderful discoveries that can be made while browsing the bookshelves, and these advanced catalog search approaches cannot replace the browsing techniques that produce such marvelous serendipity. In addition to these enhanced online browsing capabilities, libraries should always attempt to provide some form of physical browsing of collections when disciplines require such access. Until book tables of contents and indexes are included within the searchable catalog, it would be disadvantageous to remove access to the physical objects. The eventual inclusion of additional metadata (e.g., diagram and illustration descriptions) will make searches of book catalogs even more productive.

Online Full-Text Books

Advances in technology have made it possible to store and deliver full-text materials either over the Internet or via CD-ROM platforms. Individual scholars maintain local CD-ROM databases of journal archives, online dictionaries, data sets, and other personal interest items. Many organizations are creating electronic text centers to serve as clearinghouses and gateways for the coordination of full-text storage, retrieval, delivery, and user training. These full-text collections offer the promise of wonderful new analysis capabilities. Researchers are just beginning to explore and comprehend the possibilities for manipulating these data sets. Searches can include keywords, frequency analysis, linguistic analysis, and visualization analysis, to name just a few. These new tools will certainly change researcher behaviors and identify new research domains.

While the novelty value of online full text is still drawing attention, there are many issues that must be addressed before it becomes a normal part of most researchers' daily routines. A major requirement for the acceptance of full-text materials would be the creation of a seamless access interface: a one-stop search engine that covers a critical threshold collection of materials. This should be a transparent component of the normal library catalog. The unhindered use of these materials will require innovative approaches to satisfying copyright concerns. Even if the identification and delivery of materials is efficient and effective, there are issues of convenience and usability that must be considered. Even librarians must admit that the current display technology does not provide pleasing viewing for long-term online reading. Even with the newest large-screen monitors, most readers still prefer to print sections for extended reading sessions. While there are proprietary technical solutions for many user-requested capabilities, there are no satisfactory integrated systems yet on the market that allow for the following features: comfortable look and feel, portability, long battery life, durability, large storage capacity, reasonable price, online commenting and hyperlink creation, and local high-quality image generation. There are many other issues to consider before the average researcher will accept online full-text materials.

In terms of libraries, there are additional concerns with online full-text materials. One of the most important is the long-term viability of such repositories in terms of archiving. The paradigm shift from ownership of paper materials to access to remote collections of electronic resources has many implications, both intellectually and practically. New use and cost models must be developed. Cooperative collection development strategies must migrate from providing one-time on-demand delivery of locally maintained collections to the institution of a complex system for constant support of shared materials. The evolving standards for electronic formats, hardware, and software mean there is a need for text and image data migration over time. This migration will require long-term planning and funding. International standards are being developed for the archiving of the data, the metadata descriptors, the software, and the hardware.

Below are listed a few representative examples of online full-text delivery systems.

186. **Project Gutenberg**. http://www.gutenberg.net (accessed May 6, 1999).
A compilation and distribution mechanism for public-domain texts.

187. **netLibrary**. http://www.netlibrary.com (accessed May 6, 1999).
A new online book venture that is focusing on academic texts for library subscriptions and also marketed to individual readers.

188. **Rocketbooks**. http://www.rocketbooks.com/enter.html (accessed May 6, 1999).
A technology for full-text books that is currently on the market for individual readers.

Career Information

The best career information is often obtained from people already within the field. There is no substitute for experience in terms of identifying the subtle nuances of career development. It is strongly recommended that beginners consult practitioners and learn about career considerations through mentoring relationships. (This is not unlike the difference between learning to dance from an instructor or through reading.) With that caveat in mind, the following paper and online resources will provide some basic guidance. They are arranged in the following categories: job descriptions, organizations, and job opportunities.

Job Descriptions

189. **Careers in Science and Technology: An International Perspective**. Advisory Committee, Office of Scientific and Engineering Personnel and Committee on International Organizations and Programs, Office of International Affairs, National Research Council. Washington, D.C.: National Academy Press, 1995. 194p. $35.00. ISBN 0309054273.

190. **Occupational Outlook Handbook**. U.S. Department of Labor, Bureau of Labor Statistics. Washington, D.C.: GPO, 1959– . Biennial. Irregular. $22.95.
The classic book of brief career information facts (salaries, projections, etc.) put out by the U.S. government.

191. **Physics Through the 1990s**. National Research Council (U.S.). Physics Survey Committee. Washington, D.C.: National Academy Press, 1986. 8 vols.

This report outlines current trends and future directions for the sciences in terms of probable research fronts, grant opportunities, organizational support, etc.

Also see the many online tools available through various physics gateways dealing with job placement and professional development.

Organizations

There are many directories that list logical places to secure employment within the traditional physics career track. Lists of government laboratories, university and college settings, private corporate laboratories, and educational institutions can be located in a variety of paper and online resources.

Graduate Programs: Physics, Astronomy, and Related Fields. (See entry 139.)

Directory of Physics, Astronomy and Geophysics Staff. (See entry 140.)

Research Centers Directory. 2 vols. (See entry 141.)

Government Research Directory. (See entry 142.)

International Research Centers Directory. (See entry 143.)

Commonwealth of Independent States: 1996–1997 Directory of Physics and Astronomy Staff. (See entry 144.)

Job Opportunities

Job boards are available in both paper and online resources. The best general paper tools would be the Information Exchange section of the journal *Physics Today* and the Bulletin Board section of the *Chronicle of Higher Education*. Certain subject-specific journals also list job postings.

Some of the more widely recognized federated online job postings are listed in the Online Tools section under "Job Opportunities Information."

Key Textbooks

It is quite difficult to identify the most important textbooks in physics due to both the number of textbooks and the intended audience (scope of coverage, level of expertise, mathematical requirements, etc.). A core list of textbooks can be derived from scanning online syllabi requirement criteria, existing reserve lists, and bookstore lists of required and recommended readings.

Chapter 5

Online Sources

Online Internet gateways have been developed to help researchers identify some of the most frequently used electronic resources. These interfaces attempt to organize the physics-related Internet resources. Many tools are listed on all gateways. In addition to surfing the hierarchical gateways, consider "mining" the Internet by performing keyword searches using some of the search engines listed below. However, even searching all the available gateways and search engines will not provide comprehensive coverage of physics materials on the Web.

In addition to gateways and search engines, this section also lists selected examples of frequently used online physics resources. Topics include web teaching tools, funding agencies and grant information, finding people and organizations, job opportunities information, and a listing of SLAC library databases.

Physics Gateways

Below is listed a selection of popular physics gateways that provide pointers to many helpful resources. There is a great deal of overlap among these gateways at this time. Do not expect these gateways to provide comprehensive coverage of all available tools in the ever-changing Internet domain.

192. **TIPTOP (The Internet Pilot TO Physics)**. http://physicsweb.org/tiptop/ (accessed May 6, 1999).

TIPTOP was created to serve everyone with an interest in science in general and physics in particular, including students, teachers at all levels, and researchers in academe and industry. Sections include bulletin board systems for conferences, jobs, used equipment, and book reviews; Physics Calendar; Physics Chatroom; mailing lists; Physics News Flashes; Today in the History of Physics; a list of physics-related Java Applets (and some VRML and Shockwave material); and the popular Physics Around the World (PAW) resource database. TIPTOP is now part of the PhysicsWeb online gateway service provided by the Institute of Physics (IOP Publishing): http://physicsweb.org/ (accessed May 6, 1999).

193. **PhysLINK**. http://www.physlink.com/ (accessed May 6, 1999).

Attempts to provide comprehensive research and education tools to physicists, engineers, educators, students, and all other curious minds. Sections include: Cover Story, Ask Experts, Physics Jobs, Science Software, Quotations, Science Reference, Physics Departments, Physical Societies, Scientific Journals, History of Physics, Graduate Advisor, Images of Physicists, Physics News, HighTech Companies, New Theories, and Physics Fun.

194. **SciCentral Physical and Chemical Sciences**. http://www.scicentral.com/P-02phys.html (accessed May 6, 1999).

This gateway provides links to many Internet resources including parts of the other gateways mentioned in this section. The pages include: Specialty Gateway, Companies & Products, Conferences & Meetings, Career Resources, Databases, Funding Resources, Institutions, Journals, Research Communications, Discussion Groups, Dynamic Information, Specialty Directories, Educational Materials, and Search SciCentral.

195. **PhysDoc: Physics Documents in Europe**. http://www.physik.uni-oldenburg.de/EPS/PhysNet/link-lists/noframe_doc_europe.html (accessed May 6, 1999).

A fascinating project that searches for distributed documents at European and U.S. physics departments. Perhaps this is a prototype of federated search engines that will someday provide one-stop searching of distributed resources.

196. **Yahoo! Physics Subject Hierarchy**. http://www.yahoo.com/Science/Physics/ (accessed May 6, 1999).

The Yahoo! browsing hierarchy section covering physics materials. It is not comprehensive, but it is a good way to identify starting points; especially effective for non-peer-reviewed information such as discussion lists, equipment, and teaching materials.

197. **SLAC SPIRES**—Stanford Public Information REtrieval System. http://www.slac.stanford.edu/find/spires.html (accessed May 6, 1999).

The subsections are as follows:

Hepnames

Worldwide e-mail directory of persons related to particle physics. Includes SLAC physicists, personnel.

Conferences

Past and future particle physics conferences. Find the list of this month's, next month's, or next year's conferences, or cover the period Oct.–Dec. 1998, or Jan.–Mar. 1999, or Apr.–Jun. 1999, or Jul.–Sep. 1999, or make your own search. To announce a new HEP-related conference, please write to: conf@slac.stanford.edu.

Institutions

Addresses, phone and fax numbers of high-energy physics institutions. See also the SPIRES list of HEP institutions with web servers.

Experiments

Experiments in high-energy physics (source for the PDG LBL-91 Report). See also the Experiments Online document.

SLAC-Speak

Glossary of SLAC and HEP-related acronyms and terms.

Online Particle Physics Information

This guide organizes online catalogs, databases, directories, web pages, etc., that are of value to the particle physics community. It provides descriptions of each resource's scope and content to assist researchers in choosing the right source to fit their information needs. A more detailed explanation of the scope of this guide is available along with the credits.

While a substantial amount of particle physics information is Internet-accessible, most listings do not provide descriptions of a resource's scope and content, making it difficult for searchers to know which source to use for a specific information need. This compilation lists the main information sources with brief annotations and web addresses.

A resource is excluded if it provides information primarily of interest to only one institution. In some cases, multiple databases covering much the same material have been included, with the assumption that users will make subsequent choices based on Internet speeds, search system interfaces, or differences in scope, presentation, and coverage. Resources that provide information covering physics broadly have been included only if they have a significant, and somewhat unique, set of information useful to particle physics. With such broader resources, the annotation attempts to highlight the parts that specifically relate to particle physics.

Seminars

Meetings, colloquia, and seminars of interest to the broader high-energy physics community, with entries for SLAC and Stanford University along with other academic and industrial facilities in the area, including Berkeley, Lockheed, San Francisco, and Santa Cruz. Find seminars for today, tomorrow, all future dates, or make your own search.

FreeHEP

A collection of software and information about software useful in high-energy physics. You can also browse an alphabetical subject area or go to the FreeHEP home page: http://heplibw3. slac.stanford. edu/FIND/FHMAIN.HTML (accessed May 6, 1999).

A compilation of available software:

by subject area

by title

by database search

by name

tutorials on topics of common interest

hepnet.freehep discussion group

Particles

Data from the Review of Particle Physics (RPP). This database is no longer available at SLAC. Please visit the LBL Particle Data Group (PDG) web server, where the full-text Postscript version of the latest edition of the RPP is available. To search the corresponding database, use telnet to reach the PDG public access account at MUSE.LBL.GOV (or 131.243.48.11). Log in as PDG_PUBLIC. Another PDG database formerly maintained in SPIRES, the Reaction Data, is now available at the HEPDATA server in Durham.

198. **SPINweb**. American Institute of Physics. http://ojps.aip.org/
spinweb/ (accessed November 11, 1999).

Physics News Services reports important events in the physical sciences, with links to the latest information from leading physical science organizations, universities, labs, and research centers worldwide; U.S. Congress and other policy-making institutions; and the Internet at large, where SPINweb gathers high-impact information from a diverse range of sources. Each news item is presented in news-capsule style, with hyperlinks to more complete entries.

Directories of Scientists is "the ultimate online physics Rolodex." Updated regularly and cross-searchable, it provides immediate links to 150,000 scientists. Entries are drawn from the Directory of Physics & Astronomy Staff (DPAS) and the following AIP Member Society directories:

American Association of Physicists in Medicine

American Astronomical Society

American Geophysical Union

Acoustical Society of America

American Vacuum Society

Optical Society of America

Physics News Graphics is an archive of figures depicting important physics research topics and concepts.

199. **MetaPhys: The Physics Document Meta Search Engine**. http://www.physik.uni-oldenburg.de/MetaPhys/ (accessed May 6, 1999).

An interesting search overlay that serves as a unified query interface to the databases of a variety of publishers including:

Free full-text servers: Los Alamos e-print archive, APS Preprints

Distributed databases: **PhysDoc** (Department's, Institute's, or Institution's publications) (see entry 195)

Databases of commercial publishers: Springer Online, World Scientific, Kluwer Academic Publishers

200. **SLA P-A-M website**.

The website of the Physics-Astronomy-Mathematics Division of the Special Libraries Association.

http://www.sla.org/division/dpam/pamtop.html (accessed May 6, 1999).

Includes links by librarians to the best gateways and resources in the following subject areas: physics, astronomy, mathematics, and computer science.

Internet Search Engines

The following website includes descriptions and tips on web search engines: http://www.notess.com/search/ (accessed May 6, 1999).

Single-Site Search Engines

The following sites allow you to search for web pages by keyword; each search is run against a single search engine.

AltaVista.

> http://www.altavista.com (accessed May 6, 1999).
>
> A powerful search engine that has wide-ranging coverage of websites. This service has begun to post commercial entries at the top of result lists.

Excite.

> http://www.excite.com/ (accessed May 6, 1999).
>
> A powerful search engine and web gateway.

InfoSeek Ultra.

> http://ultra.infoseek.com/ (accessed May 6, 1999).
>
> Advanced keyword searching. Provides broad coverage and allows limiting by portions of HTML documents' titles, headers, and metadata.

Northern Light.

> http://www.nlsearch.com (accessed May 6, 1999).
>
> A search engine that places items in subject folders; searches free and for-fee information sources. Provides document delivery of many Special Collection items. An excellent example of integrating free and commercial databases.

WebCrawler.

> http://www.webcrawler.com/ (accessed May 6, 1999).
>
> This site provides simple keyword searching of websites; it is fast but not complete. Best used for known item searches.

Multiple Simultaneous Site Searching

The following sites allow you to search for websites by keyword; each search is run against multiple search engines. This is often less comprehensive than multiple individual search engines due to syntax concerns (truncation, adjacency, etc.).

Dogpile.

> http://www.dogpile.com/ (accessed May 6, 1999).
>
> Very broad coverage of the Internet.

HotBot.

> http://www.hotbot.com/ (accessed May 6, 1999).
>
> Provides broad coverage and allows limiting by portions of documents. See the More Search Options section for the powerful possibilities.

Inference Find.

> http://www.infind.com/ (accessed May 6, 1999).
>
> Wide-ranging coverage, and clustering of search results into subject folders.

SavvySearch.

> http://www.savvysearch.com/ (accessed May 6, 1999).
>
> All-in-one keyword search engine; this tool provides a list of many search engines and allows the researcher to select the tools to include.

Discussion Lists and Newsgroups

In addition to browsing by topic or searching by keyword, there are other ways to navigate and explore the Web. The following online tools are directories of discipline-based discussion groups. There are many physics-related entries covering topics such as teaching, research, and libraries.

201. **Directory of Scholarly E-Conferences: Discussion Lists, Newsgroups, Interest Groups**. Kovacs, Diane, ed. http://www.n2h2.com/KOVACS (accessed May 6, 1999).

An excellent listing of subject discussion arenas on the Internet. Find electronic groups by keyword or browse by subject. Locate descriptions and directions on subscribing. As of June 11, 1999, a global search of "physics" locates 44 items.

202. **TILE.NET/LISTS: The Reference to Internet Discussion & Information Lists**. http://tile.net/lists/ (accessed June 11, 1999).

A reference to Lyris, listserv, ListProc, and Majordomo e-mail discussion, announcements, and information lists on the Internet. As of June 11, 1999, a search of "physics" locates 25 lists.

Example Tools

Teaching Tools

203. **Physics Java applet demos**. University of Oregon, Department of Physics. http://jersey.uoregon.edu/vlab/ (accessed May 6, 1999).

A large collection of Java applet demos covering the areas of Atomic Emission, Cannon, High Bandwidth Cannon, Exponential Growth, FMA, Flux, Inverse Square, Kinetic Energy, Momentum, Piston, Plank Radiation Formula, Potential Energy, Spectra, Telescope, Thermodynamics, Voltage, Weather, and Work.

Equipment and Supplies

204. **Physics World Buyer's Guide**. http://physicsweb.org/net/bgprod (accessed May 6, 1999).

Part of the IoP PhysicsWeb, this resource will allow one to search the Buyer's Guide database by keyword.

205. **TIPTOP Physics Around the World: COMPANIES Section**. http://physicsweb.org/TIPTOP/paw/ (accessed May 6, 1999).

Includes the following topics: Publishers, Computer Manufacturers, Consulting, Directories, Education, Equipment, Materials, Software Companies, and Used Equipment.

Photographs

206.   **Emilio Segrè Visual Archives**. http://www.aip.org/history/esva/ (accessed May 6, 1999).

A collection of some 25,000 historical photographs, slides, lithographs, engravings, and other visual materials, the Emilio Segrè Visual Archives is part of the Niels Bohr Library of the Center for History of Physics at the American Institute of Physics. The collection focuses on American physicists and astronomers of the twentieth century, but includes many scientists in Europe and elsewhere, in other fields related to physics, and in earlier times. As of March 1999 there were 1,507 images available online. Updates are being made continuously.

207.   **The Laws List**. http://www.alcyone.com/max/physics/laws/index.html (accessed May 6, 1999).

The Laws List covers "Laws, rules, principles, effects, paradoxes, limits, constants, experiments, and thought-experiments in physics" by Erik Max Francis.

People and Organization Information

Email/Phone Directories: from other organizations on the Web. http://www.uiuc.edu/cgi-bin/ph/lookup?Query= (accessed May 6, 1999).

Four 11: phone and e-mail information. http://www.four11.com/ (accessed May 6, 1999).

InfoSpace: e-mail, government addresses, phone numbers for the United States. http://www.infospace.com (accessed May 6, 1999).

IoP PEERS e-mail directory. http://www.iop.org/cgi-bin/PEERS/main (accessed May 6, 1999).

PEERS is a free service from the Institute of Physics Publishing. It provides a moderated global e-mail directory of people working in science; a place where one can search for peers, colleagues, or any useful contacts in one's chosen scientific field.

Kapitol's International Telephone Directory. http://www.in-fobel.be/infobel/infobelworld.html (accessed May 6, 1999).

An incomplete listing, but one of the only tools of its kind available. It is worth a try.

Online Telephone Directory: the white pages for the United States. http://www.switchboard.com/ (accessed May 6, 1999).

Society Servers. http://www.lib.uwaterloo.ca/society/overview.html (accessed May 6, 1999).

A list of society-based web servers.

University Phone Books and Directories. http://acs.tamu.edu/~jimhu/edirectories.html (accessed May 6, 1999).

U.S. White Pages. http://www.555-1212.com/whte_us.htm (accessed May 6, 1999).

Includes a reverse directory (number - name/address).

Yahoo! People Search. http://www.yahoo.com/search/people/phone.html (accessed May 6, 1999).

Job Opportunities

208.   **TIPTOP (The Internet Pilot TO Physics) Jobs Forum**. http://physicsweb.org/tiptop/forum/jobs/ (accessed May 6, 1999).

209.   **IoP PhysicsJobs**. http://physicsweb.org/jobs (accessed May 6, 1999).
All the jobs, internships, and courses advertised in *Physics World* magazine are automatically placed on this server. New vacancies can also be sent directly via e-mail.

210.   **AIP CareerServices**. http://www.aip.org/careersvc/ (accessed May 6, 1999).
E-mail: csv@aip.org
Telephone: 301-209-3190
Fax: 301-209-0841

Job Opportunities is an online searchable jobs database, updated daily.

211.   **AIP Physics Careers: Information Archives**. http://www.aip.org/aip/careers/careers.html (accessed May 6, 1999).
Hundreds of physicists have posted their biographies and have answered questions about diverse areas of work outside academia.

212. **The Chronicle of Higher Education: Career Network**. http://chronicle.com/jobs/ (accessed May 6, 1999).

Each week posts hundreds of new job announcements from the latest issues of the *Chronicle*, plus other information useful to people pursuing careers in higher education. The latest week's listing requires a subscription.

213. *Science* **magazine: Job Search**. American Association for the Advancement of Science. http://recruit.sciencemag.org/jobsearch.dtl (accessed May 6, 1999).

Browse or search by discipline with a variety of parameter settings.

214. **Theoretical Particle Physics Jobs**. http://terrapin.phys. washington.edu/~calvin/ (accessed May 6, 1999).

Rumor Mill, founded in 1995, is an anonymously run site that includes the names of candidates who have been short-listed or offered positions. It also features links to other rumor sites, a satirical letter "rejecting a rejection," and other job information.

215. **Experimental Particle Physics Jobs**. http://www-hep.colorado. edu/~bbehrens/rumor.html (accessed May 6, 1999).

Rumor Mill, which originated in 1995, is run by Bruce Behrens, a research associate at the University of Colorado. His site includes job listings from *Physics Today*, information about recent appointments, and job statistics for particle physicists.

Other Example Resources

216. **Physical Reference Data**. http://physics.nist.gov/PhysRefData/ contents.html (accessed May 6, 1999).

Physical constants, units, and conversion factors; atomic spectroscopic data; molecular spectroscopic data; X-ray and gamma-ray data; etc. From NIST.

217. **Fundamental Physical Constants**. http://physics.nist.gov/ PhysRefData/codata86/article.html (accessed May 6, 1999).

The 1986 CODATA Recommended Values of the Fundamental Physical Constants. This paper gives the values of the basic constants and conversion factors of physics and chemistry resulting from the 1986 least-squares adjustment of the fundamental physical constants as recently published by the CODATA Task Group on Fundamental Constants and as recommended for international use by CODATA. From NIST.

218.   **Atomic Mass Data Center**. http://www-csnsm.in2p3.fr/amdc/ (accessed May 6, 1999).

The AMDC and its electronic bulletin aim at being a meeting place where information on masses (experimental, evaluation, or theory) can be exchanged. All those working on topics related to atomic masses can thus keep the community informed on the latest developments of their own work. There are approximately three issues of the e-bulletin per year, no more than two pages long each. To register, send an e-mail message to audi@csnsm.in2p3.fr.

219.   **Particle Data Group**. http://pdg.lbl.gov/ (accessed May 6, 1999).

The PDG is an international collaboration that reviews particle physics and related areas of astrophysics, and compiles/analyzes data on particle properties. PDG products are distributed to 30,000 physicists, teachers, and other interested people. *The Review of Particle Physics* is the most cited publication in particle physics during the last decade.

220.   **The Nuclear Data Project (NDP)**. http://www.phy.ornl. gov/ndp/ndp.html (accessed May 6, 1999).

The Nuclear Data Project (NDP) is an evaluation center that, as part of the U.S. Nuclear Data Network, is responsible for collecting and evaluating nuclear structure information. The NDP has responsibility for 56 mass chains in the mass region A>200.

221.   **Map of the Nuclides**. http://t2.lanl.gov/data/map.html (accessed May 6, 1999).

Level structures from TUNL, radioactive decay data from ENDF/B-VI, raw and interpreted neutron-data evaluations from ENDF/B-VI, Postscript plots of the cross sections, and ground-state masses and properties from Moller & Nix. From LANL.

222.   **Periodic Table**. http://www-c8.lanl.gov/infosys/html/periodic/ periodic-main.html (accessed May 6, 1999).

One of many found on the Web, this is from the Los Alamos National Labs.

Chapter 6

Other Non-Bibliographic Databases and Paper Resources

In addition to peer-reviewed journals and books and e-print/preprint materials, there are many other nonbibliographic databases that provide current information for physics researchers. In some cases the data sets (e.g., calculations, standards, conversion factors) may be in paper or online. In other cases information (e.g., equipment, supplies) may be available from commercial companies through catalogs or phone directories. There are many teaching tools and discussion groups available online. Some of these tools are discussed in the Online Tools section (see chapter 5).

A selection of popular nonbibliographic tools used by physics researchers include the following.

Patents

Physics researchers often refer to patents for technical details such as processes or materials. Some physicists use patents to stay aware of the potential commercial uses of specific materials. Finally, some physics researchers apply for patents for discoveries and inventions. While complete information about the patenting process is too complex to discuss here, there are overviews available in book, article, and online versions. For patent information within the United States, see the helpful pages created by the U.S. Patent and Trademark Office listed below (entry 224). There are numerous guides to patent procedures in other countries; one can contact a patent attorney, a librarian, or Patent Depository Library for additional details. Due to the technical legal protection requirements on applications, any serious patent application should be prepared by a trained patent attorney.

Full-Text Patents

223.   **IBM Intellectual Property Network**. http://patent.womplex. ibm.com/ (accessed May 6, 1999).

Formerly known as the IBM Patent Server, the Intellectual Property Network provides access to more than 2 million U.S. patents issued since 1971, and images of all U.S. patents issued after 1974. In addition, 1.4 million documents are available from the World Intellectual Property Office (WIPO) and ESPACE-EP-A and ESPACE-EP-B from the European Patent Office (EPO). Includes patent images.

224.   **USPTO Patent Databases**. http://patents.uspto.gov/ (accessed May 6, 1999).

Text only; AIDS patent database includes images.

The U.S. Patent and Trademark Office (USPTO) offers three separate patent databases:

1.   U.S. Patent Full Text Database, a database of the full-text content of U.S. patents starting from January 1, 1976. (Note: Drawings and images are not available online.)

2.   U.S. Patent Bibliographic Database, a database of U.S. patents front page information starting from January 1, 1976.

3.   AIDS Patent Database, a database of the full text and images of AIDS-related patents issued by the U.S., Japanese, and European patent offices.

225.   **NEXIS**.

Full-text patents (excluding images) from 1971 to the present are available from the NEXIS PATENT Library in the telnet version. This material is not included in the Academic Universe Internet version. NEXIS is a full-text news and information service that provides access to newspapers, magazines, transcripts, business and legal information, and much more. LEXIS-NEXIS, P.O. Box 933, Dayton, OH 45401-0933. PHONE: 937-865-6800 or 800-227-9597.

Patent Abstracts

226.   **U.S. Patent Citation Database** (through the Community of Science gateway). http://patents.cos.com/ (accessed May 6, 1999).

Searchable bibliographic file containing all of the approximately 1.7 million U.S. patents issued since 1975. The database includes "front page" information about each patent: number, dates, assignee, inventor, title, abstract, exemplary claims for recent years, and U.S. and international classifications. In addition, the database tracks the "lineage" of each patent—how each patent cites previous patents or is cited by subsequent ones.

227.   **European and World Patents**. http://dips.patent.gov.uk/ (accessed May 6, 1999).

The esp@cenet system is a searchable collection of patent documents published around the world during the last two years. Users may search in the following categories: United Kingdom patents, patents from other European countries, European (EP) patents, PCT (WO) patents/World International Property Organisation (WIPO), worldwide patents, and Japanese patents. Includes bibliographic details and, where available, the abstract, full text, and images of a document. See the http://www.patent.gov.uk (accessed May 6, 1999) British Patent Office esp@cenet information page for web browser requirements.

228.   **Derwent World Patents Index** (DWPI). Derwent Information.

Updated weekly. Available via the STN and Dialog online search services.

This is the premier international patent database, providing access to more than 16 million international patent documents. The records contain bibliographic data, abstracts, general indexing, and in-depth chemical and polymer indexing. Electrical and engineering drawings are present in records dating back to 1988, and chemical structure drawings are present in records dating back to 1992. Each record in the database describes a single "patent family," including the basic patent as well as any "equivalents," which are further published patents relating to that invention.

Patents from the following patent authorities are covered: Argentina, Australia, Austria, Belgium, Brazil, Canada, China, Czechoslovakia, Czech Republic, Denmark, European Patent Office, Finland, France, Germany, Germany (East), Hungary, Ireland, Israel, Italy, Japan, Luxembourg, Mexico, Netherlands, New Zealand, Norway, PCT, Philippines, Portugal, Romania, Russian Federation, Singapore, Slovakia, South Africa, South Korea, former Soviet Union, Spain, Sweden, Switzerland, Taiwan, United Kingdom, and the United States.

The database is derived from the following print publications: *Chemical Patents Index*, *Engineering Patents Index*, *DWPI Gazette Service*, *Derwent World Patents Abstracts*, and *Electrical Patents Index*.

Patent Organizations

229.   **U.S. Patent and Trademark Office**. http://www.uspto.gov/ (accessed May 6, 1999). http://www.uspto.gov/web/offices/ac/ido/opr/ptcs/ (accessed May 6, 1999). Ordering patents. http://www.uspto.gov/web/offices/pac/doc/general/ (accessed May 6, 1999). General patent information.

230. **British Patent Office**. http://www.patent.gov.uk/ (accessed May 6, 1999).

The British Patent Office is the official body for the granting of patents and for the registration of designs and trademarks in the United Kingdom (through its Designs Registry and Trade Marks Registry). It is involved with domestic and international policy on all forms of intellectual property, including copyright, design right, and other unregistered rights (through its Policy Directorates). This site leads to information about intellectual property rights and other related topics. British patents are searched in the **esp@cenet** database (see entry 232).

231. **Japanese Patent Office**. http://www.jpo-miti.go.jp/ (accessed May 6, 1999).

This site maintains many facts, policies, and procedures for Japanese copyright applications.

Japanese patents are searched in the **esp@cenet** database (see entry 232).

232. **European Patent Office**. http://www.european-patent-office.org/index.htm (accessed May 6, 1999).

The European Patent Organisation (EPO), established by the Convention on the Grant of European Patents (EPC) signed in Munich in 1973, is the outcome of the European countries' collective political determination to establish a uniform patent system in Europe. This site offers information about the organization, facts and figures, and serves as an excellent gateway to related patent information.

esp@cenet, http://www.european-patent-office.org/espacenet/info/access.htm (accessed June 17, 1999), provides free online patent searching in more than 30 million documents (EPO member states). The database includes all patents published in the preceding two years by any member state of the European Patent Organisation, as well as by the European Patent Office and the World Intellectual Property Organization (WIPO). The national offices of the member states act as service providers and offer users access via Internet home pages hosted by them. Once users are connected to the patent office of their country via the Internet, they can then access the servers of other national offices as well as the EPO.

Searches are based on the bibliographic data in patent documents, using an easy-to-operate search mask that is not, however, suitable for more complex searches. The full-text images of the documents in **esp@cenet** are available as .PDF files. Older documents are included, and equivalent patents are identified.

Obtaining Patent Documents

In addition to the full-text resources mentioned above, patent documents can be obtained from the following sources.

Public Libraries

Public libraries in each state serve as Patent Depository Libraries. The patent collections include full-text patents from 1973 to the present, as well as print and online sources for finding patents. Most collections also include sources for identifying foreign patents and trademarks. Patent documents are in microfilm or CD-ROM format. Printing facilities are often available for a fee.

233. **Lists of Patent Depository Libraries**. http://www.uspto.gov/web/offices/ac/ido/ptdl/ptdlib.htm (accessed May 6, 1999).

Commercial Document Delivery of Patents

A number of companies sell patents. Two major distributors are listed.

234. **Global Engineering Documents**—An Information Handling Services Group Company. http://global.ihs.com/ (accessed May 6, 1999).
A distributor of collections of standards, specifications, and technical publications. Global maintains an extensive collection of documents from more than 400 standards-developing organizations (SDOs) worldwide, including ASTM, ANSI, ASME, BSI, DIN, IEEE, ISO, and JIS. This enables Global to offer one-stop shopping, excellent service, and highly competitive prices.

235. **MicroPatent**. http://www.micropat.com/ (accessed May 6, 1999).
Download copies to PCs or printers from the Standard and Special Collections of 30+ million patent documents. Download in MP (.TIFF), .PDF, or Lotus Notes® format. They have two patent collections:

PatentWeb—Standard Collection

United States, 1964–current update

European applications—EP-A, 1978–current update

European patents—EP-B, 1980–current update

PCT (WIPO) applications, 1978–current update

PatentWeb Special Collection unites full patent images from the major patenting authorities of the world. Pre-1964 U.S. patents are also available.

MicroPatent USA   MicroPatent Europe
250 Dodge Avenue   235 Southwark Bridge Road
East Haven, CT 06512   London SE1 6LY, England
800-648-6787   +44 (0) 171-407-7225

Translations

Some non-English journals are translated cover-to-cover by commercial publishers. These titles and their translation titles are listed in the publication guides *INSPEC List of Journals* (see entry 35a) and *CASSI* (see entry 50).
Selected articles are translated and listed in the following.

236.   **Translations Register-Index**. [Chicago] National Translations Center.

Often non-English titles and abstracts are translated into English by the **INSPEC** database (see entry 35).
If none of these options exist there are two other approaches:

1.   Pay for a professional translation service.

Translation companies can be located using the following URL:
http://dir.yahoo.com/Business_and_Economy/Companies/Communications_ and_Media_Services/Translation_Services/ (accessed May 6, 1999).

2.   Try a free web translation service such as http://**www. babelfish.com** (accessed May 6, 1999) for a close approximation.

Reviews of the Literature

Professional reviews of subjects within the peer-reviewed literature are found in a number of publications. There are review journals, such as *Reviews of Modern Physics*, that produce lengthy review articles. Selected subject journals also produce review articles as part of their regular materials. These items can be found by limiting subject searches in A&I services (see "Abstracting and Indexing Databases" chapter) using the document type "review." In addition, many subject areas have annual and/or irregular state-of-the-art books or series. See the "Books", "Key Monographic Series" section for a selected list of annual review series titles.

A-V Materials

A detailed list of multimedia tools is outside the scope of this book, but there are a few producers of films and integrated media that should be mentioned.

237.   **PhysicsEd: Physics Education Resources**. http://www-hpcc. astro.washington.edu/scied/physics.html (accessed May 6, 1999).

The University of Washington–based NASA High Performance Computing and Communications (HPCC) Project maintains links to integrated physics data in the following areas: Courses and Topics, Curriculum Development, Resources for Demonstrations, Software, Physics Education Projects, Research in Physics Education, AAPT and Other Physics Education Organizations, Individual Physics Education Pages, Physics Textbooks, Journals and Newsletters, E-Mail Discussion Groups, Biography/History, Science Reference, Suppliers of Equipment and Software, Frequently Asked Questions, and Other Physics Links.

These physics resources are found within the larger **SciEd** site (see below).

238.   **SciEd: Science and Mathematics Education Resources**. http://www-hpcc.astro.washington.edu/scied/science.html (accessed May 6, 1999).

The broader University of Washington–based NASA High Performance Computing and Communications (HPCC) Project site (see above) providing a gateway to Science and Mathematics Education Resources.

239.   **Physics Academic Software**. http://www.aip.org/pas/ (accessed May 6, 1999).

Telephone: 800-955-8275 or 919-515-7447

Fax: 919-515-2682

E-mail: pas@aip.org

Physics Academic Software (PAS) is a software publishing project of the American Institute of Physics (AIP) in cooperation with the American Physical Society (APS) and the American Association of Physics Teachers (AAPT). PAS reviews, selects, and publishes high-quality software suitable for use in high school, undergraduate, and graduate education in physics. All software is peer-reviewed for excellence in pedagogical or research value and tested for accuracy, compatibility, and ease of use. Packages include detailed documentation for users and instructors.

Also consider browsing the many Internet gateways that cover A-V materials (see chapter 5).

Dissertations

The identification of relevant Ph.D. dissertations is not difficult. Many Ph.D. dissertations are covered in the **INSPEC** database (see entry 34) and in **Dissertation Abstracts International** (see entry 68). Obtaining these items is more difficult and can become quite a frustrating and extended experience. In some cases the granting universities' libraries will lend these items through traditional interlibrary loan (see Document Delivery, chapter 9). If ILL will not provide the desired item, the next option is the purchase of a copy by either the organization library or by an individual researcher. Bell and Howell Information and Learning (formerly known as University Microfilms International), the producers of *Dissertation Abstracts International*, will sell copies on paper or microfilm; for more information see their home page at http://www.umi.com/hp/Products/Dissertations.html (accessed May 6, 1999) or call their North American toll-free numbers 800-521-3042 or 800-521-0600, ext. 3781; Fax 800-308-1586; or international numbers 734-761-4700, ext. 3766; Fax 734-973-7007.

240. **Digital Library of ETDs.**
A new development is the mounting of online dissertations on commercial and/or free web servers. One attempt to create a free clearinghouse for dissertations is the **Digital Library of ETDs** (Electronic Theses and Dissertations) project found at http://www.theses.org (accessed May 6, 1999).

241. Marckworth, M. Lois. **Dissertations in Physics: An Indexed Bibliography of All Doctoral Theses Accepted by American Universities, 1861–1959**. Stanford, Calif.: Stanford University Press, 1961.
A bibliography of doctoral theses accepted by 97 American universities from 1861 to 1959. Entries are arranged by author and contain the following information: title, date, university, availability. The indexes are permuted subject (rotating title keywords) and numerical values. A short statistical summary table giving degrees granted by year at each university is also included.

Societies

These online gateways point to society and association information resources containing data such as biographical information, upcoming conferences, sponsored publications, job postings, and grant opportunities.

242. **Society Servers**. http://www.lib.uwaterloo.ca/society/ overview.html (accessed May 6, 1999).

The University of Waterloo maintains this excellent listing of society-based web servers.

TIPTOP (The Internet Pilot TO Physics). http://physicsweb.org/ TIPTOP/ (accessed May 6, 1999).
(See entry 192.)

PhysLINK. http://www.physlink.com/ (accessed May 6, 1999).
(See entry 193.)

SciCentral Physical and Chemical Sciences. http://www.scicentral. com/P-02phys.html (accessed May 6, 1999).
(See entry 194.)

Also consider the paper directories mentioned in the "Current Sources, Books, Directories" section.

Abbreviations

Many journal references use abbreviations. Unfortunately, these abbreviations are not standardized across fields. It may be necessary to check a number of journal listings in order to determine the full and complete title for any abbreviation.

Current Journals

The primary tool for physicists should be the **INSPEC List of Journals and Other Serial Sources** (see entry 35a).

Another wide-ranging journal list is the **Chemical Abstracts Service Source Index (CASSI)**. This multivolume tool is searched alphabetically using only the letters in bold (see entry 50).

For interdisciplinary materials, try the *Science Citation Index* journal list **Source Publications/Science Citation Index Expanded** (see entry 42).

Another tool for applied physics topics is the **Publications in Engineering: PIE: Publications Abstracted and Indexed in the . . . Engineering Information Databases** (see entry 53).

Older Material

For older materials try the following bibliographies.

243. **Union List of Serials in Libraries of the United States and Canada**. 3rd ed. Titus, Edna Brown, ed. New York: H. W. Wilson, 1965.

244. **Union List of Serials in Libraries of the United States and Canada**. 2nd ed. Gregory, Winifred, ed. New York: H. W. Wilson, 1943.

245. **Union List of Serials in Libraries of the United States and Canada**. Gregory, Winifred, ed. New York: H. W. Wilson, 1927.

The supplement may also be helpful.

246. **New Serial Titles**. Prepared under the sponsorship of the Joint Committee on the Union List of Serials. Washington, D.C.: Library of Congress. Eight monthly issues, four quarterly issues and annual cumulations that are self-cumulative through periods of 5 or 10 years. Began with January 1953.

Variant Title: Union List of Serials in Libraries of the United States and Canada. 3rd ed. Serial titles newly received. A cumulation, 1950–1970 (4 vols.) published by R. R. Bowker in 1973.

Chapter 7

Grants

Grant opportunities can be found in a variety of paper and online resources. Some grants are not widely advertised, and you must contact your local organization for historical connections to granting foundations. Below is listed a selection of tools to help researchers identify and prepare proposals for grant opportunities; contact your local librarian for additional ideas.

Paper Tools

The following books provide information on grants from government and private sources. Additional grant information can be found in the Online Sources chapter (see entries 192 and 194).

247. **Guidelines for Preparing Proposals**. Meador, Roy. Lewis Publishers, 1996. 224p. $54.95. ISBN 0873715888.
This helpful and concise book is designed to help individuals and groups organize, compile, and write effective proposals. It will be helpful for federal, state, foundation, company, and private funding source proposals. The material also covers preparation of proposals for magazine articles or books, proposals from consultants, and unsolicited proposals. The book includes several sample proposals.

248. **Grant Application Writer's Handbook**. Reif-Lehrer, Liane. Jones and Bartlett Publishers, 1995. 496p. $40.00. ISBN 0867208740.
A guide to help improve proposal-writing skills. There is a strong emphasis on NIH and NSF procedures. Sample NIH and NSF forms and associated strategies are included.

249.   **Annual Register of Grant Support: A Directory of Funding Sources**. 32nd ed. New York: R. R. Bowker, 1999. 1,400p. $199.95.

Includes grant support programs for U.S. and Canadian researchers from government agencies, public and private foundations, corporations, community trusts, unions, educational and professional associations, and special interest organizations. The interests include academic and scientific research, project development, travel and exchange programs, publication support, equipment and construction grants, in-service training, and competitive awards and prizes. Each description includes details on the type, purpose and duration, amount of funding available, eligibility requirements, geographic restrictions, areas of interest, publications available, consulting or volunteer services, representative grants in the previous year, application instructions and deadline, contact personnel and phone, fax, e-mail, and website. Divided into 11 sections; the most relevant are Physical Sciences, Life Sciences, Technology and Industry, and the Multiple Special Purpose category. The subject index is both by topic and by type of interest category (e.g., construction), with cross-references. There are also organization and program name, geographical (by state), and personnel (name) indexes.

250.   **College Blue Book: Scholarships, Fellowships, Grants and Loans**. 26th ed. New York: Macmillan, 1997.

Indentifies a wide variety of private and institutional sources committed to funding a college education. There are nine broad subject areas; the most relevant are Physical Sciences, Technology, and General (not restricted). Each entry includes organization; award title; level of education supported; number, amount, and type of award; eligibility requirements; deadline; application contacts; and additional information. Indexes are to title of award, sponsoring organization, level of education, and subject.

251.   **Directory of Research Grants**. 24th ed. Phoenix, Ariz.: Oryx Press, 1975– . Irregular. ISBN 1573560952.

Variant Title: DRG, 1981–1986.

The paper equivalent of the **GRANTS** database (see entry 264), this tool covers nearly 6,000 nonrepayable research funding programs for research projects and programs, scholarships, fellowships, conferences, and internships. Also includes a brief guide to proposal planning and writing. Each entry includes program focus and goals, restrictions, eligibility requirements, funding amounts, deadlines, and sponsor name and addresses. There is a separate listing of websites for listed organizations. Geographic restrictions are identified with a diamond beside the entry title. Indexes are to subject, sponsoring organization, grants by program type (36 categories), and geographic location.

252. **Foundation Directory**. 21st ed. Feczko, Margaret Mary and Elizabeth H. Rich, eds. New York: Foundation Center, 1999. 2,640p. $215.00; $185.00 (pa). ISBN 0879548703; ISBN 0879548746(pa).

252a. **Foundation Directory Part 2**. 1,200p. $185.00. ISBN 0879548711.

252b. **Foundation Directory Supplement**. 626p. $125.00. ISBN 087954886X.

The *Foundation Directory* features current data on more than 10,000 major foundations, those that hold assets of at least $2 million or distribute $200,000 or more in grants annually. Designed as a companion volume to the *Directory*, *The Foundation Directory Part 2* covers more than 5,700 mid-sized foundations with assets between $1 million and $2 million or annual grant programs between $50,000 and $200,000. *The Foundation Directory Supplement* is issued six months after the *Directory* and the *Directory Part 2* and provides useful updates to the information contained in those volumes.

253. **Foundation Grants to Individuals**. 11th ed. New York: Foundation Center, 1997. 630p. $65.00. ISBN 0879548835.

This title complements the **Foundation Directory** (entry 252) by covering more than 3,800 ongoing grant programs for direct grants to individuals; those grants provided through college and university programs are not included. The one exception is the group of entries listed under Awards, Prizes and Grants by Nomination. Each grant listed must be of at least $2,000 per year. Entries include addresses, contact names, financial data, application information, and program descriptions. They are arranged in three categories: educational support, general welfare, and arts and culture. The indexes are to foundation name, subject, types of support (e.g., scholarships, publishing), geographic, company employee grants, and specific educational institutions.

254. **Peterson's Grants for Graduate & Postdoctoral Study**. 5th ed. Hauppauge, N.J.: Peterson's, 1998. $32.95. ISBN 0768900190.

A combination of the previously published *Grants for Graduate Students* and *Grants for Post-Doctoral Study*, this volume is a compilation of information on fellowships, scholarships, research and travel grants, exchange programs, internships, training programs, and awards and prizes for individuals at the graduate and postgraduate level. No purely organizational grants are covered. Includes a brief introduction to the grant-seeking process, detailed profile listings, and indexes by subject and special characteristics (e.g., minorities, women, international students). Every specific award has its own entry that includes agency, title, contacts, program description, level of study, amount and number of awards, duration, renewability, eligibility requirements, and application procedures. The most relevant subject headings are Physical Sciences; Science, General/Other; Technology; Engineering (and subdisciplines); and All Fields.

255. **Grants Register 1997**. Austin, Ruth, ed. New York: St. Martin's Press, 1996. 1,300p. $110.00. ISBN 031215898X.

A survey of worldwide awards for students at or above the postgraduate level, or for those who require further professional or vocational training. There are five sections. Subject and Eligibility Guide to Awards lists awards according to the International Association of Universities subject index, which is then divided by national eligibility. Grants Register provides information on each granting organization—multiple grants are listed alphabetically within the organization. Entry information includes subject area, eligibilty, purpose, type, number, value, frequency, length of study, study establishment, country of study, application procedure/deadline, and full contact information. There are indexes to awards, discontinued awards, and awarding organizations.

Online Tools

256. **NSF Grants and Awards**. National Science Foundation. http://www.nsf.gov/home/grants.htm (accessed May 10, 1999).

This NSF site lists programs, awards, fellowships, grants information, regulations, previous awards, and the new FY1999 grant proposal guide. Example entries include:
    Division of Grants and Agreements: http://www. nsf.gov/bfa/dga/
    Grant Proposal Guide: http://www.nsf.gov/cgi-bin/getpub?nsf992
    What's New: http://www.nsf.gov/home/grants/grants_new.htm

257. **GrantsWeb** (federal and private funding sources). The Society of Research Administrators. http://web.fie.com/cws/sra/resource.htm (accessed May 26, 1999).

The SRA GrantsWeb brings viewers the merged resources of the National Research Administrators Resources Network, developed by Robert Killoren of Penn State University, and GrantsWeb, developed by Bill Kirby while he was with the National Science Foundation. This service provides an excellent gateway to grant resources and policies.

258. **FEDIX** (federal funding sources). http://web.fie.com/htdoc/fed/all/any/any/menu/any/index.htm (accessed May 26, 1999).

Federal Information Exchange (FEDIX) is a free online information retrieval service of federal opportunities for the education and research communities. This service provides instant access to federal agency information on research programs, contact information, educational programs and services, equipment grants, procurement notices, minority opportunities, and more.

FEDIX OPPORTUNITY ALERT is a free online e-mail service delivering targeted research and education funding opportunities within area(s) of interest. http://www.rams-fie.com/opportunity.htm (accessed May 26, 1999).

259.   **NIH Guide for Grants and Contracts**. http://www.nih.gov/grants/guide/index.html (accessed May 26, 1999).

A weekly electronic bulletin board containing information about National Institutes of Health (NIH) activities. Both browsing and keyword/phrase searching are available. The section covering grants is titled "Requests for Applications."

Users may also subscribe to weekly content notifications via e-mail and then access further information using the embedded URLs. Information is available at http://www.nih.gov/grants/guide/listserv.htm (accessed May 26, 1999).

Another useful NIH site is the "Funding Opportunities: Grants" page, which provides information about NIH ongoing grant programs and special initiatives. Included are application instructions and forms, guidelines for various grant programs, such as fellowships (F series), regular research projects (R series), research career development awards (K series), and identification of contacts at the NIH awarding institutes and centers. http://www.nih.gov/grants/funding/funding.htm (accessed May 26, 1999).

260.   **Federally Funded Research in the U.S.** http://fundingopps2.cos.com/ (accessed May 26, 1999).

The Community of Science, a network of scientists and research organizations, gathers award information directly from sponsoring agencies in the following disciplines: Agriculture, Food Sciences, Foods; Arts, Humanities, Cultural Activities; Behavioral or Social Sciences; Education; Energy; Engineering; Geographical Terms; Health and Safety, Medical Sciences, Biomedical; Law; Management or Commerce; and Science & Technology, Mathematics, Computer Science. Sources of these awards include federal and regional governments, foundations, professional societies, associations, and corporations. Updated daily, COS Funding Opportunities includes more than 15,000 grants from around the world. Users can also use a "Search for Related Records" option from any matching record.

This service is packaged as part of a full COS Institutional Membership (information at http://www.cos.com/members.shtml) but may also be purchased as a stand-alone information resource. As a stand-alone resource, the cost for an annual subscription ranges from $500–$1500 for most institutions and is based on the institution's annual budget. Individuals may subscribe for an annual fee of $500.

261.   **The Foundation Center**. http://fdncenter.org/ (accessed May 26, 1999).

The Foundation Center is a nonprofit service organization with a mission to foster public understanding of the foundation field by collecting, organizing, analyzing, and disseminating information on foundations, corporate giving, and related subjects. Among other publications, they produce the **Foundation Directory** (see entry 252). This site provides help information about the grant process, some limited search capability, and a listing of their other tools. The Foundation Center operates libraries at five locations. These include national collections at its headquarters in New York City and at its field office in Washington, D.C., and regional collections at its offices in Atlanta, Cleveland, and San Francisco. Center libraries provide access to a unique collection of materials on philanthropy and are open to the public free of charge. Professional reference librarians are on hand to show library users how to research funding information using Center publications and other materials and resources.

One other electronic tool they provide is *FC Search: The Foundation Center's Database* on CD-ROM , a comprehensive, fully searchable fundraising database that covers close to 50,000 U.S. foundations and corporate givers, includes more than 200,000 associated grants, lists more than 200,000 donors, and provides direct links to some 600 grant-maker websites.

U.S. Government Agencies

In addition, consider U.S. government agencies pages for funding information from individual agencies. These are easily identified using the **GrantsWeb** (see entry 257).

Browsing the Internet

Try using the **Yahoo!** subject searching method. http://www.yahoo.com/ (accessed May 6, 1999).

Type "grants" in the search box. This approach provides a wide variety of web-based grant-related information.

Listservs

262.   **GRANTS-L**. NSF Grants and Contracts e-conference. listserv@ jhuvm.hcf.jhu.edu

263.   **CFRNET-L**. Partnerships between educational institutions, corporations, and foundations. majordomo@mtu.edu

Fee-Based Databases

264.   **GRANTS**. The online version of the **Directory of Research Grants** (see entry 251). Updated monthly. Describes more than 8,700 grants offered by U.S. federal, state, and local governments, businesses, professional associations, and foundations. Available through Dialog (see entry 79) or via GrantSelect at http://www.higheredconnect.com/grantselect.

265.   **FOUNDATION GRANTS INDEX** describes more than 300,000 grants of $10,000 or more for nonprofit organizations. Available through Dialog (see entry 79).

Chapter 8

Bibliographic Management Tools

Personal Bibliographic Database Software

The ability for researchers to easily mark and download large sets of citations from bibliographic literature databases has created a need for individual researchers to organize their citation collections over time. Downloading, storing, searching, and retrieval of data sets are most logically performed using software applications known as personal bibliographic database tools. These tools were originally developed from other applications, such as database spreadsheet programs and word processors, but have recently become more sophisticated and tailored for bibliographic purposes. There are a number of competing software applications on the market, and researchers have begun to ask librarians for advice about which tool is best for their needs. Each of the products has varying strengths and weaknesses. This section attempts to explore some of the popular tools and identify the differences between them in order to provide examples and advice to researchers.

The most common personal bibliographic database software tools are **EndNote**, **Reference Manager®**, and **ProCite®**. Other tools that are add-ons or tools not specifically designed for citation storage include **BookWhere? 2000**, **InMagic**, **DB Textworks**, and **AskSAM**.

The Major Application Packages

InMagic

InMagic provides a suite of freeware programs, available only for DOS, which are no longer being developed. The older software has been replaced by DB Textworks, a much more powerful networking database tool. The DOS freeware is available at http://inmagic.com/dosfree.htm (accessed May 26, 1999). Compared to other software listed below, InMagic and DB Textworks are more complex systems than would be required for most personal applications. If you already have these programs they can be modified to provide citation database functions. The home page for this company and their products is at http://inmagic.com/index.htm (accessed May 26, 1999).

EndNote, Reference Manager, and ProCite

EndNote, *Reference Manager*, and *ProCite* are personal bibliographic software products that share a number of significant features. These common features include:

1. citation templates (work forms) for various bibliographic record formats (e.g., journal article, book, conference proceeding) with a variety of defined fields (e.g., author, article title, abstract);

2. Boolean and field searching capabilities;

3. the ability to import citations from a literature database into stored files;

4. "cite while you write" add-in features for many word processing programs; and

5. the ability to generate bibliographies in a variety of citation styles (e.g., APA, APS, IEEE) from within word processing programs.

Determining the Best Product for Your Local Needs

An important factor in determining the best tool for your needs should be the functionality of each product with your local information resources. EndNote, Reference Manager, and ProCite offer modules for importing citations from bibliographic databases directly into database files. In order to test the importing features, you would want to download records representing a variety of material types (e.g., journals, book sections, conference proceedings) from the major information databases available to your community, such as INSPEC, Science Citation Index (Web of Science), Current Contents, and your online library catalog. Many of the bibliographic database software producer web pages provide freely available filters (files that parse the item records of a particular database and interface, and transfer that data into appropriate fields in the bibliography files) for major databases and servers. While there certainly appear to be many preconfigured import filters, in a number of scenarios the appropriate filters are not provided or are not fully functional. Two of the programs evaluated, EndNote and ProCite, allow the editing of existing filters and the creation of new filters.

Local Filters

Due to the complexity of record structures and inconsistencies within some databases, it is not always possible to create filters that reliably transfer data to the correct fields within bibliographic files. Some bibliographic database producers, such as the IEE, which produces INSPEC, do not maintain a consistent record structure across their many publication types. Therefore it is not possible to design a completely accurate filter, and the user may be required to manually verify and edit certain types of citation records after the data have been imported.

Contact your local librarian for information about the compatibility of these personal bibliographic database software tools with your local systems and the creation of specific database filters.

EndNote 3.0

EndNote is one of the most popular tools used in academia to search online bibliographic databases, organize references, and create bibliographies. The software includes all of the features available in the combined Reference Manager and ProCite packages described below. A large number of preconfigured filters are supplied with the software, and users can modify existing filters or create new ones. EndNote has a "smart parsing" feature that makes creating new filters relatively easy by automatically interpreting data field delimiters. For example, the program uses algorithms to determine separations between author names, such as between multiple authors, between last and first names, and between first and middle names.

EndNote 3.0 also supports direct connections to Z39.50-compatible databases. This feature allows users to connect to and search remote databases through the EndNote software interface and removes the need for a separate search interface program. Connection files for a variety of Z39.50 library catalogs and online services are included with EndNote, and the software allows files to be modified and new files to be created. However, creating a Z39.50 connection file is significantly more complex than creating an import filter and requires knowledge of the Z39.50 client database configuration. Moreover, the EndNote search interface offers limited functionality when compared to that available from most database interfaces (e.g., Ovid, SilverPlatter, OPACs). Due to the limitations of the present Z39.50 connection, this feature can only be recommended for known item data retrieval. It is recommended that users still do their interactive and sophisticated searching using the endemic search interfaces.

EndNote Plus 3.0.0.0 (IBM, Mac) plus EndLink $299 + $99

EndNote is available for Windows NT/95/3.1 and Macintosh. Additional information, including directions for downloading a 30-day trial demonstration copy, is available from http://www.endnote.com/ (accessed May 13, 1999).

Note: As of April 15, 1999, the Institute for Scientific Information (ISI) announced the acquisition of Niles Software and the formation of a new company, ResearchSoft. Niles Software, creators of the EndNote bibliographic management program, will combine forces with another ISI subsidiary, Research Information Systems (RIS) of Carlsbad, California, to form the new organization.

ResearchSoft
800 Jones Street,
Berkeley, CA 94710
Telephone: 510-559-8592
Fax: 510-559-8683
E-mail: kimberlym@researchsoft.com

or

ResearchSoft—Carlsbad
2355 Camino Vida Roble,
Carlsbad, CA 92009
Telephone: 800-722-1227 or 760-438-5526
Fax: 760-438-5573
E-mail: sales@risinc.com

Reference Manager 8.5

The Reference Manager product is very similar to EndNote. However, there are a few significant differences that are important when selecting the most appropriate product.

First, when a preconfigured import filter is not available, the user is not able to create one. Import filters, called "capture files" in Reference Manager, cannot be modified; nor does the producer create new capture files on demand. It is thus less versatile than EndNote as a general resource. Be certain that you only use databases and services that are supported by Reference Manager capture files.

Second, a Z39.50 connection feature is not included with Reference Manager. A program called BookWhere? 2000 can be purchased separately to search remote databases and export them to Reference Manager or ProCite. Using the program's "fast export" feature, retrieved records can be moved to Reference Manager or ProCite in one step. BookWhere? 2000 is a more full-featured product than EndNote's Z39.50 connection module. The program provides connections to a wide array of library catalogs and allows multiple catalog searching. BookWhere? offers a number of record display options, including the option of displaying retrieved records by subject heading. The user can modify and create Z39.50 connection files, although this requires knowledge of the Z39.50 client database configuration. There are Z39.50 searching limitations using this generic interface as compared to endemic search service interfaces. The Z39.50 option may be important if you do a great deal of sophisticated library catalog searching and there is no sophisticated library catalog interface or if you regularly search across multiple catalogs.

Third, the program's most significant advantage is that it works extremely well with ISI's Web of Science (Science Citation Index). The producer of Reference Manager and ProCite is affiliated with ISI. A software plug-in available from Reference Manager's producer, RIS, allows users to export ISI Citation Index records directly from Web of Science to the bibliography program in one step. This advantage will probably be carried over into EndNote in the near future now that ISI has purchased the EndNote product.

Reference Manager 7.0 (IBM, Mac) plus Capture $349 + $149

Reference Manager 8.5 and BookWhere? 2000 are available for Windows 98/95/NT4. Additional information, including directions for downloading a demonstration copy, is available from Reference Information Systems, http://www.risinc.com/ (accessed May 6, 1999).

ProCite 4.03

ProCite is a far more complex database tool and has traditionally been marketed to information specialists and large database users for departmental purposes. It can be used for simple citation database functions. ProCite offers a greater number of search options, work forms, and record fields than EndNote and Reference Manager. Because of these additional features the database is more difficult to learn, and users should expect a steep learning curve.

In many user implementations, databases are often populated by manual entry of records. Therefore, the citation database module and the data capture modules are two separate programs. In order to import data from literature databases, the user needs to purchase the Biblio-Link II add-on program. Biblio-Link comes with a number of database filters, and, like EndNote, users can modify and create new filters.

Creating a filter in Biblio-Link is a much more complex process than in EndNote. There is no "smart parsing" based on position and punctuation. Biblio-Link requires the user to specifically map data elements by format and to consider the punctuation or character used to separate multiple fields. While Biblio-Link permits the user a great degree of control, even an experienced user will need to rely heavily on the user guide and spend a great deal of time in the implementation of an initial setup for most databases.

The ISI Web of Science plug-in described above in the section on Reference Manager also works with ProCite. This feature allows retrieved records to be downloaded directly into the ProCite record format. Similarly, the BookWhere? 2000 software described in the previous section works with ProCite, and retrieved records can be transferred with a "fast export" option.

The ProCite database application may be best for those with a variety of complex database requirements. It may be unnecessarily complex for those requiring only basic database search, storage, and retrieval capabilities.

ProCite 3.0.5 (IBM, Mac) plus Biblio-Links $345 + $195

ProCite 4.03 is available for Windows 98/95/NT4 and Macintosh. Additional information, including directions for downloading a demonstration copy, is available from Reference Information Systems.

RIS assistance in determining which of their products, Reference Manager or ProCite, is best for your needs may be found at http://www.risinc.com/select.html (accessed May 6, 1999).

Details about ProCite, Reference Manager, and BookWhere? 2000 are available from http://www.isinet.com/products/products.html (accessed May 6, 1999).

Reviews of These Products

Additional reviews of personal bibliographic databases and related software is available from Electronic Research @Chorus (sponsored by the College Writing Programs, University of California, Berkeley). http://www-writing.berkeley.edu/chorus/eresearch/ (accessed May 6, 1999).

Chapter 9

Document Delivery

This section discusses options for obtaining materials not available from your local library. There are a number of approaches that are possible, and the selection of a specific path is often dependent on how quickly you need the information and how much you are willing to pay. Interlibrary loan (ILL) is the cooperative loan and photocopy service provided by most public and academic libraries. Both public and commercial libraries use commercial document delivery services.

Traditional Interlibrary Loan

Traditional ILL is based upon reciprocal copying or loaning of materials among educational institutions for articles and books. Technology has made this process much faster and has allowed for better quality transmissions. While it appears that this ILL operation is free, there are actually large hidden costs in terms of staff, equipment, and researcher time. Recent improvements are attempting to reduce these costs by removing the staff intermediary delays and costs through direct end-user requests.

Given the high cost-per-use figures for many expensive and/or infrequently used journals, rapid and reliable commercial document delivery may be a better alternative for a portion of the present journal subscription base in many libraries. Some journals cannot be replaced with on-demand article delivery for a variety of reasons, such as a need for color images, user requirements for browsing, currentness requirements, and serendipity.

Economic Aspects of Copyright

The commercial aspects of information are responsible for many of the present frustrations and limitations to easy document delivery. While the commercial publishers do provide added value (e.g., editorial support, typesetting, a distribution mechanism), they can also restrict access to both academic readers and the originators of the material. When authors give away their rights and are forced to repurchase this material, it is often under quite restrictive conditions. Given the new technologies, a reevaluation of the interests and impacts of commercial publishers in the scientific process is likely.

As long as the distribution of scientific information is based on commercial conditions, interlibrary loan will require a commitment to shared repositories and a critical number of subscriptions. As libraries continue to reduce titles in response to fiscal pressures, there are a number of journal subscriptions that are becoming prohibitively expensive for the few remaining libraries that maintain these subscriptions. After a critical subscription base has been eroded, reciprocal ILL will fail to satisfy user demands.

Commercial companies now offer document delivery in a variety of methods ranging from paper delivery to two-hour fax. In addition, the per-article copyright charge for individual documents is rising rapidly. This cost increase will only become more evident as multimedia materials become a standard part of requested items, and the charging algorithms become much more complex in the near future.

Even if the requests are within the educational guidelines, all library ILL activities require Copyright Clearance Center (CCC) coordination to ensure that payments are made for organizational use beyond Fair Use regulations (five articles per journal title per year).

Copyright protection does not appear to be particularly advantageous for nontrade works such as science journal literature. The important publishing elements are validation/filtering, quality control, and wide and rapid distribution. The last of these concerns is often complicated and counteracted by commercial distribution.

Historical precedent has allowed approximately half of the most important physics journals to be commercially controlled. This has resulted in more expensive and complex access issues. The current system hinders rather than serves the best interests of the majority of authors who work under noncommercial situations. This is why the preprint systems have become so popular among physicists with high levels of computer skills and technology.

Alternative noncommercial scientific peer review distribution mechanisms are possible; however, the economic aspects will need to be dissociated from the present publish-or-perish promotion and tenure process. One example scenario, an E-Print Moderator Model, by David Stern, with text reprinted from the *Newsletter on Serials Pricing Issues*, no. 214, February 8, 1999, is presented at the end of this section.

Commercial Document Delivery Sources

266.   **CARL UnCover**. http://uncweb.carl.org/sos/sosinfo.html (accessed May 6, 1999).

> E-mail: uncovweb@carl.org
> Telephone: 800-787-7979
> Fax: 303-758-5946 (all U.S. numbers)

UnCover SOS, or Single Order Source, is a level of document delivery created for users that simply want to forward orders to UnCover. This service meets the needs of users who know what they want to order. Orders can be sent to UnCover by e-mail, fax, or phone. Receipt and status of orders will be confirmed within two hours. Turnaround times are generally within 24 hours. Currently, UnCover fills orders for journal articles from titles that are indexed in the UnCover database. Through contributing libraries and scanned image database, they provide access to 18,000+ titles. High-quality fax articles are delivered to the user. There are no fax charges for articles delivered within the United States and Canada.

267.   **CISTI**. http://www.nrc.ca/cisti/docdel/docdel.html (accessed May 6, 1999).

> E-mail: cisti.info@nrc.ca
> Telephone: 800-668-1222
> Fax: 613-993-7619

CISTI, the Canada Institute for Scientific and Technical Information, is one of the world's major sources for information in all areas of science, technology, engineering, and medicine. They provide your choice of Ariel, fax, or overnight courier document delivery from their collection (DIRECT Supply), plus priority service from the British Library Document Supply Centre (BLDSC) in England and the Science and Technology Information Center (STIC) in Taipei, China (LINK Supply), and from around the world (GLOBAL Supply). Turnaround time: DIRECT—Most documents are supplied within 48 hours; LINK—within five days; GLOBAL—within four weeks.

268.   **ISI Document Solution (IDS)**. http://www.isinet.com/products/ids/ids.html (accessed May 6, 1999).

E-mail: ids@isinet.com
Telephone: 215-386-4399
Fax: 215-222-0840 or 215-386-4343

Formerly known as The Genuine Article® (TGA), the new name is ISI Document Solution. Covers the ISI on-site journal collection as they have with TGA, plus document delivery access to any publicly available document at no additional service charge. Standard 24-hour internal turn-around time for most material, and an optional, superfast, 30-minute fax delivery. IDS offers complete "one-stop shopping" document delivery service for journal articles, conference proceedings, book chapters, technical reports, and more.

269.   **Articles in Physics**®. http://ojps.aip.org/jhtml/artinphys/aboutac. html (accessed May 6, 1999).

> E-mail: ojshelp@aip.org
> Telephone (U.S. and Canada): 800-874-6383
> Telephone (all other locations): 516-576-2262
> Fax: 516-349-9704

The AIP online document delivery service allows users to purchase and receive online any article published in their Online Journal Publishing Service—at up to 50% discount when compared to the cost of other document delivery sources. Immediate transmission of full-text .PDF files.

270.   The American Chemical Society's **CAS Document Detective Service**. Telephone: 800-631-1884 (North America), 614-447-3870 (elsewhere); Fax: 614-447-3648; Telex: 6842086 via WUI; http://www. cas.org/Support/dds.html (accessed May 6, 1999) is an example of the many other related societies that offer commercial document delivery.

E-PRINT MODERATOR MODEL, by David Stern, with text reprinted from the *Newsletter on Serials Pricing Issues*, No. 214, February 8, 1999 (ISSN: 1046-3410).
The following URL contains an abstract of this idea plus a graphic:

http://www.library.yale.edu/scilib/modmodexplain.html (accessed May 6, 1999).

The intent of this model is to allow the widest range of scientific manuscripts to be archived, searched, and distributed electronically at the lowest possible cost. The primary goal is to significantly reduce the amount of journal material distributed in a commercial manner. This would be accomplished through very minimal filtering and subsequent placement of e-prints on a noncommercial archival server by a subject-specific Moderator appointed by a society (or consortium of societies). It would function in the manner of an online ERIC Clearinghouse.
A society-appointed Editorial Board (with double-blind peer review approved by the nonprofit Peer Review Inc. organization) would then identify the most important materials from among these archived items, and the stamp of approval for these items would be included in a secondary Virtual Collection. This Virtual Collection, or other spinoffs such as enhanced abstracts, SDI services, and e-mail threads, would be easier to use

for browsing and/or having abstracts sent electronically to individual researchers. There are no direct submissions to the Editorial Board; manuscripts would be directed to the Editorial Board in one of three ways:

1. nominated by the e-print Moderator upon receipt for the archival server;

2. notification sent to the Editorial Board when a threshold number of hits is generated by any one manuscript on the archive server; and

3. nominated by readers of material from the archive; this process requires a letter of support outlining the importance of the work to the Editorial Board.

The Virtual Collection could be produced as a variety of products:

enhanced abstracts

e-mail threads (with comments)

virtual reviews of subdisciplines

SDIs (selective dissemination of information) current awareness tools

This process:

- reduces the load on Editorial Boards, which results in a faster review process;

- differentiates those items worthy of higher recognition from those worthy of archiving, making it easier for a reader to filter material, based upon a society and discipline authority (rather than commercial reasoning);

- provides for search and SDI across all materials from the archive if the user desires speed or comprehensiveness; and

- provides for search/browse/SDI from the Virtual Collection for filtered information, reducing this more expensive identification and distribution option for only those items recognized as of the highest quality.

The funding for this archiving server and Virtual Collection infrastructure would come from a blend of direct (professional societies and author page charges) and indirect (government, taxes) sources. This would reduce the cost and guarantee the judicious selection of materials for the Virtual Collection.

The support of the Virtual Collection infrastructure could be provided by a blend of commercial and noncommercial sources, depending upon the resale value of the eventual end products. Some disciplines may be attractive for commercial support of editorial boards, while other areas may only have noncommercial support. The sophistication of the end products may be related to the commercial viability of the content.

Promotion and tenure decisions would be based on both Virtual Collection and archival materials. This step would significantly reduce the need to subsidize the most expensive distribution process as the only means of meeting the publish-or-perish tenure process requirements.

The E-Print Moderator Model graphic is shown on the facing page.

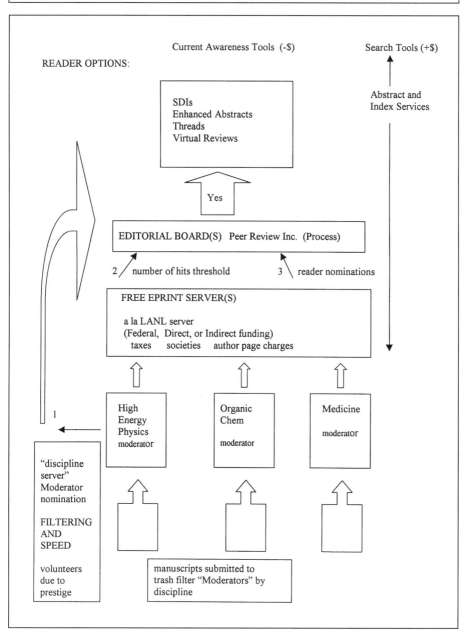

Fig. 10. Alternative Post-Release Peer Review Filtering Model

Chapter 10

Copyright and Reserves

The area of intellectual property is very complex, and this book will not attempt to interpret the laws and practices. This section highlights a few significant online tools that address these dynamic regulations in the United States. International copyright laws are far too complex for a quick overview.

The Digital Millennium Copyright Act (DMCA) became law in October 1998. This legislation addresses many significant copyright issues for researchers and research organizations. Some of the areas of concern are fair use definitions, online service provider liability, preservation allowances, copyright management information, and distance education.

The DMCA represents the most comprehensive reform of U.S. copyright law in a generation. This legislation seeks to update U.S. copyright law in addressing the new digital storage and transmission possibilities. The DMCA legislation was rushed into existence after heated debate between the publishing industry and the library and education community. The result is a compromise agreement that seeks to ensure that fair use is maintained in the digital realm while revising the U.S. copyright law in preparation for ratification of the World Intellectual Property Organization (WIPO) treaties. These WIPO treaties are far more favorable to commercial interests than are current U.S. policies.

The EDUCAUSE consortium, created to help shape and enable transformational change in higher education through the introduction, use, and management of information resources and technologies in teaching, learning, scholarship, research, and institutional management, maintains a website to help researchers understand the concerns and status of the legislation:

http://www.educause.edu/issues/dmca.html (accessed May 26, 1999).

The Association of Research Libraries also maintains a website for interested educators:

http://www.arl.org/dmca/resources.html (accessed May 26, 1999).

Answers to the Most Common Questions

Here are a few general statements that can be made:

1. It is allowable to copy a single article for personal research and/or educational purposes within a nonprofit organization.

2. It is not allowable to "systematically" copy materials in order to create a personal anthology of articles if this activity would relieve the reader from purchasing a subscription to one or more journals.

3. In almost all cases it is not allowable to reuse previously copied library Reserve Collection materials for another semester without obtaining permission from the publisher.

4. Any "Fair Use" must satisfy *all four* (not just one of the four) conditions as written in the U.S. Code, Title 17, Section 107:

    1. Spontaneous nature of the use
    2. Percentage/portion of the work in relation to the work as a whole
    3. Impact on the market for the commercial product
    4. Nonprofit nature of the research

United States Copyright Law

A quick review of copyright law for scholars is available from:

University of Texas—Crash Course on Copyright.
http://www.utsystem.edu/OGC/IntellectualProperty/cprtindx.htm (accessed May 6, 1999).

The actual legal documents pertaining to copyright, from the Legal Information Institute, are located at:

U.S. Code Title 17.
http://www4.law.cornell.edu/uscode/17/ (accessed May 6, 1999).

"Fair Use" Section of Title 17.
http://www4.law.cornell.edu/uscode/17/107.html (accessed May 6, 1999).

Special Library and Archive Rules.
http://www4.law.cornell.edu/uscode/17/108.html (accessed May 6, 1999).

Documentation of concerns are found at:

Stanford University Libraries Copyright & Fair Use Website.
http://fairuse.stanford.edu/ (accessed May 6, 1999).

University of Texas—Offsite Copyright Resources.
http://www.utsystem.edu/OGC/IntellectualProperty/offsite.htm (accessed May 6, 1999).

5.1 Legal Issues: Intellectual Property Rights.
http://info.lib.uh.edu/sepb/lcopyr.htm (accessed May 6, 1999).

University of Texas—Copyright Law and Electronic Reserves Website.
http://www.utsystem.edu/ogc/intellectualproperty/ereserve.htm (accessed May 6, 1999).

Northwestern University—Electronic Reserves System Guidelines.
http://www.library.nwu.edu/ERS/about/copyright.html (accessed May 6, 1999).

Copyright Clearance Center.
http://www.copyright.com/ (accessed May 6, 1999).

The CCC coordinates the online registration, the title database, and online interaction for requesting academic permissions and online course content service.

Negativland.
http://www.negativland.com/intprop.html (accessed May 6, 1999).

Negativland is an experimental music and art collective that has been recording and self-releasing music/audio/collage works since 1979. This site expresses their strong opinions and has some interesting links.

Chapter 11

Future Developments, Directions, and Trends

This chapter describes some new approaches to information discovery that are made possible due to the electronic nature of information databases. Topics include enhancements to the traditional A&I and full-text databases, new initiatives for full-text distribution, next-generation improvements in searching data files, the development of knowledge databases, and some logistical concerns that must be addressed.

Traditional Full-Text Data Files

Even among the traditional bibliographic and full-text databases of peer-reviewed materials, there will be significant advances in information navigation. Short-term improvements will be found in the easier searching of indexes and abstracts within and across discipline databases. Better interfaces with sophisticated analysis techniques will assist researchers in identifying relevant items. Medium-term improvements will include seamless links between indexes and full-text documents, and across full-text documents (from references to other articles). Long-term enhancements will include the ability to store selected documents and comments in personal electronic file cabinets. These virtual file cabinets can be created for individuals, research groups, classrooms, and administrative purposes. Personal preferences such as file types (e.g., .PDF, ASCII, Postscript) and default display options will be stored and automatically implemented.

Users will still have the option of searching in-depth, subject-specific indexes and online databases, interdisciplinary databases that sacrifice depth for scope of coverage, popular/core-level indexes and full-text materials, and/or non-peer-reviewed materials (e.g., Internet resources). Perhaps these searches will be run on a single gateway interface with simple limit options. Database services may be comprehensive in coverage or limited by a predetermined set of resources. Aggregators are already creating subsets of materials that are sold to populations as core collections. Some publishers market their own full-text databases as the only system necessary in order to find essential information. Regardless of the apparently impressive nature of the packages being marketed, the researcher must be aware of the limitations of these packages.

Examples of experimental information services offering some of these advanced options are the following.

SPARC, the Scholarly Publishing & Academic Resources Coalition. http://www.arl.org/sparc/ (accessed May 6, 1999).

This alliance of libraries intends to expand competition in scholarly communication through the collaboration between Association of Research Libraries (ARL) organizations and selected publishers and societies. SPARC is attempting to create new, innovative, and less-expensive alternatives to the current commercial journal publisher products. There are a few new journals appearing, and the SPARC initiative has just announced the availability of grant funds to serve as seed money for additional innovative approaches to information distribution.

HighWire Press. http://highwire.stanford.edu/ (accessed May 6, 1999).

HighWire Press, developed by the Stanford University Library, is attempting to become an innovative journal platform for society and nonprofit publishers. This operation will provide full-service online support for peer-reviewed journal material. The advantages of this arrangement are that the players in this project have the best understanding of the most appropriate technologies, the desire to implement these cost-saving and empowerment tools, and the best interests of the researchers as their prime motives.

JSTOR. http://www.jstor.org/ (accessed May 6, 1999).

JSTOR's mission is to help the scholarly community take advantage of advances in information technologies. Since January 1, 1997, some 428 U.S. institutions and 53 international institutions have become JSTOR participants. As of June 11, 1999, there are 67 participating publishers, and 92 journals are currently online. The project is attempting to create a long-term archival clearinghouse for selected journal materials. The first phase involved a package of selected journals from a variety of disciplines. Phase II will expand the disciplines.

ICAAP, the International Consortium for Alternative Academic Publication. http://www.icaap.org/ (accessed May 6, 1999).

In this somewhat radical approach, a Canadian initiative is dedicated to the development of an international alternative scholarly communication system outside of the commercial mainstream. ICAAP journals are freeware or low-cost shareware publications. In addition, the group is involved in research and development designed to demonstrate the full potential of information technology.

PDF Images and Limitations

The decision by these services to provide full text as PDF images is a short-term necessity, as most scholars cannot deal with the enhanced SGML that is produced by the publishers. If these services decide to migrate toward XML storage and retrieval in the future, they can offer many additional options for their users.

E-Prints

We will certainly continue to see an explosion of e-print servers. Some will remain primarily novelty publication tools, but others may eventually become accepted core scientific distribution tools when they enhance their timeliness advantage with the inclusion of some form of validation process. As no one server can be the clearinghouse for all material in a discipline, the seamless searching across these decentralized servers will be a great help in identifying prepublication literature. User concerns regarding standard and seamless display formats will need to be addressed. The e-print servers will probably become more closely linked with other nonbibliographic online tools for teaching, laboratory support, and general communication among physicists.

Next-Generation Developments

This section presents several important digital library theories, technologies research, and practical implication considerations. Users will experience many radical changes in the way both known and novel pieces of information are identified and obtained once these digital libraries begin to incorporate the enhancements that electronic knowledge databases offer.

One-Stop Shopping

The most beneficial option for most researchers would be the introduction of federated (broadcast) searching. The ability to simultaneously search all databases (both bibliographic and nonbibliographic) would mean that users would no longer need to spend time learning to navigate the plethora of Internet sources. A more sophisticated solution would include the additional coverage of paper and CD-ROM sources.

In order for this federated searching to occur, there will need to be a coordination and normalization of search indexes across the various databases. The historical development of widely divergent proprietary hardware and software tools has created what is called a loosely coupled system. There are few similarities and standards that can be used to help users connect and operate these tools. The alternative system design is a tightly coupled system in which the infrastructure is developed according to standards that can be easily transferred from host to host. It is not likely that the many present systems will be converted to any one standard at this late date. Therefore the seamless searching of these distributed tools will require sophisticated indexing and smart agent search technologies.

Smart Agents

Smart agents, automated intelligence programs designed for specific information-gathering tasks, will automate cross-database searching by coordinating complex operations between hosts with differing protocols. A number of smart agent technologies are being tested in digital library environments. Below are listed two websites that will help in identifying current literature and research initiatives.

LibraryAgents: Library Applications of Intelligent Software Agents. http://www.public.iastate.edu/~CYBERSTACKS/Agents.htm (accessed May 6, 1999).

Within CyberStacks, Gerry McKiernan consolidates many interesting library projects into online reviews. One of these topics covers many intelligent agent technologies. The entire Net Projects site (http://www.public. iastate.edu/~CYBERSTACKS/Projects.htm [accessed May 6, 1999]) is worth a visit.

Intelligent Software Agents. http://www.sics.se/isl/abc/survey.html (accessed May 6, 1999).

This site includes links to information about many types of agent technologies. Also included are links to readings, standards, conferences, and other web resources.

Multidisciplinary Searching

Whether searching is done within one large database or across feder-ated databases, a major issue that needs to be addressed is the development of good relational linkages between and across discipline-specific termi-nologies. Keyword searching will not be adequate for good recall, as terms and acronyms are not consistent across the sciences. The ability to map similar concepts will be an important feature. This can be done using a number of techniques such as word frequency analysis, thesauri mapping, and citation analysis. Citation analysis is discussed as an evaluation tool in chapter 3. Below are a few example approaches to providing cross-discipline searching using controlled vocabulary and subject hierarchies.

KnowledgeCite. http://www.silverplatter.com/KC/kcoverview.html (ac-cessed May 6, 1999).

This project, developed in cooperation with the SilverPlatter search service, provides a testbed for cross-database multithesaurus searching. Users enter familiar terminology, and the system presents possible subject heading matches and cross-references from a variety of database thesauri. Searching can be run across multiple databases using these headings. While this approach assists researchers in determining alternative terminologies, it involves a great deal of work on the part of the researcher to review all the possible headings and cross-references. An eventual best-guess automatic mapping option among these headings (perhaps based on word frequency analysis from a sample of selected documents) would greatly improve the utility of this tool.

Community Architectures for Network Information Systems (CANIS). http://www.canis.uiuc.edu/about.html (accessed May 6, 1999).

The University of Illinois Digital Library Initiative has a different ap-proach to cross-database searching that involves the identification of clus-ters of related documents and subject headings from within a large universe of materials. The Interspace Research Project includes a number of con-cepts, one of which is Concept Spaces. These clusters of "concept spaces" were identified by using a Cray supercomputer to analyze the INSPEC and Compendex thesauri and abstracts. The result is a mapping of the subjects covered in these two major abstracting and indexing databases. This dis-play of data elements will allow researchers to navigate the overlapping sub-ject areas without requiring the input of multiple thesauri terminology. This test of indexing capabilities is part of the larger investigation of the adequacy of enhanced index searching when compared to full-text searching of a large engineering full-text testbed. A full-scale test of this technology is proposed for the medical field (http://www.canis.uiuc.edu/medspace/).

Discovery Technologies

Alternative methods of discovering information are becoming available to researchers. Simple and complex Boolean keyword searching and thesaurus browsing is being supplemented with a variety of new electronic possibilities. The implementation of XML will allow these traditional information servers to improve access to the enormous amount of data within their domains, providing the ability to mine additional information using the metadata elements within XML (e.g., document sections, image descriptions, methodologies). The ability to display content organization using XML document tree structures will provide visual assistance in navigating within documents. The transfer of XML documents will also mean that users will have the ability to manipulate the content and the presentation; they will not be restricted to simple reading, as they are now by the .PDF format.

Another significant enhancement in the discovery process will be the introduction of new visualization techniques. Visualizations of content and relational analysis techniques are now possible across the new electronic domains. This will radically change the way researchers view and work with information databases.

Below are listed a few examples of innovative discovery technologies that will certainly change the behaviors and research methodologies of physicists in the near future.

Iodyne. http://www.canis.uiuc.edu/medspace/iodyne/ (accessed May 6, 1999).

This search interface incorporates visual metaphors and drag-and-drop techniques to provide a simple and powerful stateless icon manipulation interface. Using images, researchers can drop object icons into types of searches, historical search strategies, subject thesauri, and other customized visual tools. The stateless mode means that searches can be run simultaneously or in parallel, and combinations of objects can be created in a nonlinear fashion. This is a novel interface providing easy yet sophisticated searching within and across complex databases.

lifestreams. http://www.cs.yale.edu/~freeman/lifestreams.html (accessed May 6, 1999).

The concept behind this innovative search system is that researchers make connections between the data they have studied and the other life experiences they have at the same point in time. This system allows for time- and event-dependent indexing within a relational database. A researcher can enter "first child" and "Philadelphia" and "germanium" and the system will create a folder of documents that have some relationship with these items. This interface brings search technology into a closer relationship with human behaviors.

Visualizations

A fascinating new software development is the use of enhanced visualization possibilities for innovative analysis and display of document sets. The ability to analyze a set of documents and represent them visually can transmit new visions of data content and concept relationships. Below are a few examples by the Pacific Northwest National Laboratory (http://multimedia.pnl.gov:2080/infoviz/index.html) of visual representations that provide new techniques to describe and explore information.

Visual Text Analysis: SPIRE. http://multimedia.pnl.gov:2080/showcase/pachelbel.cgi?it_content/spire.node (accessed May 6, 1999).

This imaging system represents the distribution and density of concepts within a data set. The color, height, and distances show relationships between concepts. Visualizations of this type can identify interesting areas for exploration and concentration.

Pacific Northwest National Laboratory Visualization Technologies Page. http://multimedia.pnl.gov:2080/infoviz/technologies.html#galaxies (accessed May 6, 1999).

One example within this set of tools is Rainbows, which are multiple-line representations of embedded database concepts. Where these lines cross, the concepts intersect. This visual display allows a researcher to discover and study relationships between concepts. It may show unusual linkages that identify areas for further research. The other technologies display alternative visual representations that may lead to other cognitive pathways.

Knowledge Databases

Knowledge databases are repositories that contain all related information regarding a particular topic. These data elements may be bibliographic (citations) and nonbibliographic (full-text documents, metadata descriptions, images, data banks, software, membership information, etc.). The majority of the information in these knowledge databases is generally created by the researchers. Descriptive and organizational elements are contributed by information specialists. Technical support is provided by information technology personnel. The collaboration of these players produces a powerful, integrated, and scalable information system. Below are a few examples of these new seamless information systems.

Worm Community System. http://www.canis.uiuc.edu/wormsystem/ (accessed May 6, 1999).

This system, developed by a worldwide collaboration of biology researchers, was intended as a prototype system containing all the knowledge of the community of molecular biologists who study the nematode worm C. elegans. Included within this system are genetic information, full-text documents, images, e-mail threads, and biographical information. It has been used as the basis for many other projects by the CANIS group (discussed above).

Urania. http://www.aas.org/Urania/ (accessed May 6, 1999).

This overlay to numerous databases includes most of the information that a working astronomer would need for advanced research. Among the many tools are search engines to bibliographic data, full-text document images for the great majority of peer-reviewed journal materials, and advanced search engines for metadata (e.g., the SIMBAD database of online star catalogs that allows for alternative name and property range searching). There are seamless links between these elements, providing a researcher with an integrated information platform. This knowledge database was developed through collaborations among astronomers, national governments, and librarians. It provides a magnificent example of practical tool development, and it stands as a model for other disciplines. Of course there are still challenges for this virtual service, such as the incorporation of international document identification standards, the linkage of these materials with other information services, and the development of long-term archiving and financial strategies.

Logistical Concerns

Regardless of the final end-user tools and infrastructures involved in future systems, there are many facilitator operations that must be designed before a truly integrated information network can be implemented. Below are listed a few considerations that must be addressed in order to maximize the everyday use of these complicated options.

Validators

Seamless access to federated tools and services will require the coordination of permissions across a variety of hosts. Permission agents will become major players within the information industry. These agents will provide user validation through either subscription approvals or transactional item tracking and delivery. Agent services will store organizational and individual preferences for directing and formatting information requests across linked services using industry-wide standard protocols.

Current standards under development, such as the document object identifier (DOI), only address current scenarios and options; however, there will be many additional options that need to be explored, and many other transactional considerations that need to be transmitted (e.g., requests for subunits of documents, preferences, equipment capabilities, off-site access) in the new information paradigm.

The consolidation of all subscription information across consortia, publishers, vendors, and aggregators is only one example of the type of clearinghouse information that will be required to support a seamless delivery system.

While information organizations have been requesting IP address validation instead of passwords to make distributed access scalable, we are beginning to notice that there are times when passwords, or more likely passwords embedded into proxy servers, will be necessary to provide adequate access to off-site researchers. We will need a combination of these validation mechanisms to accommodate the complex and dynamic researcher behaviors.

Distance Education

When considering the extension of programmatic information services to off-site researchers, there is a need for improved online and real-time support. This assistance will be needed for both the technical requirements of this broad range of proprietary software packages and the instructional requirements for these ever more complex navigation and manipulation software applications.

Local Servers and Local Information

The same coordination services that are necessary in the previous validation section are also required on the local level in many organizations. There are many instances where the distribution of local electronic information will require access to personal preferences, the use of proxies for off-site user validation, and the tracking of transactional interactions for charge-back and evaluation purposes. A scaled-down version of the above agent software might be a logical tool for local validation and permissions.

An example scenario of this local need would be the tracking of high-use materials such as those used in a reserve collection. This technology could also provide valuable information about usage for both financial and pedagogical analyses.

Multiuser Requirements

Current information network technologies and protocols allow for the delivery of items across the Internet from a remote server to an individual researcher. Future developments must consider the additional requirements for practical implementation of these processes to working groups of researchers, be they in laboratories, classrooms, or physical or virtual consortia. The ability to share electronic search strategies, documents, commenting capabilities, and other communication techniques will be a part of the normal work flow of researchers in the near future. Information network designers must develop powerful infrastructures and interfaces for both individuals and groups of researchers.

Facilities and Staffing Redesign in Relation to New Options

Rapid changes in researcher information-gathering behaviors have resulted in increased pressures on present library operations. The success and spread of these new and popular remote discovery and distribution options, with their associated complex and expensive automation tool requirements, are forcing information organizations to reassess and revise their services. Libraries must consider reallocating staff and redesigning facilities to better service the present and near-future needs of this growing population of remote users. Perhaps fewer (or less-expensive) branch facilities are necessary as more information can be delivered directly to researcher desktops from central repositories. Even central library facilities may have significant changes in layout due to changing requirements and processes in service points and technical support operations.

Changing Library Staff Tasks

As libraries perform new operations and discontinue older processes, there is a need to retrain existing staff and hire staff with nontraditional skills. The new electronic information center will still require all of the old paper-based skills for some time to come, but new challenges exist in many areas.

As many traditional public service library activities are distributed to remote users, the library may not find itself marginalized as many outsiders are predicting. Instead, it will focus on central processing concerns such as materials and services analysis, acquisition, and payment; the provision of centralized computing and printing capabilities for those without personal or shared equipment; and the identification, storage, and purchase of non-bibliographic data sets.

Another task that will become more important for all members of organizations as the information tools become more complex and diverse is that of centralized instruction. It is no accident that libraries have often been the leaders in web instruction; they are perfectly situated to service the cross-disciplinary needs of organizations. A logical product of this centralized support position is the development of well-designed and consistent population-specific navigation tools. This is particularly important for the many interdisciplinary researchers who could waste enormous amounts of time and energy learning each unique discipline gateway tool.

The same principles required to design central navigation tools are used to design powerful knowledge databases. Librarian collaboration with researchers and information technology staff will produce sophisticated local subject tools that can be used for research and teaching support across disciplines.

As the information tools become more powerful, and byproducts provide new possibilities, the library presence will be expanded to include additional support for an organization's administrative services. There are many untapped information resources that will become everyday tools as information mining becomes more accessible to organizational administrators.

Employees now require higher levels of technical skill in order to provide adequate support. Some advanced skills may be better provided through outsourcing to organizations that are better able to provide state-of-the-art equipment and staff. Some technical processes can also generate savings by creating economies of scale through consortial operations.

Consolidate or Diversify Across Vendors

When turning to outside vendors, is it wise to consolidate as much as possible into a few vendors, or should organizations diversify? There are advantages and disadvantages to both approaches. Consolidation often makes interfacing easier as there are fewer protocols and training issues involved. Diversification provides advantages in terms of maintaining the ability to develop improvements through competition and protection from becoming completely crippled if your one system crashes. The best approach is often a blend of these options. Only time will tell if the rapid aggregation of present services will produce so few information providers that this point is moot.

Remote Hosts or Local Loading

The rapid state of development of nonstandard information server hardware and software makes a decision about the implementation of loading resources locally quite complex. Certain operations, such as online catalogs, remain best at the local or small consortial level, with federated search capabilities for larger domain searching. Other operations, such as loading full-text journals, may be in too embryonic a stage for the serious commitment of required resources by any but the largest and most flexible organizations. This is true especially if the organizations intend to continue providing the inevitable and desirable complex interactive capabilities that electronic networks make possible. The best approach at present is often a blend of these options within larger consortial initiatives.

Invest Now or Wait for Standards

Should libraries expend their precious resources on present technologies or wait for the next technologies that incorporate the developing industry standards? This is always a difficult question, and it is made more complex by the need to maintain expensive parallel paper-based and electronic systems. Once again the best course is probably to invest in those tools that provide the most desirable services for your user populations, but to prepare for rapid replacement and upgrades for the immediate future. Look for long-term approaches and solutions when selecting an electronic tool; flashy tools today can quickly become obsolete if they are not based on a solid design foundation (such as SQL relational techniques). Not every electronic tool that is released has an eager user population; many tools are not high-priority items, and decisions should be media-blind and based on content.

Stay Neutral or Become Involved in the Information Process

Should librarians and information centers remain simple purchasers and archivers, or should they become more active developers, designers, and partners in the information process? Traditionally, libraries have not been actively involved in influencing the direction of the information creation and distribution process beyond addressing cataloging and preservation concerns. This is beginning to change as prices drive information creators and administrators into a position of higher accountability for escalating budgets. The following examples show how libraries are becoming more involved in the entire information creation and distribution process.

Recent library and university administrator conferences have actively worked for changes in the publish-or-perish scenario and the entire tenure process. Even federal agencies such as the NSF have changed their criteria to be less quantitative and more qualitative. This constant pressure to publish, and the copyright giveaways that force the purchase of scientific materials from commercial enterprises, are now major objects of attention.

For years there have been complaints from science faculty that an unreasonable portion of their university overhead fees have gone to support nonscience operations. Libraries have been nervous about discussing this in a public arena, as it would require universities to identify priority disciplines. A new approach that has been mentioned is the migration toward direct federal funding for library operations as opposed to relying on the current indirect (overhead) and commercial funding sources. This would be a major change in philosophy, but the new centralized options available through technology make this a far more cost-effective and attractive possibility.

Libraries have become far more influencial in designing the creation processes and final information products. The industry-wide push toward standard electronic document formats such as SGML and .PDF has demonstrated new power for libraries in the development and acceptance of the best long-term scenarios and tools. This industry and library cooperation on designing XML and DOI standards is the beginning of a more responsible and proactive approach to systems design by the library community.

The development of free open-source alternatives to previously commercial library products and services is a new and interesting movement in the library community. While still in its infancy, this activity could make the entire information process much more flexible, responsive and less expensive.

The **Open Source Digital Library System** (http://osdls.library.arizona. edu/) is a project to develop an open-source, next-generation library system. This system can be implemented by a wide range of libraries—from small public libraries to large academic ones. It is hoped that the project will also bring together in cooperation a diverse group of librarians and libraries who share a similar interest—having a freely available, fully functional library system.

Explore and Develop Proactively

As users explore these new tools and technologies, they will undoubtedly demand many new applications that will require additional complexities for linkage between and among tools. The sooner we start to consider these developments, the easier it will be to create flexible and powerful standards and infrastructures to support these needs.

In this new electronic information age, minimally supported research communities and special interest groups create helpful gateways to complex information domains. One such group is discussed here.

Future Horizons-Advanced Technology. http://www.futurehorizons.net/ (accessed May 26, 1999).

Future Horizons-Advanced Technology is a small research and development group dedicated to making secret, suppressed, and controversial information accessible to interested individuals. Their mission is to develop new advanced technologies and concepts and help move mankind into the twenty-first century and beyond. They cover the following areas: Free Energy, Antigravity, Psionics, Time Travel, Alternative Fuels, Space-Age Weapons, UFOs, New Age Medicine, Bionics, High Voltage, Strange Science, Ultrasonics, Lasers, Robotics, Surveillance, and Pyrotechnics.

Surely the library element within the information industry, armed with advanced information theory and significant funding resources, can combine our talents to provide helpful navigation techniques and information knowledge systems.

If not, there are many commercial organizations waiting to cash in on the promise of easy access to information for any and all researchers. One example of an innovative product and approach can be seen from Ask Jeeves, Inc.

Ask Jeeves. http://www.askjeeves.com/ (accessed May 26, 1999).

In this free service, users type a question for Jeeves "just the way you would phrase it if you were asking a particularly knowledgeable friend," and Jeeves immediately navigates through hundreds of millions of websites and delivers the results in the form of questions for you to select. Ask Jeeves combines a unique natural-language engine with a proprietary knowledge base that gets smarter over time, as its knowledge base expands with each question asked and each answer delivered. Essentially, the Ask Jeeves staff has pre-searched the Internet and has found appropriate sites to answer a wide variety of questions.

"Powered by Jeeves" (http://www.askjeeves.com/docs/about/poweredBy.html) licenses the Ask Jeeves cutting-edge technology to corporate websites so that customers may ask plain English questions and quickly find the information they need. Jeeves acts as a customer service agent, a technical service agent, a sales agent, and a navigation agent all in one.

To demonstrate the satisfaction with this approach for information mining, and the continuing development of nonlibrary solutions to corporate and individual researcher needs, the following partnership and strategy comments are taken from the About Ask Jeeves site (http://www.askjeeves.com/docs/about/poweredBy.html):

> (Berkeley, California)—October 16, 1997: Ask Jeeves, Inc. announced today that two major websites, Infonautics Corporation's Electric Library online research service and InfoSpace, Inc.'s directory service, have licensed Ask Jeeves' "Question Answering" search engine and knowledge base.

> Infonautics' Electric Library service (http://www.elibrary.com) is an online research service that provides its members with immediate access to high-quality information using a discrete database of more than one billion words and thousands of images.

Users can launch a comprehensive, simultaneous search through hundreds of full-text newspaper and magazine sources, international newswires, classic books, hundreds of maps, thousands of images, as well as major works of art and literature. Joshua Kopelman, executive vice president of Infonautics, states "Other search engines locate sites that contain certain keywords, but Ask Jeeves finds a specific site that answers a particular question. Our users want to find answers; they don't want to spend time surfing through irrelevant sites."

InfoSpace, Inc., (http://www.infospace.com) is a content aggregator providing information from sources such as the yellow pages, white pages, and detailed business information directories including company websites, toll-free numbers, fax numbers, and e-mail addresses, and local city information including weather, traffic, and apartments. Naveen Jain, president of InfoSpace, says "Ask Jeeves' question-answer approach allows our customers to access our directories using simple English queries such as 'Where can I find a florist in Phoenix?'. Also, unlike other search technologies, the Ask Jeeves engine can easily map user queries into database lookup requests, which is important for a service such as ours."

In order for libraries to successfully compete with outside information providers, be they commercial or researcher-based initiatives, new tools must be developed that provide adequate scope, depth, and granularity. The same interface must work for researchers searching for free energy diagrams or for information about favorite hobbies.

Further Reading

Many of the latest ideas on the potential, prototypes, initiatives, and designs for these new knowledge networks can be identified through regular reviews of the literature identified at the following locations.

Scholarly Electronic Publishing Bibliography. http://info.lib.uh.edu/ sepb/sepb.html (accessed May 6, 1999).

An impressive online bibliography, compiled by Charles W. Bailey, Jr., of selected articles and books from the digital literature. Covers a broad range of subjects and is organized into subject categories.

UC Berkeley Digital Library SunSITE. http://sunsite.berkeley.edu/ (accessed May 6, 1999).

An online gateway providing a clearinghouse for digital library literature and pointers to the latest projects and initiatives.

Chapter 12

Important Works in the Development of Physics, 1600–1900

by Kristine K. Fowler

The classical era of physics is bracketed by the pivotal works published in 1600 and 1900 by William Gilbert and Max Planck. Gilbert's *De Magnete* was a systematic exploration of the phenomena of magnetism and electricity, which set the example of experimentation as the basis of scientific knowledge. The next 300 years brought the establishment and progressive development of the fields of mechanics, heat, sound, light, and electricity and magnetism. Planck's 1900 article on the quantization of energy was the cue for another radical shift in thinking, of which quantum mechanics would be the result. The bibliography in this chapter presents brief annotations of major books and articles that spurred the development of physics during those three fertile centuries.

This bibliography is intended to encourage the physicist and the student of physics or physics history to read the original presentations of important works, as modern textbooks usually contain only distillations. As Bern Dibner notes, "To go to original sources in science is to place the discovery or contribution in its proper time and framework—in its proper coordinates." Annotated citations for first publication of the works are given here in chronological order. To aid in locating accessible copies, fields a and b give information (not comprehensive) about where a particular work appears in compilations and in English translation, respectively. In some cases such suggestions were not needed: Newton's *Opticks*, for example, originally appeared in English and has been widely reprinted. In other cases, such as d'Alembert's *Traite de Dynamique*, no complete English translation is apparently available.

A preliminary version of this collection was created as an exhibit for the Physics/Astronomy Library of the University of Illinois at Urbana-Champaign, at the suggestion of then Librarian David Stern and Professor Manfred Raether.

1. William Gilbert. *De Magnete, Magneticisque Corporibus et de Magno Magnete Tellure*, 1600.

    a. *Landmarks of Science.* New York: Readex Microprint, 1967–1975.

    b. i. P. Fleury Mottelay. *On the Loadstone and Magnetic Bodies, and on the Great Magnet the Earth.* New York: J. Wiley, 1893.

        ii. Silvanus Phillips Thompson. *On the Magnet.* London: Chiswick Press, 1900.

One of the first works to use the method of experimentation, it investigated the properties of magnetic materials. Gilbert proposed that the Earth is a large magnet. *De magnete* also described some effects of electricity generated by friction, making it the first published work on electricity.

2. Simon Stevin. *Wisconstighe Ghedachtenissen [etc.]*, 1608.

    a. *The Principal Works of Simon Stevin.* Vol. 1: Mechanics. Amsterdam: C. V. Swets & Zeitlinger, 1955–1966.

    b. C. Dikshoorn, trans.; Ernst Crone et al., eds. *The Principal Works of Simon Stevin.* Vol. 1: Mechanics, 1955–1966. [facsimile of Dutch original facing English translation].

Highlights of Stevin's varied contributions included introducing the parallelogram of forces for a body on an inclined plane, and calculating the hydrostatic pressure of a liquid in a container.

3. Johannes Kepler. *Epitome Astronomiae Copernicanae*, 1618–1621.

    a. *Gesammelte Werke*, vol. 7. Munich, 1937.

    b. Charles Glenn Wallis. *Epitome of Copernican Astronomy, Books IV and V.* Annapolis, Md.: St. John's Bookstore, 1939. Reprinted: *Great Books of the Western World*, vol. 15. Chicago: Encyclopaedia Britannica, 1952.

This textbook included Kepler's three laws of planetary motion: (i) the orbit of each planet is an ellipse with the sun at one focus; (ii) the line from the sun to the planet sweeps out equal areas in equal times; (iii) the squares of the periods of the planets are proportional to the cubes of their mean distances from the sun. These were later instrumental in Newton's development of the law of gravitation.

4.   Rene Descartes. *Discours de la Methode*, 1637.

   b.   *Discourse on Method*, [various].

This influential philosophical work, advocating mathematical proof of scientific phenomena, included supplements that applied the method: La Dioptrique, Les Meteores, La Geometrie. It contained the first publication of Willebrord Snell's law governing the angle of refraction of a light beam moving from one medium to another and used the law to explain the position, although not the colors, of the rainbow. (In the long-lived debate over the measure of a body's "quantity of motion," Descartes' argument—that the quantity was proportional to velocity—is contained in his *Principles of Philosophy* [1644].)

5.   Galileo Galilei. *Discorsi e Dimostrazioni Matematiche, Intorno a Due Nuove Scienze [Attenenti alla Mecanica & i Movimenti Locali]*, 1638.

   a.   *Le Opere di Galileo Galilei*, vol. 8, pp. 39–448. Firenze: G. Barbera, 1929–1939.

   b.   H. Crew and A. de Salvio. *Dialogues Concerning Two New Sciences*. New York: Macmillan, 1914.

Galileo here developed the law of inertia—that an object at rest tends to stay at rest and an object in motion tends to stay in the same motion unless otherwise forced—as well as general principles for the accelerated motion of the pendulum, balls rolling down inclined planes, falling bodies, and projectiles. These ideas, basically intact, were to become Newton's first two laws of motion.

6.   Evangelista Torricelli. *De Motu Gravium [Naturaliter Descendentium et Projectorum Libri Duo]*, 1641.

   a.   *Opere*, vol. 2, p. 185– . Faenza, 1919.

   b.   [partial translation] W. F. Magie. *A Source Book in Physics*, pp. 111–13. New York: McGraw-Hill, 1935.

Best known for his invention of the barometer, Torricelli here presented the discovery of the theorem of fluid motion named for him: liquid pours from a hole with a velocity equal to that of a body falling freely from the free surface of the liquid to the hole.

7.   Robert Boyle. *New Experiments Physico-Mechanicall, Touching the Spring of the Air, and Its Effects*, 1660.

   a.   T. Birch, ed. *Works*. London, 1744.

Boyle's Law appeared in the second edition (1662): the volume of a quantity of gas is inversely proportional to its pressure, as long as the temperature is constant.

8.   Blaise Pascal. *Traites de l'Equilibre des Liqueurs et de la Pesanteur de la Masse de l'Air*, 1663.

    a.   *Oeuvres Completes*, vol. 2, pp. 1036–1101. Paris: Desclee de Brouwer, 1964– .

    b.   I. H. B. and A. G. H. Spiers. *The Physical Treatises of Pascal: The Equilibrium of Liquids and the Weight of the Mass of the Air*, pp. 3–67. New York: Columbia University Press, 1937.

Pascal's Law was enunciated here: pressure exerted at any point upon a confined fluid is transmitted equally throughout the fluid in all directions.

9.   Francesco M. Grimaldi. *Physico-mathesis de Lumine, Coloribus et Iride*, 1665.

    a.   *Landmarks of Science II*. New York: Readex Microprint, 1976– .

    b.   [partial translation] W. F. Magie. *A Source Book in Physics*, pp. 294–98. New York: McGraw-Hill, 1935.

Grimaldi discovered the diffraction of light by a straight edge.

10.   Otto von Guericke. *Experimenta Nova (ut Vocantur) Magdeburgica de Vacuo Spatio*, 1672.

    a.   *Landmarks of Science*. New York: Readex Microprint, 1967–1975.

    b.   Margaret Glover Foley Ames. *The New (So-Called) Magdeburg Experiments of Otto von Guericke*. Dordrecht: Kluwer Academic, 1994.

One of von Guericke's experiments is among the most famous in the history of science. He produced a vacuum between two hemispherical shells, which two teams of horses could not then separate; when air was allowed into the sphere, the halves fell apart. He had invented and informally reported the air-pump, which made these experiments possible, before 1650, and it had been used by Boyle in his investigation of gases. This book also contained von Guericke's important electrical advances, such as the invention of a device that generated electric charges by friction (although it lacked a condenser).

11.   Christiaan Huygens. *Horologium Oscillatorium [Sive de Motu Pendulorum ad Horologia Adapto, Demonstrationes Geometricae]*, 1673.

     a.   *Oeuvres Completes*, vol. 18. La Haye: M. Nijhoff, 1888–1950.

     b.   Richard J. Blackwell. *Christiaan Huygens' the Pendulum Clock*. Ames, Iowa: Iowa State University Press, 1986.

Huygens's invention of a clock controlled by a pendulum was announced in 1657, but this later book explained the dynamics involved. These included theorems on centrifugal force, as he called it, and his calculation of the length of a simple pendulum equivalent to a compound pendulum, which had important bearing on the development of gravitational mechanics.

12.   Ole Roemer (or Olaus Romer). "Demonstration Touchant le Mouvement de la Lumiere Trouve par M. Romer," *Journal des Scavans*, pp. 233–36, Dec. 7, 1676.

     a.   [facsimile] I. B. Cohen. "Roemer and the First Determination of the Velocity of Light (1636)," *Isis*, vol. 31, pp. 373–76, 1940.

     b.   i.   [not an exact translation] "A Demonstration Concerning the Motion of Light," *Philosophical Transactions of the Royal Society*, vol. 12, pp. 893–94, June 1677. Reprinted: I. B. Cohen. "Roemer and the First Determination of the Velocity of Light (1636)," *Isis*, vol. 31, pp. 377–78, 1940.

        ii.   Harlow Shapley. *Source Book in Astronomy*, pp. 70–71. New York: McGraw-Hill, 1929.

This was the first demonstration that light has a definite velocity, shown by the delay between the calculated and observed eclipses by Jupiter of its moons.

13.   Robert Hooke. *Lectures de Potentia Restitutiva, or of Spring, Explaining the Power of Springing Bodies*, 1678.

     a.   i.   *Lectiones Cutlerianae*. London, 1679.

        ii.   R. T. Gunther. *Early Science at Oxford*, vol. 8. Oxford, 1923–1945.

De Potentia Restitutiva presented Hooke's Law: the length of extension of a spring (within its elastic limit) is directly proportional to the force used to extend it. Hooke also saw the similarity between the dynamics of an oscillating spring and a swinging pendulum, and did some of the first work on simple harmonic motion.

14.   Edme Mariotte. *Essay de la Nature de l'Air*, 1679.

    a.   *Oeuvres*, vol. 1, pp. 148–82. Leiden, 1717.

    b.   [partial translation] W. F. Magie. *A Source Book in Physics*, pp. 88–92. New York: McGraw-Hill, 1935.

Mariotte discovered the relationship between pressure and volume of a gas, which he first announced in 1676, independently of Boyle; it is sometimes called Mariotte's Law.

15.   Gottfried W. Leibniz. "Brevis Demonstratio Erroris Memorabilis Cartesii et Aliorum Circa Legem Naturae, Secundum Quam Volunt a Deo Eandem Semper Quantitatem Motus Conservari, Qua et in re Mechanica Abutantur," *Acta Eruditorum*, March 1686.

    a.   *Mathematische Schriften*, vol. 6, pp. 117–23. Halle, 1860.

    b.   L. E. Loemker. "A Brief Demonstration of a Notable Error of Descartes and Others Concerning a Natural Law, According to Which God Is Said Always to Conserve the Same Quantity of Motion; A Law Which They Also Misuse in Mechanics," *Leibniz' Philosophical Papers and Letters*, vol. 1, p. 455– . Chicago: University of Chicago Press, 1956.

This was the Leibnizian side of the great debate with the Cartesians over the measure of "quantity of motion." Leibniz proposed the *vis viva*, which is proportional to the square of the speed.

16.   Isaac Newton. *Philosophiae Naturalis Principia Mathematica*, 1687.

    b.   Andrew Motte. *Sir Isaac Newton's Mathematical Principles of Natural Philosophy and His System of the World*. London, 1729.

This monumental work presented a comprehensive and powerful system of mechanics that continues to dominate treatment of the macroscopic world. Newton drew his first two laws of motion from Galileo and added the third: To every action there is an equal and opposite reaction. See the 1713 second edition for a succinct statement of the law of gravitation, which was thematic throughout the *Principia*: "the power of gravity . . . operates not according to the quantity of the surfaces of the particles upon which it acts (as mechanical causes use to do), but according to the quantity of the solid matter which they contain, and propagates its virtue on all sides to immense distances, decreasing always in the duplicate proportion of the distances."

17. Christiaan Huygens. *Traite de la Lumiere*, 1690.

  a. *Oeuvres Completes*, vol. 19. La Haye: M. Nijhoff, 1888–1950.

  b. Silvanus P. Thompson. *Treatise on Light*. London: Macmillan, 1912.

A mine of interesting new ideas, Huygens's *Traite de la Lumiere* is most notable now for expounding the theory (which he had first announced in 1678) that light was a wave propagating through ether. Reflection, refraction, and polarization (which he discovered) were explained using Huygens' Principle: every point of a wave can be considered as the center of a new wave, and the superposition of all such waves results in a wave identical with the original. The wave theory of light remained unaccepted, in the face of Newton's corpuscular theory, for more than a century.

18. Joseph Sauveur. "Systeme General des Intervalles des Sons, et son Applications a tous les Systemes et a tous les Instrumens de Musique," *Memoires de l'Academie Royale des Sciences, Paris*, pp. 297–460, 1701 (published in 1704).

  a. i. *Collected Writings on Musical Acoustics* (Paris 1700–1713). Utrecht, Netherlands: Diapason Press, 1984.

  ii. *Principes d'Acoustique et de Musique: ou, Systeme General des Intervalles des Sons*. Geneva: Minkoff Reprint, 1973.

  b. Robert E. Maxham. *Contributions of Joseph Sauveur (1653–1716) to Acoustics*, vol. 2. Thesis: University of Rochester, 1976.

An important contributor to the science of acoustics, Sauveur explained the relationship among tones on the musical scale and his discovery of overtones.

19.   Guillaume Amontons. "Discours sur Quelques Proprietes de l'Air, et le Moyen d'en Connoitre la Temperature dans Tous les Climats de la Terre," *Memoires de l'Academie Royale des Sciences, Paris*, pp. 155–74, June 18, 1702.

> b.   [partial translation] W. F. Magie. *A Source Book in Physics*, pp. 128–31. Cambridge, Mass.: Harvard University Press, 1963.

Amontons developed a thermometer that measured temperature by air pressure, which depends on the relationship between volume and temperature of a gas published by Gay-Lussac a hundred years later.

20.   Isaac Newton. *Opticks [or, a Treatise of the Reflexions, Refractions, Inflexions and Colours of Light. Also Two Treatises of the Species and Magnitude of Curvilinear Figures]*, 1704.

Much of Newton's work on light first appeared as papers published in the *Philosophical Transactions of the Royal Society* between 1672 and 1676 before being comprehensively treated in this book. In it he described his demonstration of the composite nature of white light and explained the formation of the rainbow. In his attempt to explain diffraction, Newton postulated the corpuscular theory of light, which would dominate the field for a century. He described the occurrence of Newton's rings, the alternating dark and light bands observed when light was shown on a convex lens placed on top of a flat lens; his corpuscular explanation of the phenomenon was incorrect, but established the periodic nature of light. The supplementary treatises were intended to assert Newton's priority to the discovery of calculus over Leibniz.

21.   Stephen Gray. "A Letter . . . Containing Several Experiments Concerning Electricity," *Philosophical Transactions of the Royal Society*, vol. 37, pp. 18–44, 1731–1732.

Gray discovered that materials can be classified as electric conductors or nonconductors and was the first to show that electricity could be transported from one body to another over some distance using a metallic wire.

22.   Charles Francois de Cisternay du Fay. "A Letter . . . Concerning Electricity," *Philosophical Transactions of the Royal Society*, vol. 38, pp. 258–66, 1734.

Du Fay proposed the theory that electricity comprises two fluids, which he named the vitreous and the resinous, in order to explain electric attraction and repulsion. This was the earliest important theory of electricity.

23.   Daniel Bernoulli. *Hydrodynamica [Sive de Viribus et Motibus Fluidorum Commentarii]*, 1738.

    a.   *Die Werke von Daniel Bernoulli*, vols. 4–5 [to appear]. Boston: Birkhauser, 1982– .

    b.   Thomas Carmody and Helmut Kobus. *Hydrodynamics*. New York: Dover Publications, 1968.

This first treatise on hydrodynamics applied the principle of the conservation of *vis viva* to the solution of hydrodynamical problems. It presented the basic ideas of the kinetic theory of gases.

24.   Jean le Rond d'Alembert. *Traite de Dynamique*, 1743.

    b.   [partial translation] W. F. Magie. *A Source Book in Physics*, pp. 55–58. Cambridge, Mass.: Harvard University Press, 1963.

D'Alembert finally resolved the dispute between the Cartesians and the Leibnizians over the measure of "quantity of motion," by pointing out that it was only a semantic question. (The Cartesian quantity of motion proportional to velocity corresponds to our "momentum"; the Leibnizian *vis viva*, proportional to the square of the velocity, corresponds to our "energy.") The treatise also included d'Alembert's Principle, which drew the corollary from Newton's Third Law that internal stresses balance each other and can therefore be neglected.

25.   Benjamin Franklin. *Experiments and Observations on Electricity, Made at Philadelphia in America* [2 vols.], 1751–1753.

    a.   *Works*, vol. 5. Boston: Hillard Gray, 1836–1840.

Franklin proposed the one fluid theory of electricity, giving the term "positive" to the condition of excess of the fluid and "negative" to the condition of deficit. Much of Franklin's electrical work, including the account of the famous kite experiment, was communicated by letter to the Royal Society in London, and some were published in the *Philosophical Transactions of the Royal Society* before being collected in these volumes.

26.   Henry Cavendish. *The Electrical Researches of the Honourable Henry Cavendish, F. R. S., Written Between 1771 and 1781* (posthumously edited by James Clerk Maxwell, 1879).

    a.   *Scientific Papers of the Honourable Henry Cavendish*, vol. 1. Cambridge: University Press, 1921.

A few of Cavendish's papers were published contemporaneously in the *Philosophical Transactions of the Royal Society*, but the majority

waited for Maxwell to rediscover. Maxwell judged that "the leading idea which distinguishes the electrical researches of Cavendish from those of his predecessors and contemporaries, is the introduction of the phrase 'degree of electrification' with a clear scientific definition, which shows that it is precisely equivalent to what we now call potential. . . . Thus Cavendish not only anticipated Faraday's discovery of the Specific Inductive Capacity of different substances, but measured its numerical value in several substances."

27.   Charles Coulomb. "Sur l'Electricite et le Magnetisme," *Memoires de l'Academie Royale des Sciences, Paris*, pp. 569–638, 1785, and pp. 67–77, 1786.

   a.   *Collection de Memoires Relatifs a la Physique*, vol. 1. Paris: Societe Francaise de Physique, 1884.

   b.   [partial translation] W. F. Magie. *A Source Book in Physics*, pp. 408–20. Cambridge, Mass.: Harvard University Press, 1963.

Coulomb invented the torsion balance and used it to determine the law of electric force (Coulomb's Law), that the attraction or repulsion between two charged bodies is directly proportional to the amount of charge on each and inversely proportional to the square of the distance between them. He determined that the inverse square relation holds for magnetic force as well.

28.   Joseph Louis Lagrange. *Mecanique Analytique*, 1788.

   a.   *Oeuvres*, vols. 11–12. Paris, 1867–1892.

   b.   Auguste Boissonnade and Victor N. Vagliente. *Analytical Mechanics*. Boston: Kluwer Academic, 1997.

In this work, Lagrange established a system for expressing any problem of mechanics in equations, independent of diagrams (which was a radical departure from the prevailing synthetic method, as used by Newton). Its foundation was his principle of virtual velocities. He is one of the originators of the concept of potential, which he applied to gravitation problems.

29.   Luigi Galvani. "De Viribus Electricitatis in Motu Musculari Commentarius," *De Bononiensi Scientiarum et Artium Instituto atque Academia Commentarii*, vol. 7, 1791.

   a.   Margaret Glover Foley. *Commentary on the Effects of Electricity on Muscular Motion*, pp. 97–156. Norwalk, Conn.: Burndy Library, 1953.

   b.   Margaret Glover Foley. *Commentary on the Effects of Electricity on Muscular Motion*, pp. 43–96. Norwalk, Conn.: Burndy Library, 1953.

A professor of medicine, Galvani noticed convulsions in the legs of a dissected frog under varying circumstances related to electric sparks. He established that the necessary conditions involved a chain of two metals touching the frog at different points. He attributed the effect to "animal electricity." Sending a copy of his paper to Volta produced a different explanation.

30.   Alessandro Volta. "On the Electricity Excited by the Mere Contact of Conducting Substances of Different Kinds [in French]," *Philosophical Transactions of the Royal Society*, vol. 90, pt. 2, pp. 403–31, 1800.

   a.   *Opere*, vol. 1, pp. 563–82. Milan, 1918.

   b.   i.   "On the Electricity Excited by the Mere Contact of Conducting Substances of Different Kinds," *Philosophical Magazine*, vol. 7, pp. 288–311, 1800.

         ii.   Bern Dibner. *Alessandro Volta and the Electric Battery*, pp. 111–31. New York: F. Watts, 1964.

Volta explained the effect Galvani had observed as due to contact electricity: he had found that electricity would flow from one metal to another merely by touching them together. He produced a direct current of appreciable size by using a series of alternating zinc and copper plates separated by wet paper: the Voltaic pile, which then led to the Voltaic battery.

31.   Joseph Black. *Lectures on the Elements of Chemistry*, 1803.
The first to make the distinction between temperature and heat, Black discovered specific and latent heat.

32.   Thomas Young. *Lectures on Natural Philosophy* [or *Course of Lectures on Natural Philosophy and the Mechanical Arts*], 1807.
This work contained various important contributions, such as the term "energy" for Leibniz's "quantity of motion," the definition of elastic modulus, and the first explanation of the working of the lens of the eye. Its primary significance lay in Young's discovery of the interference of light, and his resuscitation of the wave theory to explain it.

33.   John Dalton. *A New System of Chemical Philosophy* [2 vols.], 1808–1810.
The chief significance of this work for physics was the presentation of the atomic structure of matter.

34.   Etienne-Louis Malus. "Sur une Propriete de la Lumiere Reflechie par les Corps Diaphanes," *Memoires de la Societe d'Arcueil*, vol. 2, pp. 143–58, 1809.

> b.   *Nicholson's Journal of Natural Philosophy*, vol. 30, pp. 95–102, 1812.

This paper recounted the discovery of the polarization of light by reflection.

35.   Joseph von Fraunhofer. "Bestimmung des Brechungs- und Farbenzerstreuungs- Vermogens virschiedener Glasarten, in Bezug auf die Vervollkommnurg achromatischer Fernrohre," *Denkschriften der Koniglichen Akademie der Wissenschaften zu Munchen*, vol. 5, pp. 193–226, 1817.

> a.   E. C. J. Lommel, ed. *Gesammelte Schriften*. Munich, 1888.

Fraunhofer discovered certain dark lines in the solar spectrum, which had immediate application in calculating precise diffractive indexes, and which had greater significance once Kirchhoff successfully interpreted them.

36.   Hans Christian Oersted. "Experimenta circa Effectum Conflictus Electrici in Acum Magneticam," *Journal fur Chemie und Physik*, vol. 29, pp. 275–81, July 1820.

> a.   [facsimile] *Isis*, vol. 10, pp. 437–44, 1928.
>
> b.   i.   "Experiments on the Effect of a Current of Electricity on the Magnetic Needle," *Annals of Philosophy*, vol. 16, pp. 273–76, October 1820. Reprinted: R. A. R. Tricker. *Early Electrodynamics*, pp. 113–17. Oxford: Pergamon, 1965.
>
> ii.   Karen Jelved et al. *Selected Scientific Works of Hans Christian Oersted*, pp. 413–16. Princeton, N.J.: Princeton University Press, 1998.

This short paper, translated and published in several languages within months, announced the discovery of a magnetic field surrounding a current-carrying wire.

37.   Andre Marie Ampere. "Sur les Effets des Courans Electriques" and "De l'Action Mutuelle de Deux Courans Electriques," *Annales de Chimie et de Physique*, ser. II, vol. 15, pp. 59–76, 170–218, 1820.

> a.   i.   *Memoires sur la Theorie Mathematique des Phenomenes Electrodynamiques, Uniquement Deduite de l'Experience*, 1826.

      ii. *Memoires sur l'Electrodynamique*. Paris: Societe Francaise de Physique, 1885–1887.

  b. i. [partial translation] *Philosophical Magazine*, vol. 57, pp. 47–49, 1821.

      ii. [partial translation] O. M. Blunn, trans.; R. A. R. Tricker, ed. *Early Electrodynamics*, pp. 140–54. Oxford: Pergamon, 1965.

In a rapid series of papers on the heels of Oersted's announcement, Ampere established the relationships for the forces exerted by two current-carrying wires on each other, laying the foundation for the field of electrodynamics.

    38.   Jean Biot and Felix Savart. "Note sur le Magnetisme de la Pile de Volta," *Annales de Chimie et de Physique*, ser. II, vol. 15, pp. 222–23, 1820.

    a.   *Melanges Scientifiques et Litteraires*, vol. 1. Paris, 1858.

    b.   O. M. Blunn, trans.; R. A. R. Tricker, ed. *Early Electrodynamics*, pp. 118–19. Oxford: Pergamon, 1965.

Here Biot-Savart's Law was presented: the magnetic field around a current-carrying wire varies inversely as the distance from it.

    39.   Augustin J. Fresnel. "Memoire sur la diffraction de la lumiere," *Memoires de l'Academie des Sciences, Paris*, vol. 5, pp. 339–475, 1821–1822 (published in 1826).

    a.   *Oeuvres Completes*, vol. 1, pp. 247–382. Paris: Imprimerie imperiale, 1866–1870.

    b.   [partial translation] H. Crew. *Wave Theory of Light*. New York: American Book Company, 1900.

Fresnel established the wave theory of light, using Huygens' Principle and Young's interference phenomenon to explain diffraction.

    40.   Jean Baptiste J. Fourier. *Theorie Analytique de la chaleur*, 1822.

    a.   *Oeuvres*, vol. 1. Paris: Gauthier-Villars et Fils, 1888–1890.

    b.   Alexander Freeman. *Analytical Theory of Heat*. Cambridge, Mass.: Cambridge University Press, 1878.

Fourier established the law of conduction—that heat flows between two touching bodies in proportion to the difference in their temperatures—amid important new methods of analysis for theoretical physics, such as the theory of the dimensions of physical quantities.

41.   Thomas J. Seebeck. "Magnetische Polarisation der Metalle und Erze durch Temperatur-Differenz," *Abhandlungen der Preussischen Akademie der Wissenschaften*, pp. 265–373, 1822–1823.

    a. i.   *Annalen der Physik und Chemie*, vol. 6, pp. 1–20, 133–60, 253–86, 1826.

        ii. *Ostwald's Klassiker der exakten Wissenschaften*, no. 70. Leipzig, 1895.

    b. [partial translation] W. F. Magie. *A Source Book in Physics*, pp. 461–64. New York: McGraw-Hill, 1935.

Despite its title, the effect announced in this paper was thermoelectricity: in a ring of two different metals joined together, an electric current is produced in the ring if one of the junctions is at a different temperature than the other.

42.   Sadi Carnot. *Reflexions sur la Puissance Motrice du Feu*, 1824.

    b. R. H. Thurston. *Reflections on the Motive Power of Heat.* New York: Macmillan, 1890. Reprinted: E. Mendoza, ed. *Reflections on the Motive Power of Fire by Sadi Carnot and Other Papers on the Second Law of Thermodynamics by E. Clapeyron and R. Clausius*, pp. 1–59. New York: Dover Publications, 1960.

One of the foundations of thermodynamics, this work considered the maximum amount of work to be obtained from an amount of heat, and concluded that this is produced by an engine cycle in which each of the operations is reversible.

43.   Georg S. Ohm. "Bestimmung des Gesetzes, nach welchem Metalle die Contaktelektricitat leiten, nebst einem Entwurfe zu einer Theorie des Voltaischen Apparates und des Schweiggerschen Multiplicators," *Journal fur Chemie und Physik*, vol. 46, pp. 137–66, 1826.

    a. i.   E. Lommel, ed. *Gesammelte Abhandlungen*, pp. 14–36. Leipzig, 1892.

        ii. *Die Galvanische Kette, mathematisch bearbeitet*, 1827.

    b. i.   N. H. de Vaudrey Heathcote. "A Translation of the Paper in Which Ohm First Announced His Law of the Galvanic Circuit, Prefaced by Some Account of the Work of His Predecessors," *Science Progress* 26(101), pp. 51–75, July 1931.

ii.   [translation of *Die Galvanische Kette*] William Francis. "The Galvanic Circuit Investigated Mathematically," *Scientific Memoirs, Selected from the Transactions of Foreign Academies and Learned Societies and from Foreign Journals*, vol. 2, pp. 401–506. London: Taylor, 1841.

In a work little appreciated at the time, Ohm established the relationship among quantities in an electric circuit, i.e., Ohm's Law: the current is directly proportional to the electromotive force, and inversely proportional to the resistance.

44.   Robert Brown. *A Brief Account of Microscopical Observations Made in the Months of June, July, and August, 1827, on the Particles Contained in the Pollen of Plants; and on the General Existence of Active Molecules in Organic and Inorganic Bodies*, 1827.

a.   i.   *Philosophical Magazine*, vol. 4, pp. 161–73, 1828.

ii.   *Miscellaneous Botanical Works of Robert Brown*, vol. 27, p. 1– . London, 1866.

The biologist observed under the microscope the eponymous Brownian motion of particles suspended in a liquid, explained by Einstein in 1905 as the result of the motion of molecules in the liquid.

45.   Karl Friedrich Gauss. "Intensitas Vis Magneticae Terrestris ad Mensuram Absolutam Revocata," *Annalen der Physik und Chemie*, vol. 28, pp. 241–73, 591–614, 1833.

a.   *Werke*, vol. 5, pp. 293–304. Leipzig-Berlin, 1863–1933.

b.   [partial translation] W. F. Magie. *Source Book in Physics*, pp. 519–24. New York: McGraw-Hill, 1935.

In proposing to measure the magnetic field of the Earth, Gauss created a system for measurement in absolute units that had ramifications for every field of physics.

46.   Michael Faraday. *Experimental Researches in Electricity* [3 vols.], 1839–1855.

a.   *Experimental Researches in Chemistry and Physics*. London: Taylor & Francis, 1859.

This classic work collected the long series of Faraday's experimental researches in electricity published in the *Philosophical Transactions of the Royal Society* between 1831 and 1854. It included many important developments, such as the discoveries of electromagnetic induction and of diamagnetism, and a demonstration that a magnetic field will rotate the plane of polarization of light.

47.   Julius R. Mayer. "Bemerkungen uber die Krafte der unbelebten Natur," *Annalen der Chemie und Pharmacie*, vol. 42, pp. 233–40, 1842.

    a.   *Die Mechanik der Warme.* Stuttgart, 1867.

    b.   G. C. Foster. "Remarks on the Forces of Inorganic Nature," *Philosophical Magazine*, ser. 4, vol. 24, pp. 371–77, 1862. Reprinted: Stephen G. Brush. *Kinetic Theory*, vol. 1, pp. 71–77. Oxford: Pergamon, 1965–1972.

Mayer formulated the idea of the equivalence of heat and mechanical work, calculating a value for the work needed to compress air from its rise in temperature.

48.   James P. Joule. "On the Calorific Effects of Magneto-Electricity, and on the Mechanical Value of Heat," *Philosophical Magazine*, vol. 23, pp. 263–76, 347–55, 435–43, 1843.

    a.   *Scientific Papers*, vol. 1, pp. 123–59. London, 1884–1887.

Independently of Mayer, Joule developed the equivalence between heat and mechanical work and convincingly demonstrated it by experiments based on the heat generated in an electric circuit (Joule's Law governing this process was established in a previous paper.) This was one of the founding works in the principle of the conservation of energy, also disposing of the prevailing idea that heat was a material substance ("caloric").

49.   Hermann L. von Helmholtz. *Uber die Erhaltung der Kraft*, 1847.

    a.   i.   *Wissenschaftliche Abhandlungen*, vol. 1. Leipzig, 1882.

       ii.   *Ostwald's Klassiker der exakten Wissenschaften*, no. 1. Leipzig, 1889.

    b.   John Tyndall. "The Conservation of Force," *Scientific Memoirs, Selected from the Transactions of Foreign Academies of Science, and from Foreign Journals: Natural Philosophy*, pp. 114–62. London: R. and J. E. Taylor, 1853. Reprinted: Stephen G. Brush. *Kinetic Theory*, vol. 1, pp. 89–110. Oxford: Pergamon, 1965–1972.

Helmholtz applied mathematical arguments—including his definition of the energy of motion as one-half the product of mass and the square of velocity—to a variety of mechanical processes, and thereby firmly established the principle of the conservation of energy.

50.   Armand H. Fizeau. "Sur un Experience Relative a la Vitesse de Propagation de la Lumiere" and "Sur l'Experience Relative a la Vitesse Comparative de la Lumiere dans l'Air et dans l'Eau," *Comptes Rendus Acad. Sci. Paris*, vol. 29, pp. 90–92, 1849, and vol. 30, pp. 771–74, 1850.

      b.   [partial translation] W. F. Magie. *A Source Book in Physics*, pp. 341–42. New York: McGraw-Hill, 1935.

Fizeau made the first successful absolute measurement of the speed of light (i.e., not dependent on astronomical observations).

51.   Rudolf J. Clausius. "Uber die bewegende Kraft der Warme," *Annalen der Physik und Chemie*, ser. 2, vol. 79, pp. 368–97, 500–24, 1850.

      a.   i.   *Ostwald's Klassiker der exakten Wissenschaften*, no. 99. Leipzig, 1898.

          ii.   *Die Mechanische Warmetheorie*, 1864.

      b.   i.   W. F. Magie, trans.; E. Mendoza, ed. "On the Motive Power of Heat, and on the Laws Which Can Be Deduced from It for the Theory of Heat," *Reflections on the Motive Power of Fire by Sadi Carnot and Other Papers on the Second Law of Thermodynamics by E. Clapeyron and R. Clausius*, pp. 107–52. New York: Dover Publications, 1960.

          ii.   [translation of *Die Mechanische Warmetheorie*] W. R. Browne. *Mechanical Theory of Heat*. London: Macmillan, 1879.

One of the founders of the kinetic theory of gases and of thermodynamics, Clausius conceived the Second Law of Thermodynamics in these terms: it is impossible for an isolated process to remove heat from a reservoir at one temperature and deliver an equal quantity of heat to a reservoir at a higher temperature.

52.   William Thomson, Lord Kelvin. "Dynamical Theory of Heat," *Philosophical Magazine*, vol. 4, pp. 8–21, 105–17, 168–76, 424–34, 1852.

      a.   *Mathematical and Physical Papers*, vol. 1, pp. 174–210. Cambridge, 1882.

Kelvin independently stated the Second Law of Thermodynamics: it is impossible for an isolated process to draw a given amount of heat from a reservoir and perform an equivalent amount of work (i.e., it is impossible to construct a perfect heat engine). This paper also contained Kelvin's proposal for an absolute scale of temperature as it is now used.

53. Gustav R. Kirchhoff. "Uber den Zussammenhang zwischen Emission und Absorption von Licht und Warme," *Monatsbericht der Akademie der Wissenschaften zu Berlin*, pp. 783–87, 1860.

   a. i. *Gesammelte Abhandlungen*, pp. 566–71. Leipzig, 1882.

       ii. *Ostwald's Klassiker der exakten Wissenschaften*, no. 100. Leipzig, 1898.

   b. D. B. Brace. *Laws of Radiation and Absorption*. New York: American Book Company, 1901.

Kirchhoff, a founder of spectrum analysis, was the first to clearly distinguish between, and correlate, emission and absorption spectra. He used this relationship to explain the Fraunhofer lines as the absorption spectra of elements in the outer regions of the sun.

54. James Clerk Maxwell. *A Treatise on Electricity and Magnetism* [2 vols.], 1873.

This classic work presented a cohesive dynamical system of electricity and magnetism. It was the fuller development of some previous papers, such as "A Dynamical Theory of the Electromagnetic Field" (*Philosophical Transactions of the Royal Society*, vol. 155, pp. 459–512, 1865), in which he adduced evidence for light being an electromagnetic wave.

55. Johann J. Balmer. "Notiz uber die Spectrallinien des Wasserstoffs," *Annalen der Physik und Chemie*, ser. 3, vol. 25, pp. 80–87, 1885.

   b. i. J. B. Sykes, trans.; W. R. Hindmarsh, ed. "A Note on the Spectral Lines of Hydrogen," *Atomic Spectra*, pp. 101–7. Oxford: Pergamon, 1967.

       ii. H. A. Boorse and L. Motz. "A Note on the Spectral Lines of Hydrogen," *The World of the Atom*, pp. 365–68. New York: Basic Books, 1966.

This paper announced the formula for the Balmer series of hydrogen's spectral lines, the first of its kind.

56. Albert Michelson and Edward Morley. "On the Relative Motion of the Earth and the Luminiferous Aether," *Philosophical Magazine*, ser. 5, vol. 24, pp. 449–63, Dec. 1887; or *American Journal of Science*, ser. 3, vol. 34, pp. 333–45, 1887.

   a. Kenneth Schaffner. *Nineteenth-Century Aether Theories*, pp. 144–60. New York: Pergamon, 1972.

This famous experiment used a delicate interferometer to test whether the speed of light was affected by the motion of the Earth through the ether; the negative result was eventually accepted as disproving the ether's existence, and it also had implications for the theory of relativity.

57.   Heinrich Hertz. *Untersuchungen uber die Ausbreitung der elektrischen Kraft*, 1892.

    a.   *Gesammelte Werke*, vol. 2. Leipzig, 1894.

    b.   D. E. Jones. *Electric Waves*. London: Macmillan, 1893.

In a series of papers originally published in the *Annalen der Physik* between 1887 and 1890, Hertz reported the results of his experiments confirming Maxwell's theory that light is an electromagnetic wave.

58.   Wilhelm Röntgen. "Uber eine neue Art von Strahlen," *Sitzungsberichte der Physikalisch-medicinische Gesellschaft zu Wurzburg*, pp. 132–41, Dec. 1895, and pp. 11–19, 1896.

    a.   *Annalen der Physik und Chemie*, vol. 64, pp. 1–17, 1898.

    b.   George Frederick Barker. *Rontgen Rays*, pp. 3–18. New York: Harper, 1899. Reprinted: *American Journal of Physics*, vol. 13, pp. 284–91, 1945.

Here was the account of the discovery of X-rays, for which Röntgen would be awarded the first Nobel Prize in physics.

59.   A. Henri Becquerel. "Sur les Radiations Emises par Phosphorescence" and "Sur les Radiations Invisibles Emise par les Sels d'Uranium," *Comptes Rendus Acad. Sci. Paris*, vol. 122, pp. 420–21, 689–94, 1896.

    a.   "Recherches sur une Propriete Nouvelle de la Matiere," *Memoires de l'Academie des Sciences, Paris*, vol. 46, 1903.

    b.   Alfred Romer. "On the Radiation Emitted in Phosphorescence," *The Discovery of Radioactivity and Transmutation*, pp. 8–9, 13–18. New York: Dover Publications, 1964.

These reports detailed the discovery of radioactivity in uranium.

60.   Ludwig Boltzmann. *Vorlesungen uber Gastheorie*, 1896–1898.

    a.   *Gesamtausgabe*, vol. 1. Graz, 1981.

    b.   Stephen G. Brush. *Lectures on Gas Theory*. Berkeley, Calif.: University of California Press, 1964.

One of the founders of statistical mechanics, Boltzmann presented in this work important developments in the kinetic theory of gases, particularly mathematical formulas for entropy.

61.   J. J. Thomson. "Cathode Rays," *Philosophical Magazine*, ser. 5, vol. 44, pp. 293–316, 1897.

   a.   Stephen Wright. *Classical Scientific Papers—Physics*, pp. 77–101. New York: American Elsevier, 1965.

This paper announced the discovery of the electron, the first known subatomic particle, and included a measurement of the ratio of its charge to mass.

62.   Pierre Curie and Marie Curie. "Sur une Substance Nouvelle Radio-Active, Contenue dans la Pechblende" and "Sur une Nouvelle Substance Fortement Radio-Active, Contenue dans la Pechblende," *Comptes Rendus Acad. Sci. Paris*, vol. 127, pp. 175–78, 1215–17, 1898.

   a.   i.   *Oeuvres de Pierre Curie*, pp. 335–38, 339–42. Paris, 1908.

      ii.   Marie Curie. *Prace/Oeuvres*, pp. 46–48, 57–59. Warszawa: 1954.

   b.   H. A. Boorse and L. Motz. "On a New Radio-Active Substance Contained in Pitchblende," and "On a New Substance, Strongly Radio-Active, Contained in Pitchblende," *The World of the Atom*, pp. 432–34, 434–36. New York: Basic Books, 1966.

These two similarly titled papers recounted the discoveries of polonium and radium, respectively, both much more strongly radioactive than the uranium of Becquerel, with whom the Curies shared the 1903 Nobel Prize in physics.

63.   Max Planck. "Zur Theorie des Gesetzes der Energie verteilung im Normalspectrum," *Verhandlungen der Deutsche Physikalische Gesellschaft* 2(17), pp. 237–45, 1900.

   a.   i.   Stephen G. Brush and D. ter Haar. *Planck's Original Papers in Quantum Mechanics* (*Classic Papers in Physics*, vol. 1), pp. 6–14. London: Taylor & Francis, 1972.

      ii.   *Vorlesungen uber die Theorie der Warmestrahlung*, 1906.

b. D. ter Haar. "On the Theory of the Energy Distribution Law of the Normal Spectrum," *The Old Quantum Theory*. Oxford: Pergamon, 1967. Reprinted: Stephen G. Brush and D. ter Haar. *Planck's Original Papers in Quantum Mechanics* (*Classic Papers in Physics*, vol. 1), pp. 38–45. London: Taylor & Francis, 1972.

Planck revolutionized the world of physics with this paper, in which he explained certain black-body phenomena with the idea that energy was not continuous but came in discrete amounts, or quanta, proportional to a value that has come to be called Planck's Constant.

Selected Bibliography

Brush, Steven G., ed. *Resources for the History of Physics. Part II: Guide to Original Works of Historical Importance and Their Translations into Other Languages*. Hanover, N.H.: University Press of New England, 1972.

Cajori, Florian. *A History of Physics in Its Elementary Branches Including the Evolution of Physical Laboratories*, rev. and enlarged ed. New York: Macmillan, 1938.

Crew, Henry. *The Rise of Modern Physics*, 2nd ed. Baltimore, Md.: Williams and Wilkins, 1935.

Dibner, Bern. *Heralds of Science: As Represented by Two Hundred Epochal Books and Pamphlets in the Dibner Library, Smithsonian Institution*, 25th anniv. ed. Norwalk, Conn., and Washington, D.C.: Burndy Library and Smithsonian Institution, 1980.

Gillispie, C. G., ed. *Dictionary of Scientific Biography*. New York: Scribner's, 1970.

Home, R. H. *The History of Classical Physics: A Selected, Annotated Bibliography*. New York: Garland, 1984.

Magie, William Francis. *A Source Book in Physics*. New York: McGraw-Hill, 1935.

Author/Title/Editor/Electronic Resource Index

Note: Reference is to entry number or page number; page numbers are italicized.

Subject Index

*Note: Reference is to entry number or page number;
page numbers are italicized.*